'Down with the Crown'

PICTURING HISTORY

Series Editors
Peter Burke, Sander L. Gilman, Ludmilla Jordanova, Roy Porter,
†Bob Scribner (1995–8)

'Down with the Crown'

British Anti-monarchism and Debates about Royalty since 1790
(1999)

Antony Taylor

REAKTION BOOKS

To my parents, John and Nora Taylor

Published by Reaktion Books Ltd
79 Farringdon Road, London EC1M 3JU, UK

First published 1999

Series design by Humphrey Stone

Printed and bound in Great Britain by Biddles Ltd,
Guildford and King's Lynn

British Library Cataloguing in Publication Data

Taylor, Anthony.
    'Down with the crown' : British anti-monarchism and debates
    about royalty since 1790. – (Picturing history)
    1. Monarchy – Great Britain – Public opinion 2. Monarchy –
    Great Britain – Public opinion – History 3. Republicanism –
    Great Britain 4. Republicanism – Great Britain – History
    I. Title
    321.8´7´0941

ISBN 1 86189 049 4

Contents

Acknowledgements

I would like to thank all those who have helped me in the preparation of this volume. I first undertook some of the research that led to this book as part of a broader project on the structural differences between London and Manchester radicalism in the post-Chartist period. This was subsequently presented at Manchester University for the degree of Ph.D. in 1992. I would particularly like to thank Iorwerth Prothero for supervising this early stage of my research, and for his inexhaustible supply of references on mid-century British politics. A special mention must also go to John Breuilly for his advice on comparative history, which I hope I have followed in chapter 5.

Early on I encountered some scepticism about the validity of a study of ideas commonly held to play only a tiny part in the popular politics of the nineteenth century. I am particularly grateful to James Vernon for encouraging me to persevere in an understanding of mid-century opposition to the monarchy, and to Michael Bush for pointing out the value of an entire study devoted solely to this subject. His enthusiasm for and knowledge of many of the books and authors cited has contributed substantially to the final form of the volume. I would also like to thank Luke Trainor, formerly of the University of Canterbury, Christchurch, New Zealand, for insights into Australian/British comparisons during the nineteenth century, and his unparalleled patience with a relative novice in Australian history. Subsequently, he has enriched my ideas on subjects as diverse as Blairism and Antipodean voting systems. My thanks, too, to those who have commented on some of the ideas in this book, either at conferences or in correspondence. I am particularly indebted to David Nash, Owen Ashton, Rohan McWilliam, Martin Hewitt, Nicky Richards and Mark Hampton for their suggestions for improvements. I would also like to thank the University of Warwick for financial support from the Research and Innovations Fund and the Institute of Education OSIS account, without which much of the research in this volume would have been impossible.

This study grows out of my recent published work in this area. It draws particularly on my articles '*Reynolds's Newspaper*, Opposition to Monarchy and the Radical Anti-Jubilee: Britain's Anti-Monarchist Tradition Reconsidered', *Historical Research*, LVVIII (1995), pp. 318-37 and 'Republicanism Reappraised: Anti-Monarchism and the English Radical Tradition 1850-1872, in *Re-reading the Constitution: New Narratives in the Political History of England's Long Nineteenth Century*, ed. James Vernon (Cambridge, 1996), pp. 154-78. Chapters 4 and 2 are extensively revised versions of these earlier draft pieces. I thank the publishers concerned for permission to reproduce extracts from the earlier articles here.

This is above all a Manchester book. I would especially like to thank the staff of the Social Science Room, Manchester Central Library for their constant support and good humour, and their willingness to tackle the most obscure references and requests. Unparalleled technical guidance, bibliographic expertise and friendship has been provided throughout by Nick Weaver and Fergus Wilde. A special mention must also go to Laurence and Keren for their unfailing enthusiasm for my early journalistic exploration of some of the ideas expressed in the following pages.

My greatest debt must be to my partner, Marsha Healy; she knows how much I owe her.

List of Abbreviations

BI	Bishopsgate Institute
BL	British Library
HC	George Howell Collection
MCRL	Manchester Central Reference Library
SDF	Social Democratic Federation
SNP	Scottish National Party
SPD	German Social Democratic Party

Frontispiece Sean Read, *Happy and Glorious* (see illus. 79).

Introduction

Now that the fairy-tale of the British monarchy's relationship with the public is over, and a debate about the future of the House of Windsor has at last opened up, it is perhaps time to consider whether the recent disillusionment with the throne is a unique event or part of a recurrent pattern of decay and renewal in the life cycle of the throne. This is an area that has received very little attention from historians of popular politics who tend to see republicanism in Britain as the dog that does not bark.[1]

It is the purpose of this book to examine the absence from historical writing of a perceived current of opposition to the throne from the high-Victorian period onwards. It analyzes the attitudes not of the apologists and proponents of the British monarchy, but rather of its critics and detractors. It concludes by considering the reasons for their failure to establish a political movement dedicated solely to the removal of royal authority.

Monarchy is inextricably intertwined with the history of the British Isles. Moreover, the royal history of Britain is one in which the themes of continuity and stasis are paramount. The monarchy survived the seventeenth-century power struggle between Crown and Parliament, emerging from the Restoration of the Stuart kings in 1660 with its prestige and popularity enhanced, despite the upheavals of the English Civil War. The experience of Oliver Cromwell's short-lived republic, however, dictated that the strength of the throne was tempered by notions of consent in government. Consultation remained an important part of the governing compact between Crown, Parliament and people. Consent, it was believed, acted as a brake on arbitrary rule, and was invoked both by the Parliamentarians and the supporters of William of Orange in 1688 to justify their actions. The overthrow of James II in that year confirmed the rights of the 'Freeborn Englishman', enshrining the principle of parliamentary sovereignty in the relations between Crown and Parliament.[2]

The Revolution Settlement was rooted in classical notions of republican thought. Classical republicanism is not necessarily hostile to the idea of monarchy, only despotic kingship. It proposes instead a balanced form of government with a separation between the executive and legislative powers. There is no doubting the strength of popular attachment to this system and to the monarchy based on it. For many Englishmen the Settlement was a supreme example of the success of a balanced form of government between king, lords and commons at a time of entrenched royal absolutism on the Continent. In later years the British governing system was invested with a semi-mystical pedigree. The conservative theorist Edmund Burke saw the ancient constitution as organic, inimical to tyranny, and expressive of the notions of liberty at the heart of British government. Retrospectively 1688 was placed in a tradition of Anglo-Saxon liberties before the Norman Conquest and confirmed by the great Magna Carta between king and barons in 1215.

The French Revolution of 1789, however, changed perceptions of liberty. Whether as a simple slogan or as a doctrine of rights, the Revolution altered the political landscape of Europe, releasing humanitarian, regicidal and reformist instincts in equal measure. Such sentiments highlighted the limitations of public liberty in Britain and raised questions about the British freedom from enslavement under the Crown. French Revolutionary impulses echoed the doubts frequently expressed about English liberties in Europe in the eighteenth century when even enthusiasts for English democracy like Voltaire were critical of the 'titled plunderers' and 'ecclesiastical tyrants' who acted as the guardians of professed liberties.[3]

In Britain the past century has witnessed a rapid shift of power away from a traditional aristocratic elite and the creation of a more meritocratic society, yet there has been no accompanying diminution in the wealth and splendour of the monarchy that emerged from the Glorious Revolution of 1688. Moreover, in Britain the population are still subjects of the Crown, not citizens in their own right. Given this, it remains puzzling that in the last hundred years occasions when calls for the complete abolition of the monarchy have reached a wider audience have been few and far between.

Existing explanations for the apparent inertia of reformers on the constitutional questions emerging from the Crown's position range across familiar territory. Much of the analysis of republican failure draws on an established view of the national past. The success of the Revolution Settlement of 1688, and its centrality in creating a system of monarchist-inspired constitutional intangibles safeguarding the royal element in the constitution, is often seen as explanation enough for the narrowing of the space occupied by republican alternatives.

Herein, it is argued, lay the monarchy's ability to be all things to all men, radicals included.[4]

The role of the media in Britain is also often highlighted and the suggestion made that it proved hugely successful at discrediting the anti-monarchist cause in the nineteenth century by linking monarchy with patriotism and national stability in the public mind. Moreover, the British monarchy is often regarded as protean and endlessly capable of reinventing itself at times of crisis. Hence the royal family has shown an infinite ability to modernize, so confounding, and by implication neutralizing, their critics.[5] Even the agenda of 'national character' is sometimes still raised to suggest that the British are quite simply too deferential and socially conservative to tolerate the notion of an elective non-hereditary head of state.[6]

None of these explanations will do at a time of crisis in the fortunes of the current Queen. It is more likely that the opposition that has surfaced to royalty in recent centuries has simply been overlooked by historians. In this sense there has been a marked vacuum in the historiography of the royal state. British history indeed has been hijacked and reduced to the level of a procession of kings and queens.[7] This is a point made strongly by David Norbrook, who points out that many British intellectuals and men of letters have traditionally been 'republican' by instinct and inclination.[8] This raises complex questions about the nature and dynamics of historical writing, the relationship of the current 'national history' to the British past, and the direction taken by social history at the end of the twentieth century.

Equally to be avoided are excessive claims in the other direction. In 1990s Britain 'republicanism' is a novel notion, and the first truly original concept to enter the public domain for some years. Nowadays we hear much about its rediscovery. At *The Times/Charter 88* debate on the monarchy in 1993 Christopher Hitchens argued for a resurrection of mummified English traditions of republicanism rooted in Cromwell's Commonwealth and driven underground by long years of royal ascendancy.[9] There are remnants of a Whig historical perspective here, reflected in the notion of inherited constitutional freedoms passed down through the generations. This is as much a caricature of traditional English opposition to the throne as the alternative argument that postulates a total plebeian compliance in and popular enthusiasm for that institution. Moreover, the very concept of an underground tradition confirms the link in the popular mind between the 'unrespectable', the 'subterranean' and a small handful of opponents of the throne.

While not entirely inappropriate for a consideration of British republicanism, implicit in such sentiments are still notions of liminality and the marginal. The emphasis radicals themselves have traditionally placed on the loneliness of the position they occupy outside the mainstream of political debate has also contributed to a vision of them as 'outsiders'. Constitutional reformers have drawn their strength from the notion of a 'suppressed tradition'. In fact, in some periods like the 1870s, their views have been central to political debate, rather than outside it.

Most troubling of all, we still have no real definition of the elusive term 'republicanism' in British history. Used quite arbitrarily it is rapidly becoming a catch-all for any criticism of monarchy at all. Indeed the provenance of the word colludes in this process. There have always been self-styled 'republicans' in the English political landscape, but they have consistently failed to define the term, or give an outline of any potential republican platform. In fact, the word is more helpful to the defenders of monarchy than to its opponents. In England it carries with it connotations of the un-English Cromwellian Commonwealth, the violence surrounding the Irish Republican Movement, and, after the creation of the Irish Free State and the emergence of the Scottish National Party in the 1920s and 1930s, the potential dissolution of the Union. It is no coincidence that the years between the General Strike in 1926 (the year of the current Queen's birth) and the coronation of 1953 marked the emergence of a recognizably modern cult of monarchy and conferred the patina of 'Englishness' on the throne that still surrounds royalty. As Ben Pimlott has noted in his recent biography of the Queen, the concerns of Elizabeth II regarding the Commonwealth and national unity echo contemporary debates about 'Englishness' emerging in the 1920s at a time of imperial decline and national self-examination.[10] Republicanism therefore can sometimes connote 'anti-Englishness'.

In recent years the condescension of those radicals who have laboured to devise alternative non-monarchical constitutions towards those who articulate a simple visceral aversion for monarchy has further obfuscated the term. Constitutional reformers insist on maintaining the fiction that they are indifferent to the personality or character flaws of the reigning monarch, suggesting rather that it is the institution of monarchy itself that is at fault. Yet the fact remains that without the public opposition prompted by royal failings, constitutional reformers would gain no public hearing for their position.

The imperative for British republicanism is generally seen as deriving from continental precedent.[11] Closer inspection, however, reveals fewer tangible continental links than is often supposed. Chapters 2, 3 and 5 explore not only the lack of interest of many anti-monarchists in European parallels, but also suggest that British opposition to the throne in the nineteenth century was grounded firmly in a nativist historical current and local traditions of perceived royal wrongdoing. This was a battle fought primarily over the soul of the British past and only infrequently over imported French sentiments of universal liberty as manifested in the US or Europe. Radicals often misread the European or American examples, and were endlessly disappointed by their excesses.

As chapters 4 and 5 demonstrate, imperial, rather than European examples, often provided a better guideline for the reform community as to the future or imminent demise of the monarchical state. Indeed apparent connections between British anti-monarchists and the French Jacobin tradition harmed rather than aided the anti-monarchist cause and played into the hands of loyalist satirists; so much so that some radicals warned against the Continental associations of the word 'republican' and its tendency to evoke memories of the Terror. G. J. Holyoake wrote of George Julian Harney's publication the *Red Republican* in 1850:

We are not at this time prepared to express an opinion as to the merits of the *Red Republican*, but we are prepared to assert that the name we conceive is not happily chosen; and it is our deliberate conviction that, however talented and true the articles may be that are therein written, no genius or energy can bear up against its unhappy cognomen, which must tend to deter vendors from exhibiting or pushing it, and we doubt not actually make timid republicans chary of applying for the paper. As true friends of the cause of human progress we regret what we believe to be a fatal error, and if these lines should reach the eyes of the editor of the *Red Republican* we express the hope he will rechristen his publication at the earliest possible moment.[12]

At the heart of this book then is an attempt to re-write the history of opposition to the throne in Britain between the 1790s and 1999. As part of this process it probes the space Jane Connors has described as somewhere 'between resistance and idiocy'.[13] Above all, it seeks to clarify the confusions surrounding the terminology of opposition to monarchy in England by explicating the notion of anti-monarchism as a more satisfactory substitute for the hazy label of 'republicanism'. It is also a plea for Victorian anti-monarchism to be taken seriously. Recent historical scholarship has tended to dismiss anti-monarchist sentiments as 'crude republicanism', while giving serious consideration to 'crude monarchism'.[14] This is to diminish anti-monarchism's centrality within mainstream radical thought and its importance as part of the long-standing radical critique of corrupt practice in government known as 'Old Corruption', which has itself been reassessed as a populist anti-statist credo.

Indeed, there are significant resonances of William Cobbett's 'regaling tax-eaters' in the rhetoric employed by mid-century opponents of monarchy. Precisely because popular anti-monarchism trades in complaints about royal finances and expresses disgust at immorality in court circles, it has been seen as merely tinkering with the edges of royal privilege, rather than going to the heart of the matter by proposing the blue-print for an alternative constitution. This is to unfairly relegate these sentiments about monarchy to the sidelines in Victorian debates about royalty. As in Europe, where a similar rhetoric was employed by European socialists and Liberals before and during the Great War to engender a sense of crisis in the state, anti-monarchism's strength in Britain is its ability to portray the Old Order as irredeemably flawed and the royal superstructure as in imminent danger of collapse.

With these considerations in mind, this book reprises the English tradition of anti-monarchism in the nineteenth century. As part of this process it seeks to rehabilitate the submerged current of popular opposition to the throne that features in the radical journalism of the period, and to re-define it in terms of the populism that is now recognized as central to an understanding of mid-century radical politics.[15] Here, as in other recent re-examinations of radicalism, the keynote is continuity rather than disjuncture with earlier movements of political protest from the 1790s onwards. The anti-monarchism that surfaced in movements such as Chartism and its successor agitations in the 1860s and 1870s drew together the same strands of radical patriotism and hostility to feudalism that had persistently characterized radical responses to the royal state from the post-Napoleonic War period onwards. This book is therefore not just about opposition to the monarchy, it is also part of a broader attempt to understand the nature of radical continuities, and to bridge the period 1848–1900 during the caesura of popular radicalism and at the highpoint of Gladstonian Liberalism. This was a period not of truce and equipoise between Liberalism and the shade of an older radical tradition, but instead one of sustained political unrest. In the 1870s in particular industrial and agricultural depression, the extension of the franchise, the Irish Home Rule Bills, and concerns for the purity of the constitution expressed by opponents of reform galvanized a radical constituency constructed around the disavowal of loyalist readings of kingship.[16] Such radicalism was more complex than recent revisionism has sometimes implied.[17]

Periodic criticism of monarchy was frequently expressed in the nineteenth century, occurring in unlikely places and in organizations conventionally portrayed as part of a passive Liberal constituency. A random example chosen from the temperance movement shows the degree to which images of unrestrained kingship acted as a popular frame of reference in many campaigns linked to (and in part derived from) an earlier phase of popular radicalism. A rhyme, 'Hail King Gin!', in *The Popular Temperance Reciter* published in the royal jubilee year of 1887 draws a comparison between the role of gin as an exaction on the pockets of the poor, and kingship as a financial encumbrance on the state:

> So you see, He *is* a king,
>   For he does the royal thing:-
> He maintains his regal station,
>   By the process of taxation.
> Who this palace enters in,
>   May learn this lesson from King Gin:-
> Kings are not ashamed to tax
>   Shoeless feet and shirtless backs.[18]

Here a correlation emerges between the notion of the moral failings of kings and a defective political order dependent upon the brewing interest. This image remained an important motif. Later in the 1890s satirical French cartoons portrayed Queen Victoria as a drink-sodden alcoholic, addicted to gin. Gin occupied an important place in the folk-lore of the nineteenth century as 'Mother's Ruin'. The implications were clear to contemporaries. Queen Victoria was an inadequate mother, whose poor nurturing skills had created a dysfunctional family, with the Prince of Wales fulfilling the role of a delinquent son. So, too, it seemed the kingdom might fall into ruin.[19] Here the boundaries between the traditional political nation and a more robust and irreverent style of popular politics blur. Moreover, I suggest that memories of Chartism and an older radical tradition, rather than simply being the exclusive preserve of Liberalism, were of a great and frequently contested significance. Such a view thereby offers a route for reconnecting Chartism and Labourism around a non-Liberal vision of the recent political past.

Locating opposition to the throne in the context of these attitudes, this study suggests that anti-monarchism fulfilled an important social and cultural function within radicalism. It was articulated on the occasion of royal ceremonial in a genuine attempt to undermine the royal state, but also sought to express alternative counter-cultural forms that made radicals recognizable to each other, while placing them outside, and in opposition to the civic polity and person of the monarch. Sensational exposures of royal scandal in the radical press could never by themselves destroy the throne, but such coverage did de-mystify the Victorian monarchy and allow radicals to convey the hollowness and moral bankruptcy of the Crown. A similar phenomenon occurred in Germany where the alleged association of Kaiser Wilhelm II with a court circle of homosexuals provided his enemies with ammunition and did much to undermine his position in the years before the Great War.[20]

In the nineteenth century the debate about monarchy was accordingly a rambunctious one, polarizing opinion and prompting extremes of invective and counter-argument from both defenders and opponents of monarchy. At times during the 1870s a discourse of disillusionment with royalty seriously tested the defenders of the throne and gained much wider public currency at the height of the protests about Victoria's seclusion in 1870–71. In addition, working with recent reappraisals of mid-Victorian radicalism this book suggests that the anti-monarchist rhetoric of journals like *Reynolds's Newspaper* or of organizations like the SDF (Social Democratic Federation) in the 1880s enables such bodies to be rescued from the fringes of political activity and placed instead in the radical constitutionalist mainstream. When in 1887, during Victoria's golden jubilee, SDF and socialist clubs protested against 'fifty years of royal flunkeydom' they located themselves within a long and well established tradition of hostile royal comment.[21]

These ideas are developed by scrutiny of the campaign waged by *Reynolds's Newspaper* against the throne in the 1870s during the so-called 'republican crisis'; in 1876 at the time of the Royal Titles Bill; and subsequently during the set-piece royal occasions of the late Victorian and Edwardian periods. It concludes with an examination of Labour's failure to grasp the nettle of constitutional reform in the 1920s and 1930s despite manifest grassroots support for this course of action, and assesses the more recent significance of anti-monarchism during a period of crisis in the fortunes of the royal family.

As part of this analysis the book draws on recent and historical images of monarchy and subjects them to searching analysis to contextualize the prevailing nineteenth-century representations of the throne, and to understand the meanings of monarchy for both defenders and critics of the Crown. Such images were central to the appeal of monarchy in the nineteenth century and, as the book shows, could be interpreted in a series of subversive and unconventional ways to ridicule and deride, rather than to praise and adulate royalty.

This book is emphatically not an addition to the avalanche of studies charting the recent slump in popularity of the House of Windsor in the years since 1992. Rather it represents a contribution to the current

literature on the subject of the royal state and the long-standing historical failure of British 'republicans' to contest it effectively. While there
are numerous studies of the ceremonial surrounding royalty in print,
there is still no single accessible study of opposition to the throne in
England. There is now an urgent need for a non-monarchical account
of 'republican' readings of the British constitution. It is hoped that this
study's combination of historical rigour and topicality makes it of
interest to both the general reader and a specialist academic audience.
In addition, it also provides an opportunity to contribute to a current
and very lively debate in British politics and culture. With the rationale
of once-fashionable 'national' history of the kind which has always
elevated monarchy currently undergoing re-examination, and a crisis
in the royal state itself, this study seeks to place the current extensive
public dissatisfaction with the Crown in context.

The book is organised into seven chapters, each dealing with a separate theme in the history of anti-monarchism in Britain between 1837
and 1999. It begins with the crisis in the royal state of the 1790s and
scrutinizes the prevailing images of the royal family from George IV to
Queen Victoria in the popular press, and in the world of satire and caricature. At the core of the book, however, is a close study of the 1870s
which seeks to place nineteenth-century opposition to the monarchy in
context.

Chapters 2, 3 and 5 explore alternative readings of 'republicanism'
to those conventionally put forward by historians in an attempt to
explain the vitality of a current of opposition to the throne in the
1870s, both in the United Kingdom and in the broader context of the
empire. As part of this approach, chapter 4 reconsiders the role of the
radical press during Queen Victoria's jubilees of 1887 and 1897 to
locate hitherto submerged currents of opposition to the throne. The
book concludes with an analysis of the significance of the Liberal peers
v. people campaign of the period 1909–11 and of the failure of anti-
monarchism to establish a constituency within Labourism following
the Labour Party's assumption of office in 1924, and its steady absorption into the establishment after 1929. The concluding chapter relates
the current crisis in royal fortunes to previous periods of disillusionment with monarchy and the 'royal constitution'.

1 Equivocations of Liberty 1800–1837

> Yesterday, going through one of the parks, I saw the poor little Queen. She was in an open carriage, preceded by three or four swift red-coated troopers; all off for Windsor just as I happened to pass. Another carriage or carriages followed with maids-of-honour etc.: the whole drove very fast. It seemed to me the poor little Queen was a bit modest [...a] nice little lassie; blue eyes, light hair, fine white skin; of extremely small stature; she looked timid, anxious, almost frightened; for the people looked at her in perfect silence; one old liveryman alone touched his hat to her: I was heartily sorry for the poor bairn.
>
> (THOMAS CARLYLE, letter to his mother, 12 April 1838)

> George the First was reckoned vile,
>   Viler still was George the Second,
> And what mortal ever heard,
>   Any good of George the Third?
> When to hell the Fourth descended,
>   Heaven be praised, the Georges ended!
>
> (WILLIAM THACKERAY, on the death of George IV, 1830)

To the Victorian public, the best known contemporary image of Queen Victoria was the painting *The Secret of England's Greatness* by T. Jones Barker (illus. 1). Completed in the early 1860s, it shows Victoria presenting an open Bible to an unidentified African chief who kneels subserviently before her. Behind her stand Prince Albert and the court, while prominent politicians of the day, including Lord Palmerston, the chief custodian of British interests abroad, observe from the sidelines. The backdrop is shadowy, but the opulent curtains and furnishings, and the presence of Lord Palmerston in his role as prime minister, suggest a royal building used for formal state occasions, possibly St James's Palace, Buckingham Palace or Windsor Castle. We do not known whether the painting was intended to commemorate a particular event. The National Portrait Gallery, which currently owns the work, speculates that it records a reception held in the Audience Chamber of

1 *The Secret of England's Greatness* by T. Jones Barker, an enduring image of Queen Victoria and 19th-century royalty, was widely exhibited and reproduced as a print.

Windsor Castle. What we can say for certain, however, is that it is a faithful reconstruction of many similar occasions when visiting foreign and imperial dignitaries were presented at court to the queen.

The Secret of England's Greatness has featured regularly in historical scholarship and continues to provoke discussion. In *Queen Victoria's Secrets*, Adrienne Munich has demonstrated that the painting remains central to our understanding of the high-Victorian mind-set.[1] She reads it both as an important representation of the emotional and political underpinnings of Victorian monarchy, and as a symbol of the essential unity of the royal personage, church and third estate. Historians of imperialism have taken it as a generic allegorical representation of the role of Britain in the wider world and in relation to her 'Black' overseas possessions. It is still frequently reproduced in school and university text books as a stock emblem of the heyday of empire, and as a short-hand that conveys a set of precise meanings about the relationship between the Crown, state and empire in the nineteenth century.[2] Finally, Clare Midgly uses it as visual confirmation of the importance of women and femininity within the cultural experience of empire.[3]

Jones Barker's painting was extremely popular in its day. It toured the provinces at the time of the diplomatic and economic crisis surrounding British neutrality during the American Civil War and was widely reproduced as part of the commemorative literature marking Victoria's 1897 Diamond Jubilee celebrations. The presence of a phantasmagoric image of the Prince Consort gave the painting an added poignancy. He died of typhoid in 1861, shortly before the painting went on display. The image thus rapidly entered the mythology surrounding the royal family. In the weeks after his death Albert was hailed as a martyr who had spent the last days of his life engaged in exhausting diplomatic negotiations to ensure that Britain remained aloof from the damaging civil war raging in the former United States. Several obituaries suggested that the strain of this activity had weakened his resistance to disease.[4]

In later years the painting's patriotic, religious and familial elements led to its appropriation by Conservatives and the loyalist Orange Lodges of the north of England. The image of Victoria, Bible in hand, consolidated a vision of the queen as a guarantor of inherited Protestant liberties. The slogan, 'The Secret of England's Greatness', and a facsimile of the painting were prominently displayed on the banners paraded by Manchester's Orange Lodges to welcome Disraeli to the city in 1872.[5] It was at the city's Free Trade Hall that he made his famous pronouncements on the shape and direction of foreign and domestic policy under Disraelian Conservatism. Now regarded less as a manifesto for a future Tory Democracy than a defence of the constitutional verities of monarchy and the dignified aspects of the constitution, Disraeli's speech sought to rebut republican critiques at a time when the public reputation of the royal family was at a low ebb.[6] Significantly Disraeli also remained keen throughout his life to annex the shade of a sage Palmerstonianism protective of Britain's interests abroad, the presence of which is also very marked in the painting.

The Secret of England's Greatness is therefore interwoven with the fabric of British political life in the 1860s and 1870s. Despite that, there is much about the painting that unsettles and fails to harmonize with the conventional view of the work as a hymn of praise to 'altar, throne and cottage'. It is sometimes pointed out that the strongest figure in the painting is not the queen but the native chieftain offering his fealty. He is vividly drawn with strong muscle tones and an elaborate head-dress. In contrast, the image of Victoria is insipid, even dowdy. She seems an incongruous overlord and unlikely emblem of a British nation taming the savage breast to royal authority. Several historians of the empire have concluded that this symbolism contains an unintentional acknowledgement of the potential for independent colonial growth, and perhaps ultimately foreshadows the eventual separation of the colonies from the motherland.[7]

These conflicting elements in the painting were noted by contemporaries. Among those who saw the canvas when it was exhibited at

Newcastle was the young W. T. Stead (1849–1912). The son of a strongly republican family on Tyneside, he was later to distinguish himself as a radical journalist and social crusader.[8] In later life he reflected on the contradictory messages that emerged from the painting for members of the Nonconformist churches. As he pointed out, the image of the open Bible in the picture posed problems for the notion of kingship as understood in purely biblical terms. In the Old Testament, which figured significantly in Nonconformist culture, the rule of kings was seen as a debased form of government imposed as a divine punishment on the wandering tribes of Israel. By reference to Old Testament lore, kings could be portrayed as contravening natural impulses towards democracy:

The attraction of Barker's canvas for the secluded Puritans of the north was its subject. All our culture was Hebraic. The Bible was our literature, our lawgiver, the guide of daily life and the storehouse of political and social wisdom. There were family prayers morning and evening, the chapter to be privately read every day, two week-night services to be punctually attended, while the whole of Sunday was to be filled up with a series of Sunday school sermons, prayer meetings and Bible classes. To this saturation in the Hebrew scriptures was due somewhat of the austerity with which we regarded kingship. Whatever texts there were about honouring the king, the whole drift of the sacred volume, as we were taught it, went against kingship, priestcraft and every institution that came between the individual man and the Infinite personal God. 'I gave them a king in my wrath' seemed to come very near to a brand of the Divine displeasure on the monarchy, and I do not remember ever so much as entertaining even a passing doubt that we should have made a long stride towards establishing the Kingdom of God and His righteousness if Britain were to be restored to the primitive simplicity of republican institutions [...] To us, in the ardour of our juvenile republicanism, it seemed that the logical consequence of any real homage to the Bible would have been for Her Majesty to step down from the throne and out from the Monarchy, terminating once and for all the institution of kingship.[9]

Stead's response to the canvas demonstrates the potential for a radical re-evaluation of the symbols of monarchy within Nonconformist culture. His views were echoed by other critics of monarchy who attributed their hostility to the throne to their own Nonconformist roots. In his *The Right Divine of Kings to Govern Wrong*, the radical William Hone (1780–1842) wrote of the elevation of Saul to the kingship of Israel:

And is a Tyrant King your early choice?
  'Be Kings your plague!' said the Eternal's voice;
And with this mighty curse he gave the crown,
  And Saul, to Israel's terror, mounts the throne.[10]

Central to such images were memories of the militant Protestantism of the Reformation and of the exclusion of Dissenters from Parliament and civic office-holding during the seventeenth and eighteenth centuries. For a while in the eighteenth century the inclination of extreme Protestantism towards republicanism was considered more dangerous than the ambition of many Catholics to restore the link with the Papacy.[11] The repudiation of all worldly authority conveyed by the biblical story of Saul was taken quite literally by some Dissenters. Complaints that public feasting and rejoicing to celebrate the good health of princes amounted to blasphemy were common among the Nonconformist churches throughout this period.[12]

The radical engraver William Hone typified this reflective inward-looking Protestant tradition, which he later recalled as a strong feature of his own Congregationalist upbringing.[13] While acknowledging the Bible as one of the cornerstones of English liberty in his radical squib 'The Political House that Jack Built', he also displayed a healthy disrespect for all religious and royal display, and subverted its loyalist accretions in a series of radical depictions of English political institutions. In 'The Political House that Jack Built', the Bible appeared next to Magna Carta, the Bill of Rights and Habeas Corpus as a central

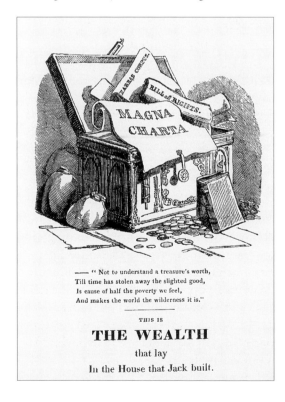

—— " Not to understand a treasure's worth,
Till time has stolen away the slighted good,
Is cause of half the poverty we feel,
And makes the world the wilderness it is."

THIS IS

THE WEALTH

that lay

In the House that Jack built.

2 William Hone equates the riches of the British constitution with radical readings of the Bible, Magna Carta, the right of Habeas Corpus and the 1689 Bill of Rights.

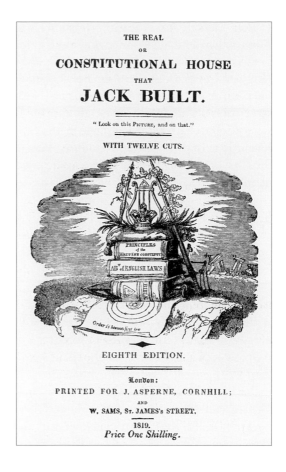

3 A loyalist counter-blast to Hone exalts the traditional function of the Bible as the foundation stone of monarchy, the legal process and the ancient constitution.

THE REAL
OR
CONSTITUTIONAL HOUSE
THAT
JACK BUILT.

" Look on this Picture, and on that."

WITH TWELVE CUTS.

Order is heaven's first law

EIGHTH EDITION.

London:
PRINTED FOR J. ASPERNE, CORNHILL;
AND
W. SAMS, St. JAMES's STREET,
1819.
Price One Shilling.

component of the ancient constitution (illus. 2). In his portrayal of the state, Hone sought to recapture the radical meanings of Nonconformist scripture. His depiction of the Bible intentionally undermined its role in the coronation oath, as well as its use as an image of the Church of England in its function as a state church.

In answer to Hone, the emblem of the Bible frequently reappeared in a Conservative guise to reinforce declarations of loyalism and to reaffirm anti-Jacobin sentiments (illus. 3). Biblical scholarship thus became contested terrain. There was, however, an elasticity about the language of biblical exegesis that made it common to many other contemporary criticisms of monarchy. For radicals from a secular or freethought background, the Bible was also able to serve as a symbol of opposition to the throne. In the nineteenth century radicals frequently reclaimed the early history of Protestantism, seeing the Lollards and Anabaptists who had faced persecution from heresy laws implemented by royal and clerical authority, as early martyrs for freedom of thought and expression.[14]

Both radicals and Nonconformists were united in their hostility to Anglicanism and questioned the validity of a state church under-pinned by royal authority and closely linked to landed society and the House of Lords. Both also ultimately hoped for the disestablishment of the Church of England. Depictions of the Bible were thus a frequent resort of radicals in search of an appropriate image with which to scourge church and state. Writing in 1848 during the first flush of the revolutions that were soon to topple many of Europe's royal houses, the Chartist leader Ernest Jones predicted: 'The age of monarchism has passed – the era of republics has arrived. The book of kings is fast closing in the great Bible of humanity. Why a republic is a plant not peculiar to France, it has grown elsewhere too [...] even in the cold atmosphere of England with a Cromwell and a Hampden.'[15] Jones's writings played with biblical metaphor, gleefully exploiting and twist-ing the textual material, while perfectly capturing the self-righteous cadences of the evangelical Bible-thumpers. In 1884 the Scottish radi-cal J. Morrison Davidson drew upon the same body of biblical representations. His best-selling *New Book of Kings* manipulated a parody of biblical imagery to reinforce an attack on the royal house. In the preface to the 1897 edition, he resorted to apocalyptic images of the Anti-Christ in the tradition of the Reformation, describing the throne under Victoria as an 'Anti-Christ institution'.[16]

The inclusion of Lord Palmerston in *The Secret of England's Greatness* is also problematic. Palmerston was the epitome of overseas expansionism and the defence of British interests.[17] At the same time, as many contemporaries realized, he experienced numerous and highly public difficulties in his relationship with Victoria and Albert. Although Palmerston was by no means a republican, these disagree-ments, combined with his well-known sympathy with continental rebels against the despotic tendencies of Europe's ruling houses, enabled radicals and reformers to claim him as an unlikely ally who expressed popular disillusionment with monarchy.[18]

During the 1850s Palmerston resigned twice as a result of royal pressure: in 1851, when Victoria articulated her displeasure at his meeting with the visiting Hungarian revolutionary Lewis Kossuth; and again in 1853, over Albert's attempts to avert the Crimean War by opening negotiations with the Russian court. On both occasions Palmerston portrayed himself as a victim. Such episodes provoked campaigns in the press against the malign influence of Albert on the queen and the role of Albert's German relatives in undermining Palmerston's trusteeship of British interests in Europe. Radical news-papers portrayed the royal relatives as conspirators determined to erode British opposition to continental despotism.[19] These controversies reflected badly on the royal family. During the Crimean War Albert's loyalty remained suspect, and it was commonly believed that he was incarcerated in the Tower of London for the duration of hostilities (illus. 4). The subject of his perceived treachery became the theme of popular street ballads like 'Lovely Albert':

4 Albert, in casual pose, was instrumental in initiating an informal style of monarchy, but was never able to escape jibes that he came from a long line of 'German sausage makers'.

The Turkish War both near and far,
    Has played the very deuce then
And little Al, the royal pal,
    They say has turned a Russian;
Old Aberdeen, as may be seen
    Looks woeful pale and yellow,
And Old John Bull has his belly full,
    Of dirty Russian tallow.

We'll send him home and make him groan,
    Oh, Al you've played the deuce then,
The German lad has acted bad,
    And turned tail with the Russians.[20]

Victoria's public reputation suffered badly from this association with an interfering Albert, and for a while in the 1850s she was nicknamed 'Queen Albertine'.

Whatever the interpretation of Thomas Jones Barker's The *Secret of England's Greatness* by contemporary critics of monarchy, the artist himself never embraced their views. There were no cryptic republican messages encoded within it. Quite the reverse, the now largely forgotten Jones Barker celebrated the defining moments of mid-Victorian patriotism with conventional images of self-sacrifice and devotion, such as *The Return Through the Valley of Death*, *The Relief of Lucknow* and *The Meeting of Wellington and Blucher*. His last painting, *The Death of the Princess Elizabeth, Daughter of Charles I, at Carisbrooke*, portrayed the royal blood line of the Stuarts in sentimental terms. In 1848 his painting of the *Death of Louis XIV*, which had been commissioned by Louis-Philippe, was burnt by a Parisian mob for its conventional and nostalgic representations of the French monarchy.[21] Above all, Thomas Jones Barker was a rank sentimentalist about English history. He portrayed it as a pageant of kings, queens and generals, ignoring usurpations, dynastic changes and civil wars. Nevertheless, his images opened a window on a contentious and divisive past that provoked debate about the course of English history.

It is clear that *The Secret of England's Greatness* and other paintings like it do not mirror an unchanging English identity but rather provide images of a fluid and inchoate sense of a national past, which have been used by supporters and opponents alike to either praise or undermine monarchy. By uncovering their alternative meanings to religious and radical communities who drew upon them, it is possible to think in different terms about how historical representations and memories were used by both the defenders and opponents of monarchy. Such analysis opens the door to a reconsideration of the opposition to the throne in Britain and the ways in which such opposition might have been articulated, and of the historical myths and precedents radicals pressed into service to bolster their hostility to kingly rule.

Recent research on the origins of English national identity has emphasized the continuities of thought that characterized the English experience of monarchy and the perceived centrality of the throne to inherited historical liberties.[22] Such notions were enshrined in the experience of 1688, when the Catholic James II was deposed, and were validated by the subsequent Revolution Settlement of 1689, which elevated William and Mary to the throne and secured the future of the Protestant Succession. Contemporaries read the events of 1688–9 as a broader metaphor for English liberty and included the Glorious Revolution as one of the highpoints of English historical memory. This was part of a common historical landscape that integrated the Anglo-Saxon *folk-moot*, the Norman Conquest of 1066 and the Magna Carta of 1215.[23] Moreover, memories of 1688 reasserted the right of popular resistance, English Anglo-Saxon liberties and freedom of religious conscience. At the same time they explicitly renounced the 'popery, brass money and wooden shoes' of imported Catholic monarchy. In public display and commemoration, these experiences formed a living tableau of sacrifice and deliverance reaffirmed at the centennial commemorations in 1788–9.[24]

Linda Colley sees monarchism, the defence of Protestant liberties and the hostility to an invasive extra-English 'other' expressed in the events of 1688–9 as central to an understanding of the English culture of loyalism in the eighteenth and early nineteenth centuries.[25] During this period they were transmuted into a royalist myth that celebrated the same values of altar, throne and cottage present in the representations of Englishness that cohered around memories of 1688–9 and pre-Norman England. In addition, Colley argues that the second half of George III's reign marked a 'royal apotheosis' during which the monarchy established the basis for a broad popular patriotism rooted in palace buildings, national pageantry and the cult of national heroes of the Napoleonic Wars.[26] The king thus became the symbol of the nation-at-arms and an emblem of Protestant militancy against alien Catholic incursions from the Continent or Ireland. This expansion in popular loyalism was rooted in revived historical memories of kingship, but was also a response to defeat in the American colonies and the threat of a revolution along the lines of the French model of 1789.

The lack of a clear Hanoverian succession in 1817 after the death of Princess Charlotte, the only legitimate offspring of George IV and Queen Caroline, as well as an embarrassment of candidates to fill the vacancy, hardened anxieties about the future of the throne. For radicals like Percy Bysshe Shelley and Lord Byron, the death of the popular Princess Charlotte represented more than the demise of a royal heir, it also symbolized the death of hopes for renewal within the royal family.[27] The wider public, moved by the princess's many charitable ventures, shared this mood. The elegies and public displays that surrounded her burial established new codes of conduct and behaviour in public mourning, which prefigured the extravagant displays that accompanied the deaths of Princess Alexandra and Lady Diana Spencer.[28] Monarchism was thus an improvised phenomenon in the 1800s. Uncertainty and panic in response to events abroad were frequently present in the search for rituals of unity and a popular culture of loyalism.

Even at the height of the patriotic backlash against the French Revolution and the English Jacobins between 1790 and 1800, there was an ambivalence about the cult of kingship in Britain and the national myths used by the royal family to bolster its position. Indeed ambiguity was at the heart of the experience of 1688. The events of that year could be interpreted either as a loyalist defence of the principles of 'true kingship' or as an assertion of the role of the people in the compact between kings and commoners. There were even republican elements to the myth. The frieze of the *Life of Julius Caesar* by Louis Laguerre in the entrance hall of the Duke of Devonshire's mansion at Chatsworth House, commissioned to mark its rebuilding in 1692–4, refers explicitly to 1688 and evokes a classical republican precedent. Drawing upon the Whig civic humanist tradition, it graphically portrays the assassination of Julius Caesar with clear intimations of the role of the Duke of Devonshire in unseating James II.

Above all 1688, 'The Year of Liberty', imbued the unwritten constitution with a vocabulary of anti-tyranny. In her zeal to uncover the origins of British patriotism, Colley has largely overlooked the ambiguities of meaning that were very marked in the process of establishing royal ceremonial both during and after the eighteenth century. Traditionally, the exaltation of kingship was reflected by a system of feast days, calendars and almanacs that mirrored the ritual cycle of the rural year. The emphasis was on a shared heritage that propagated the myth of a timeless, unchanging monarchical continuity. In marked contrast, as Ronald Hutton has demonstrated, the dynastic and religious changes of the period 1640–88 created an industry of reinvention, leading to the rejection or replacement of many of the existing rituals of loyalty.[29] This process forged strong links with the carnivalesque culture of Georgian Britain that surrounded traditional pastimes and celebrations.[30]

At the time of the restoration of Charles II in 1660, for example, a new public holiday was instituted on 29 May, named 'Royal Oak Day' after the tree in which the king took refuge during the flight from the battle of Worcester in 1651. The emblem of the festival was a cluster of oak leaves, and those who refused to wear this buttonhole were taunted or mobbed. Despite its associations with the deposed Stuarts, the ceremony survived into the nineteenth century, and in Tiverton in Devon involved the public humiliation of a dupe, shackled and dressed like Oliver Cromwell.[31]

Far from expressing timelessness, however, the majority of the traditional revels surrounding monarchy were in fact highly unstable and protean in their meanings. Even festivals that were linked to specific dynastic changes were seldom merely generic celebrations of loyalism. Remembrances of the Duke of Monmouth and the 1685 rising in the West Country, for example, celebrated the assertion of Protestant militancy against the Catholic James II, but were still characterized by retrospective nostalgia for an illegitimate heir with little real claim to the throne. Nevertheless, 'King' Monmouth, 'The Protestant Duke', remained an icon of Protestant solidarity in opposition to the debauched Hanoverians into the nineteenth century.[32] Here conventions of pedigree and heredity within the royal succession were suspended. In addition, the Monmouth rising failed to fit into a view of English history that exalted the peaceful transfer of power.

In contrast, too strict a reading of the inherited element within monarchy could debase the coinage of Hanoverian kingship altogether. In Scotland, nostalgia for the Stuarts and a sentimental cult of Jacobitism opened the way for an examination of the legitimacy of Hanoverian authority and, sometimes, the foundations of royalty itself. In the 1740s Jacobite propaganda frequently stressed the alien and Germanic character of the Hanoverians. As a result, Scottish radicals of the 1790s managed to combine both Jacobitism and Jacobinism.[33] B. H. Bronson wrote of the North-East radical Joseph Ritson: 'Jacobitism offered a convenient stick with which to beat a dog. And having found your current sovereign a usurper you can later give reign to your democratic inclinations without compunction.'[34] The popular revels surrounding memories of both the Stuart and Hanoverian dynasties could therefore subvert, as well as exalt, the existing monarchical order and the public persona of the nation's rulers.

In the eighteenth century the opposition to monarchy that expressed itself under these circumstances defiantly exalted Protestantism over Catholicism and thrived during periods in which the morality of Britain's rulers came under question. James II became the living embodiment of a kingship debased through exposure to Catholicism. Such sentiments set the tone for the strong note of public hostility to George, Prince of Wales, in 1784 when rumours of his marriage to the Catholic Mrs Fitzherbert became widespread. Under the terms of the clandestine marriage, Mrs Fitzherbert's and any issue from the union renounced their claims to the Prince's titles. Despite this, the marriage confirmed the Prince's reputation as a philandering, untrustworthy husband and as an unreliable defender of the traditional Protestant liberties his station made it essential for him to uphold. Subsequently such images and popular memories became the yardstick of bad kingship in Britain.

After the outbreak of war between Britain and Revolutionary France in 1793, the ceremonies that surrounded loyalism were improvised and developed locally on an *ad hoc* basis.[35] From their inception they were open to reinterpretation and debate. In the eighteenth and early nineteenth centuries the contemporary preoccupation with royalty was as a consequence rarely wholly subservient and passive. Moreover, by opening the rituals of royalty to public involvement and sanction at a sensitive time in the history of the English throne, the architects of monarchism made the Crown vulnerable to a polity capable of both condemning and acclaiming the affairs of kings. Loyalism was frequently a negotiated phenomenon, conditional on the wise exercise of power and justice by the ruler and on the good behaviour of the court. Often there was a selective approach to kingship, in which some royal figures were preferred to others. In the popular literature of the day, bad monarchs and poor kingship were represented as capable of dishonouring the nation as a whole. Public ceremonial for the recovery of George III from his illness in 1789 and the royal jubilee to mark his fifty years on the throne in 1809 reflected this sentiment; both festivals can be interpreted as expressions of relief that George III's recovery prevented the widely disliked Prince Regent from succeeding to the throne.[36] During the Regency the prince was routinely booed when attending theatrical performances in London, whereas other members of the royal family, notably the Duke of Gloucester, were warmly received.[37]

The amorphousness of the revels connected with monarchy conspired to obscure their meanings and frequently subverted demonstrations of loyalism by imbuing royal events with radical undertones. Radicals themselves realized the potential for disruption of staged royal events by reference to these encoded double meanings. At the time of the coronation of George IV in 1821, spoof royalist ballads ridiculed the uncritical loyalism surrounding the event. These squibs used both the metre and form of the patriotic ballad tradition to convey a radical meaning. A Newcastle example satirized the patriotic feasting on roasted oxen and urged a radical boycott of the event:

> They saw with grief, the roasted beef,
> By saucy swine neglected!
> No grateful Beast extoll'd the feast,
> Nor loyalty respected,
> Their swinish nature sure is changed!
> O! What an alteration!
> Time was when Pigs would grunt and squeal,
> To grace a coronation.[38]

The ballad elevated the 'swinish multitude' over the royal person of the king, while references in other versions to the horns of the slaughtered oxen revived memories of the many sexual indiscretions of the Prince Regent and the cuckolded husbands of the court ladies he had seduced.

Radicals also realized the potential for criticism of royalty present in the popular literature of the day. This was frequently ribald and disrespectful in its treatment of monarchy even at the height of the loyalist 'white terror' of the 1790s. From an early stage critics of the throne drew on the traditional role of monarchs in nursery rhymes and children's literature to convey a vision of a throne tottering under the weight of a farcical and risible royal dynasty. The fairy-tale element in monarchy lent itself well to this kind of treatment.[39] Nursery and children's nonsense rhymes expressed a carnivalesque image of a topsy-turvy world of graceless buffoons caught in ludicrous and unlikely situations. Here the high were brought low and the low elevated to a higher social station. The central characters were frequently, but not exclusively, kings and queens. In the hands of radicals, such associations diminished the stature of royalty and clerics and also punctured the gravitas of solemn royal ceremonial.

The two figures most strongly associated with the satirical print culture of the period 1817–30 were James Catnach and William Hone. Under their auspices, the popular-print medium evolved from the rough etchings accompanying street ballads to small shilling pamphlets lavishly illustrated with far superior wood block engravings that nevertheless retained earlier stylistic conventions. As Diana Donald has pointed out, Hone was influenced by the iconographic traditions of Reformation artists like Albrecht Dürer who also worked with simple woodcut forms. These stark depictions were particularly well adapted to the portrayal of acts of government terror like the Peterloo Massacre of 1819; prints by Hone depicting the event achieved wide currency in the 1820s.[40] Both Catnach and Hone worked extensively with the established vocabulary and metaphor of popular street literature. Catnach in particular had considerable experience of producing children's readers and illustrated nursery-rhyme collections in the earlier part of his career.[41]

The images of royalty such literature conveyed were in the vein of the stark black-and-white woodcut reproductions of the chap-book and almanac traditions. In the period between 1819 and 1830 they became an important visual frame of reference in radical circles. Hone's pamphlet 'The Political House that Jack Built', produced in 1820 with illustrations by the engraver George Cruikshank, typified the genre.[42] The form and metre of the well-known nursery rhyme made the verses easy to memorize and recite. Such was its impact that the pamphlet's depictions of the Prince Regent became a lasting part of the mythology surrounding him. The coat-tails drawn together between his legs in the shape of a phallus and his exaggerated backside were a staple of radical memories of the Regency and cemented his image as a ridiculous bloated character from folk-tale (illus. 5). Hone inspired a host of imitators. Similar illustrations of George as king, which suggested a bloodthirsty ogre of prodigious appetites and lusts, elevated reformers into radical 'Jack the Giant Killers', capable of taking on and defeating the giants of Crown, state and church.[43] George's relationship with his estranged wife, Queen Caroline, which became a major public issue in 1820–21, was also presented in knockabout terms in Hone's 'The Queen's Matrimonial Ladder', again illustrated by Cruikshank. As with his other works, there were strong elements of children's literature present in the pamphlet, which was illustrated in the style of a child's board game.[44]

During the highpoint of Tory ascendancy after 1815, Queen Caroline became the radical emblem of the constituency of the rejected.[45] After the death of the much-loved Princess Charlotte, she metamorphosed into a potent sacrificial symbol, pitied both as a grieving parent and as a victim of her husband's obsessive philandering. Radicals embraced her repudiation by the court and saw her as an outsider like themselves.[46] The pamphlet 'A Frown from the Crown or the Hydra Destroyed' implored radicals to defend the queen's honour against the duplicity and tyranny of the king, the clerical hierarchy and the establishment, who were represented as offshoots of the same hydra-headed beast of state corruption (illus. 6). Echoes of St George, the patron saint of England and hero of the almanac tradition, and his battle against an emblematic dragon of evil, clearly provided the inspiration for the motif on the front cover. In the engraving, St George's squire carries a banner marked 'Libertas' surmounted by a cap of liberty. The background to the case meant that emblems of royal excess were also apparent in popular treatments of the pro-Caroline cause.

The Prince Regent and Queen Caroline were above all comic oppositional figures, driven by the ebb and flow of public opinion, and seeking to outdo one another in outrageous pranks designed to settle

5 Hone and Cruikshank's vision of George IV as a bloated, licentious villain became established in early 19th-century political caricature.

———————— " Great offices will have
Great talents."

This is THE MAN—all shaven and shorn,
All cover'd with Orders—and all forlorn ;

6 Queen Caroline as wronged victim of her husband's excesses. Conventional images of chivalry deployed in defence of her reputation were a frequent feature of the radical campaign on her behalf.

old scores.[47] Such traditions persisted into the high-Victorian period. Victoria and Albert were often represented as the royal equivalents of Punch and Judy in the popular ballad literature of the 1850s. In the street ballad 'The Rogue Who Insulted the Queen', issued to celebrate the escape of Victoria from an assassination attempt by a former lieutenant of the Tenth Hussars, domestic violence between husband and wife features in the action and is presented in comic form throughout. Gender roles are reversed when Victoria beats Albert about the head and body to bring him into line, but this inversion only serves to reaffirm the existing patriarchal structures of power and sexuality. Male violence towards women, however, only transgresses the established boundaries in the case of a male subject striking the queen:

> If Englishmen may beat their wives,
>   It plainly may be seen,
> They must not take the liberty,
>   To strike the British Queen.[48]

The tradition established by Catnach and Hone during George IV's reign created precedents that remained influential for the critics of monarchy into the 1830s. A whiff of Regency dissoluteness clung to the Hanoverian court of William IV in which the young Victoria grew up, which many still saw as an alien Germanic institution. Moreover, Victoria's father, the Duke of Kent, was a well known philanderer. As a General in the army he was a notorious martinet, noted for his addiction to flogging. Hostile contemporaries saw his methods as the importation of the unfeeling discipline of Prussian military drill into an English setting. In 1803 he was widely blamed for a mutiny on Gibraltar during his tenure as governor.[49] Shortly before his death he featured prominently in Hone's pamphlet 'The Political A, Apple Pie', which takes the form of a child's spelling aid, as one of the greedy pensioners queuing up to receive a slice of the patronage available from the royal pie.[50] In much the same manner as her Hanoverian relatives, the young Victoria led a life of indolent pleasure, riding at every possible opportunity, dancing and attending the best society functions. Accordingly, some of the earliest satirical depictions of Victoria show her as a petulant child, surrounded by aged roués and court pederasts.[51]

Among radical opponents of the throne there were personal memories of court corruption under the Regency that gave the myth of George IV's debased and immoral kingship an additional longevity into the middle years of the nineteenth century. Major Charles Jones, father of the Chartist leader, Ernest Jones, was equerry to the Duke of Cumberland, Queen Victoria's uncle and later King Ernest I of Hanover. Ernest Jones (1819–1869) accordingly grew up surrounded by the trappings of kingship in the Hanoverian court. At the time of his birth the Duke of Cumberland consented to act as his godfather and remained deeply interested in his career throughout his life. Ernest Jones was named after him, and there were persistent rumours that he was the Duke's illegitimate son. Before he embraced radical politics, Jones benefited from the Duke of Cumberland's patronage, and in 1841 he was introduced to Queen Victoria at the Court of St James's.

In later years the influence of Ernest I cast a long shadow over the Jones family. He remained a deeply disliked figure in Regency England, surrounded by rumours of scandal, immorality and sexual perversion. In 1811 the murder of his footman, Sellis, in the Duke's royal apartments in London raised the possibility that the Duke was a victim of blackmail because of his involvement in an underground homosexual network.[52] It was widely believed that the Duke had murdered Sellis in a fit of rage to prevent him from revealing these activities. The episode became a radical *cause célèbre* epitomizing the excesses of the royal relatives and the corruption of the court.[53] The influence of this episode coloured the later history of the Jones family. In 1827 Major Jones admitted in a private journal that the Duke of Hanover had confessed to him that he was the murderer of Sellis. He wrote in his memoir: 'From that fatal night in which he made the confession I have never known peace of mind since; in fact HRH had thrown the black secret of his guilt from his own into my breast. From this time I became gloomy, lost all spirit and energy, was unwilling to meet the Duke and invented all sorts of excuses to be absent from his table.'[54] When Major Jones shot himself in 1843 while cleaning a pistol, it was believed by the family that the Duke's confession had weighed so heavily on his conscience that he had committed suicide.[55] These events had ramifications for Ernest Jones's own brand of radicalism. Although stopping short of a full republican position and remaining on cordial terms with the Duke of Cumberland, Ernest Jones always opposed the influence of the small German courts on the royal family and the presence of impoverished German relatives in the country. In 1856 he attacked 'Albertism' in Britain, fulminating against the marriage of Princess Victoria to a German prince, as well as the unruliness of Hanoverian troops stationed at Gosport: 'Albertism is in the ascendant. An English Princess is to carry £70,000 per annum of our money to German Princes. German interests and German policy are making progress, and will do so, until Englishmen vindicate their right to govern England.'[56] However, Ernest Jones's relationship with monarchy was ambivalent. Jones was not above using his royal connections to shore up his social respectability, particularly when he became a Liberal in the 1860s, but he also used images of corrupt kings and courtiers after 1848 to further a radical vision of a corrupt 'Old Order' incapable of reforming itself.[57]

The street ballad preserved many of the key elements that had provided ammunition against the Regency. For a popular audience such images still had strong resonances. Moreover, coded allusions to the Regency remained a way of criticizing the current incumbent of the throne, while circumventing treason, sedition and the blasphemy laws.[58] Here the rhetoric of revolt masqueraded as a history lesson. As in eighteenth-century print culture, loyalty and deference were never in-built in the British ballad tradition. Ballads greeting the accession of Victoria and her marriage to Prince Albert in 1840 were numerous, but expressed only a grudging admiration for the prince. Some were overtly hostile, portraying him as a German pauper intent upon securing access to the royal coffers and defrauding John Bull of the fruits of his labours which were his as a rightful recompense. One ballad hawker is recorded by James Catnach's biographer as stating that, in his experience, the best-selling ballad about the royal marriage ran as follows:

Here I am in rags,
    From the land of all dirt,
To marry England's Queen
    And my name it is Prince Al-bert.[59]

Much of the criticism of Victoria in the early years of her reign was veiled behind a veneer of loyalty and was again expressive of the ambiguities surrounding the idea of kingship in the first half of the nineteenth century. The episode relating to Victoria that found the liveliest place in mainstream ballad lore was the entry into Buckingham Palace of an adolescent pauper boy named Edward Jones in 1838. The intruder hid in the palace undetected for a day, but after being ejected repeated the feat on two subsequent occasions. On the second occasion in 1841 he was arrested with a sword stolen from a courtier.[60] The picaresque elements of the story rapidly elevated Jones to the status of a hero of the street ballads, in which he was immortalized as 'The Boy Jones'. In part 'The Boy Jones' fulfilled the public's wish for voyeurism. Readers of the ballads about his experience in the palace enjoyed the vicarious pleasure of spying on the royal family, of sleeping underneath the throne and of listening outside the queen's private apartments.

Here was a direct experience of Victoria's domestic life in its most intimate moments. It is the 'childish' nature of the feat that strikes us so forcibly. As a child 'The Boy Jones' had no respect for the personages involved or for the authority upon which he had intruded.

At one go, therefore, the tale removed the layers of regal mystery and public ceremonial separating Victoria's subjects from the throne, and ultimately the person of the monarch herself. The ballad relaying the experience performed the same feat for the reader. Once deprived of status and position, the mystery was stripped away from the monarch, who became vulnerable as merely 'one of us'. In addition, there was a pronounced undercurrent of social envy to the tale. One of the most popular ballads about the event, 'The Boy That Was Found in the Palace', portrayed Jones as a social leveller whose motive for breaking into Buckingham Palace was to find an instant route to status and riches by replacing Albert as Royal Consort:

> Prince Albert, you all know, is in a decline sirs,
>   And the young Queen must look out again, it is clear –
> So I wanted to ask if she would be mine, sirs
>   I should like the identical thousands a year.[61]

Jones assumed the form both of pretender and of social rebel. Indeed his punishment of hard labour on the treadmill seemed more appropriate for a radical than a simpleton. Again the image of monarchy that emerged from the Jones case was a mixed one. On one hand, the episode reinforced the sanctity of royal privacy and separation from the populace; on the other, it flouted principles of deference and deprived royalty of its appropriate social station.[62] The public were suitably divided in their response. Some thought the boy was to be pitied rather than punished, and he received offers of help after asserting in the dock that incarceration in Bedlam or in gaol would be better than his current life.[63]

Such ambiguous readings of the exploits of 'The Boy Jones' translated directly into the popular printed material of the 1840s. From the 1830s chap-books and penny pamphlets were steadily superseded by the new printed medium of weekly journals and periodicals. New technology provided the potential for high-quality publications addressing topical issues. This material catered to the tastes of a new literate, sometimes aspirational culture that found its voice in journals like *Punch* and *Figaro in London*. In its early phase *Punch* in particular provided a cross-over point between the older processes of ballad production in areas like Seven Dials in London, and the new reading public of the high-Victorian period. The first edition of *Punch* in June

1841 was edited by the social investigator and popular scribe, Henry Mayhew.[64] In the early part of the nineteenth century a large number of bohemian radicals like Mayhew still lived on the margins of metropolitan literary culture. Iain McCalman has spoken of a 'literary underground' populated by scribblers and hacks who had connections with reform opinion and the Chartists.[65] These circles were central to the enormous outpourings of popular printed matter that characterized the period. For a time in the 1840s there was a fusion of satirical and radical thought around irreverent organs like *Punch*, which took a provocatively anti-establishment line under the editorship of Douglas Jerrold.[66] During these years *Punch* delighted in the appropriation of the flamboyant, disrespectful culture of bohemian London. Above all, the magazine preserved the ambiguous relationship with monarchy that had characterized the culture of the balladeers and the radical print circles of the 1820s.

Initially the popular satirists and ballad-mongers shared the immense public goodwill displayed towards Queen Victoria on her accession in 1838. In the earliest days of her reign she evoked sympathy and compassion. Victoria marked an important stage in the feminization of the monarchy. As Dorothy Thompson has pointed out, she reaped the benefits of distancing herself, both geographically and socially, from her rowdy and debauched Hanoverian uncles.[67] At the start of her reign the young queen was seen as a challenge to both Toryism and male political dominance; the early popular affection for Victoria was tinged by relief that the hated Duke of Cumberland had not succeeded to the throne in her place. Moreover, her accession stirred memories of other young queens who had acted as the safeguards for traditional Protestant liberties. At the time of her coronation there were comparisons with Elizabeth I, Lady Jane Grey, Queen Anne, Queen Caroline and Princess Charlotte.[68] Such speculations were drenched with romantic nostalgia. In a study of royal visits to Wales, Edward Parry created a spurious Celtic pedigree for Victoria, claiming that she was descended from Cadwalader, last king of the Britons, and seeking to connect her with romanticized images of Boudica. The association led to a revival in the long-forgotten Boudica's popularity.[69]

Both Queen Caroline and Princess Charlotte, who were also regularly invoked as precedents for the young Victoria, had strong Whig and radical connections, enabling the radical constituency to find a point of contact within the monarchical tradition. For a time Victoria fulfilled the role of a 'Just Monarch'. In many illustrations she is shown as overturning the decisions of male law-makers in the Privy Council and injecting a note of female compassion into the affairs of state. In engravings from children's picture books of the queen's life, the young Victoria is pictured as a solitary woman in otherwise exclusively male company. In one she is presented in stark contrast with the Duke of Wellington, who, as prime minister of the Tory government of 1831–2 during the Reform Bill crisis, was notorious for his masculine confrontational style and misunderstanding of the rules of governance (illus. 7). The popular ballads reflected this element of her appeal, showing a queen receptive to petitioners and eager to redress the wrongs of society exposed by their representations, making her into a royal exponent of notions of popular sovereignty:

7 'The Queen's First Council'. Victoria was often represented as an icon of tranquil femininity in a world of men.

And when I open parliament,
    Then you'll find I do enough,
I'll take the duty off the tea,
    Tobacco, gin and snuff

I will make some alterations,
    I'll gain the people's rights,
I will have a radical parliament,
    Or they don't lodge here tonight.[70]

This image was reinforced by Victoria's connection with philanthropy and welfare.[71] In depictions of her relations with poorer neighbours like Kitty Kear on the Balmoral estate, she became an icon of charitable concern for the deserving poor. The vision of the young Victoria visiting her poorer tenants was replicated in numerous popular engravings and paintings. The most common representation of Victoria as the 'good neighbour' anticipated the image of *The Secret of England's Greatness* in a scene of the queen handing over a Bible or prayer book to a supplicant Kitty Kear. Once more the connection with religious values and the correct order in church and state is very marked, while the social hierarchy, cemented by monarchy and the deferential posture of the poor, is reaffirmed (illus. 8).

The youthfulness of the queen lent itself well to this kind of treatment. Before the advent of cheap mass photography the public's main source of information about the monarch's appearance was through the medium of line drawings and etchings, which flattered her still further. During the honeymoon period of her reign artists and cartoonists tended to sentimentalize and romanticize the young Victoria. Most of these representations drew upon conventional female images of devotion, dedication and passivity, common in the treatment of both royal and non-royal female figures. In the earliest *Punch* cartoons she is represented as a pre-pubescent girl. A cartoon of 1841 portrays her as Little Red Riding Hood, menaced by wolf-like caricatures of placemen and Tory politicians, among them Sir Robert Peel, on her walk through the forest of state.[72]

In other contemporary representations she is appreciated for her youthful fecundity following her marriage to Prince Albert in 1840. At the time of the Cawnpore massacre during the Indian Mutiny of 1857 she was portrayed as a grieving wife and mother like any other. There were echoes here of the monarch as 'everyman', sharing the joys and privations of the entire kingdom. Such notions originated with paternalistic eighteenth-century representations of George III as 'Farmer George', accessible to all while out riding or touring his estates. Victoria's youthful glamour was slow to fade and notions of her as a 'Just

8 'The Queen Visiting Her Poorer Neighbours'. In scenes of conventional Victorian philanthropy, the young queen became an emblem of charitable enterprise and care for the deserving
poor.

Monarch', rooted in the cult of King Alfred, persisted into the early 1850s. Images of Victoria from her coronation in 1838 represented her in the iconographical tradition of Anglo-Saxon kingship. The throne was girt around with these echoes of Anglo-Saxon freedoms. They fused strongly in contemporary representations of the coronation, which traced the ritual of the throning ceremony back to the crowning of German tribal kings. During the 1848 revolutions in Europe satirists showed Victoria as a female embodiment of Anglo-Saxon liberties whose sympathies were shared with the people in a project for sensible and graduated reform that would avert the threat of revolution.[73] In 1848 *Punch* depicted her as a wise female King Canute, demonstrating the pointlessness of the resistance of Lord John Russell's Whig government to a reform tide that lapped against the very foot of the throne itself. Here she appeared to confound the apparent conspiracy of Whig governments and the court to deprive the people of their liberties during a period of social and political upheaval (illus. 9). Even some radical opinion reflected this view. The Chartist leader Henry Vincent (1813–1878) commented in a speech at Manchester during the revolutions on the continent: 'For none would smile more graciously than Queen Victoria in granting the people those privileges which God

QUEEN CANUTE REPROVING HER COURTIERS.

9 This cartoon draws on Anglo-Saxon history to demonstrate the fallibility of the anti-reform cause during the continental upheavals of 1848. The image of Victoria as the people's saviour is still apparent.

intended them to enjoy and which, having, they would transmit unimpaired to their posterity, proving that the Crown was the slave of the people, and not the prop of the aristocracy.'[74]

Nevertheless, the treatment of monarchy by the satirical journals was again characterized by an attitude of ambivalence. The uncritical adulation of the early part of Victoria's reign was tempered by a growing scepticism of throne and court that reflected the dual identity of royal figures. It might be argued that by invoking the royal presence,

A ROYAL NURSERY RHYME FOR 1860.

" There was a Royal Lady that lived in a shoe,
She had so many children she did n't know what to do."

10 Victoria as 'The Old Woman That Lived in a Shoe', failing to control both her fertility and the behaviour of the royal offspring.

46

the satirists merely reinforced the centrality of monarchy in the constitution. On many occasions in the 1840s, however, *Punch* built up the royal image simply to knock it down again. The serio-comic journals were always half-mocking, half-fawning, but against a background in which the blatant disrespect for monarchy that characterized the Regency period had largely dissipated, they were able to act as a safety valve, pointing up the follies that occurred during periods of royal excess and maintaining a close scrutiny of the Crown's financial and political failings. This provides some evidence for a kind of 'social contract' with the cartoonists that reveals just how conditional much support for the monarchy really was.

These twin representations of monarchy are typified in the person of Victoria herself. The comic journals praised her in her role as 'domestic exemplar', as a wife, mother of nine children and dutiful widow of Albert whom she mourned for many years.[75] But when her behaviour fell short of the standards usually expected of Victorian women, as with her affair with John Brown and her neglect of royal duties during her period of seclusion, she was mercilessly pilloried. Almost all the prevailing elements and motifs of monarchy were vulnerable to criticism in this manner. When Victoria gave birth to royal heirs there was popular rejoicing, and the death of royal children was always publicly mourned with a particular poignancy.[76] However, too many royal children were perceived as a burden on the state, and Victoria's growing family was criticized by *Punch* as a drain on John Bull's pockets. In 1844 the magazine used the nursery-rhyme imagery familiar from Hone to portray the queen and her numerous offspring as 'The Old Woman That Lived in a Shoe'. Depicting the imagined royal family of 1860, it provided a dire prophecy of expensive royalty and escalating court costs (illus. 10). This reflected widespread popular concern, expressed through street ballads and squibs, about the expense involved in providing for a rapidly burgeoning royal family:

> While Vic and all looks gay and glad,
>   Poor old John Bull seems very sad,
> And cries oh dear what love and joy,
>   Lots of little girls and boys.[77]

The early child-like element in the appeal of Victoria was similarly malleable in this way. The image of Victoria as a capricious and wilful child was frequently invoked to symbolize the unrestrained power that remained in royal hands under the dignified part of the constitution. In 1839 her refusal to dismiss her Whig ladies-in-waiting to make way for retainers who mirrored the political complexion of the incoming Tory government under Sir Robert Peel prolonged the life of Lord Melbourne's Whig ministry and raised questions about 'domestic' rule by a young queen untutored for power. Victoria's resolute defence of the convention that the queen should select her own household companions tested the tolerance of both politicians and the public for royal interventions in everyday political life. Peel maintained that without some sign of royal favour he could not contemplate forming a ministry. Learning the lessons of the crisis, *Punch* showed Victoria as a naughty schoolgirl, knocking down the Palace of Westminster in the form of a house of cards at the time of the state opening of Parliament in 1847 (illus. 11). In the queen's later life this image was revived. In 1892 *Fun* viciously satirized Victoria's continuing influence in politics, showing her as a spoilt child treating the members of Gladstone's incoming cabinet like dolls. Critics of monarchy like Henry Labouchère (1831–1912), whose inclusion in the cabinet Victoria opposed, are in a box marked 'declined with thanks' (illus. 12). Such criticism was of a piece with the bad feeling surrounding Victoria's refusal to elevate John Bright, whom she saw as a dangerous revolutionary, to the Privy Council in 1859.

There was often a hard edge to this sort of caricature, particularly when the Prince of Wales was the target. In part, this suggests that the attitude of the Victorian public was far more finely balanced than recent historical scholarship has suggested. On occasion, such attitudes could tip over into downright hostility towards the throne. While the comic journals were still dominated by the young metropolitan literati of the 1840s, with their strong radical connections, this ambivalence was maintained. It changed only when Mark Lemons, a former inn-keeper, took over the editorship of *Punch* in 1851. He moved it away from its radical traditions and mellowed the tone of the journal towards royalty

THE QUEEN DISSOLVING PARLIAMENT.

11 Note the element of compulsion often present in drawings of royal power like this one.

48

THE QUEEN AND HER DOLLS.

LATEST ADDITIONS TO HER COLLECTION.

[See *Cartoon Verses*, p. 137.

12 Victoria as a childish delinquent dispensing with unwanted ministers during a change of government. Her extreme age at the time of the cartoon made the image of a bad-tempered child even more comic.

and royal dowries. In 1857 the magazine welcomed the betrothal of Victoria's eldest daughter, Princess Vicky, to the future German Emperor, Frederick III (illus. 13).

The concept of monarchy in Britain has always proved problematic for both defenders and critics of the throne. Critics revel in the defects of royal personages, while defenders of the royal state are embarrassed by the failures of individual monarchs to live up to the high standards of

THE DOWRY OF THE PRINCESS ROYAL.

Mr. Bull. "THERE, MY CHILD! GOD BLESS YOU—AND MAY YOU MAKE AS GOOD A WIFE AS YOUR MOTHER!"

13 John Bull expresses approval of Princess Vicky's wedding: 'There, my child! God bless you — and may you make as good a wife as your mother.' By this stage royal dowries were seldom challenged by the press.

morality and public behaviour commensurate with the position and status of the Crown. Flaws in the royal character were capable of evoking one of two responses. Where royal behaviour was judged immoral or wilfully wayward, as in the case of George IV, the monarch was held to have fallen below the threshold of what was publicly acceptable, even by the standards of Hanoverian England. For radicals then and subsequently, his death was a relief.[78] George IV remained the yardstick of bad kingship, even for defenders of the throne. A children's coronation manual of 1911 described him as a 'weak, changeable, pleasure-loving person' and hoped that George V would be nothing like him.[79] On the other hand, the physical or emotional flaws of particular monarchs have sometimes evoked sympathy, even pity for the throne. Frailty has the power to soften and humanize monarchy. Such was the case with Queen Charlotte who died young and in labour. In our own century there was immense public indulgence for George VI, who was thrust unwillingly into the position of king and forced to overcome numerous physical and emotional defects to maintain the status of the Crown.

Loyalism in Britain has therefore always been conditional. Respect for monarchy is not given uncritically but earned. Sometimes, as in the case of George IV, it is not forthcoming at all. Foreign visitors to

Britain sensed this intuitively in the nineteenth century. Americans in particular were struck by the remnants of feudal privilege in British society. Most commented on the ambivalence of the feelings displayed towards the royal family. Some, such as the educationalist Ralph Waldo Emerson, embraced the criticisms of the royal state expressed by many radicals and fulminated on the inequalities and barriers to meritocratic achievement present within British society. In common with other visiting Americans, he blamed the Crown for setting the tone for deference and subservience that he believed characterized the English and their attitudes to their social superiors.[80] The American traveller Richard Grant White realized that nineteenth-century monarchism in the United Kingdom was a variegated phenomenon and confessed himself baffled by the attitude of the British public to the throne:

The tone in which I heard the Queen and her family discussed caused me to puzzle myself with the question what is loyalty in England nowadays [...] I could find no evidence in English society of the existence of such a sentiment. Among the higher classes no one speaks with much respect of the family which has furnished the British throne with four Georges and a William, nor with personal regard or admiration of the present sovereign or of her children, although there seems to be no little ducking and deference to the Prince of Wales. I did, however hear royalty spoken of with admiration because of the dignity and picturesqueness which its functions and its accomplishments bestow upon society. This, however, isn't loyalty; nor was I able to discover any origin of that feeling which makes a theatre full of Britons thrill with a deep, sober and genuine enthusiasm when the royal box is occupied and 'God Save the Queen' is sung, other than the self-conscious glorification of John Bull and the contemplation of majesty made flesh.[81]

White captured perfectly the ambiguousness of English 'loyalism' and the complexities of the national attachment to the person of the reigning monarch. Monarchy could mirror the national mood by providing a positive image of kingship, or, on occasion, as in the case of George IV, face rejection. Such ambiguous responses were woven into historical memories surrounding the throne and were themselves a negotiated part of its relationship with the public. It was in these mixed emotions that radical opponents of monarchy found fertile ground for criticism of the royal state.

2 Republicanism Reappraised: Anti-monarchism and the English Radical Tradition 1830–75

> The old Plantagenets brought us chains; the Tudors frowns and
>   scars,
> The Stuarts brought us lives of shame; the Hanoverians wars;
> But his brave man, with his strong arm, brought freedom to our
>   lives –
> The best of Princes England had, was the Farmer of St. Ives
>
> (Lines on OLIVER CROMWELL written in Ramsay Churchyard,
> Huntingdonshire, 1848. From Edwin Paxton Hood,
> *Lays and Legends of Puritan Heroes* (London, 1880)

In recent years the view that English plebeians are relatively unsophisticated 'monarchists' has become one of the stereotypes of political culture commonly held by historians. For E. P. Thompson, the absence of any significant current of opposition to monarchy is a defining feature of the 'Peculiarities of the English' that measures the success of the political system created by the governing accord between aristocracy and industrialists.[1] The presentation of such crude monarchism as the all-pervading attitude of the nineteenth-century audience precludes any discussion of plebeian criticism of monarchy when it occurred, and closes off the very conception of a republican-style movement *per se*.

Although opposition to monarchy was a strong feature of nineteenth-century political protest and the British radical tradition, it has received relatively little attention from historians.[2] The literature that does exist is either outdated or dismisses British critics of the throne as entirely marginal to the political mainstream.[3] Partly this is a fault of the model used to define the position of those who criticize monarchy itself. British historians writing on this subject have looked to the French example, and sought in particular an equivalent to the French republican tradition in the British context. Working backwards from the involvement of Charles Bradlaugh (1833–1891) in the republican campaign of the 1870s, and grounding their ideas in Thompsonian orthodoxy, Edward Royle and Fergus D'Arcy associate criticism of monarchy almost exclusively with the ideas of Thomas Paine, who was the British radical most strongly inspired by the French example.[4] In this sense, they have accepted uncritically the loyalist propaganda of Paine's contemporaries, who sought to portray all opponents of the throne as foreign-inspired theorists of the doctrine of Natural Laws.[5] By assuming an 'ideal type' of republican thought, their argument takes on a 'Whig' aspect that does not allow for other forms of anti-monarchist display.

This vision is supported by the work of nineteenth-century satirists who frequently sought to minimize the form and content of hostility to the throne. In a cartoon from *Fun* in 1872 British republicans are represented as angry midgets, scorned by the majesty of Queen Victoria and her ministers (illus. 14). British republicanism has therefore been made marginal by association. Traditionally, pure Paineism, as it survived into the later nineteenth century, has been discounted as nothing more than an attenuated, sect-like creed. According to this view, its emphasis upon doctrines of Natural Rights, the cult of citizenship and a written non-monarchical constitution on the French model never translated effectively into a radical medium that, rather than providing a blueprint for change, sought instead the alleviation of immediate, short-term grievances.[6] Seen in these terms, republicanism can be represented as merely an offshoot of the freethought/infidel legacy, rooted originally in the Paineite tradition, passed down through Carlileism and ultimately rendered marginal by its connections with Bradlaughite secularism. This perception has been upheld by recent work that emphasizes the incompatibility of Paineism with agitation that adopts a popular constitutional mode of political expression.[7]

Dissatisfaction with this view of Paine's legacy has led to a reassessment of his influence that now emphasizes the diverse interests of his followers, and the intersections of Paineism with the broader currents of British radicalism. Against this background, older notions of the Paineite movement as an insulated sect have broken down.[8] Existing definitions of British republicanism therefore require considerable reworking. Republicanism read purely and simply as Paineism is now clearly inapplicable. Once freed from this misconception, it becomes necessary to look elsewhere for the basis of British opposition to monarchy.

At the 1993 Charter 88 Conference on the monarchy, traditional British opposition to the throne was labelled 'vulgar' or 'crude' republicanism,[9] but the term 'anti-monarchism' captures its essence as well as any other. In keeping with the long established spirit of British

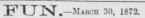

LILLIPUTIAN REPUBLICANS, OR "MANNIKIN TRAITORS."
"WHAT ODD LITTLE CREATURES! HOW ALARMING!"

14 An evocation of the figurative marginalization of republicanism in 19th-century politics.

radicalism, anti-monarchism has no blueprint for change, nor does it present a broader agenda for the overhaul of the constitution. Its opposition to the throne is based simply upon a stock of long-standing radical images of corrupt practice in British politics. By drawing attention to these, it suggests that aristocratic and kingly rule is irredeemably flawed by the sloth, intrigue and dissoluteness of a leisured and pampered lifestyle. In platform rhetoric this conception is amplified as a broader metaphor for bad government in general. Moreover, it exposes the court as a place of scandal, sexual indiscretion and the misuse of wealth and power.

Although such anti-monarchist images have occurred in other political contexts,[10] they lie at the heart of the British radical tradition. They also demonstrate the profoundly populist roots of many British radical forms. Their provenance can be traced back to the seventeenth century, and they display a durability that allowed their persistence into the 1890s and beyond.[11] The same sentiments that inspired William Cobbett to describe the panoply of aristocratic rule as 'the Thing' continued to infuse all the major mid-century movements of political protest. The Chartist press, in particular, exemplified this trend and, like its predecessors, traded heavily in anti-aristocratic lampoons and caricatures. It regularly made use of such events as royal weddings and christenings to highlight the broader inequalities of wealth and power underpinning society. In 1843 the *Northern Star* prefaced a description of the finery on show at the marriage of Princess Augusta, daughter of the Duke of Cambridge, to the Grand Duke of Mecklenberg with the comments:

Who could imagine it possible that in the country where all this glitter and show is made, this ostentatious parading of costliness and gilt, handloom weavers, those who produce the richest white silk and the rich pink silk, who could imagine after harkening to this detail of Peacockism that those who made all the finery to deck the royal wedding are pining to death on four shillings and six pence a week.[12]

This critique of monarchy was heavily reliant upon the regular exposure of royal scandal to sustain itself. Details of marital infidelities, sexual intrigue and financial corruption ran like a thread throughout such rhetoric and provided a salacious, semi-voyeuristic quality intended to titillate and entertain a wider audience. As part of this process, the staple features of previous celebrated scandals were endlessly rehearsed and re-examined. In the first half of the century radicals made much play of the strong anti-Hanoverian images of the later eighteenth century, alluding in particular to the many clandestine affairs of George IV, his divorce from Queen Caroline in 1820 and the evil reputation of Victoria's uncle, the Duke of Cumberland, suspected of the murder of his footman.[13] During Victoria's reign, however, most radicals transferred their attention to the heir to the throne, Albert Edward, Prince of Wales ('Edward the Caresser', as he was dubbed by the popular press). His exploits resurrected strong memories of George IV's minority and enabled the many images of Regency dissoluteness to be re-cycled. In 1869–70 such sentiments crystallized around Edward's apparent involvement as co-respondent in the Mordaunt divorce case. Although the prince was exonerated of any direct involvement with Lady Mordaunt, the case spawned a considerable ballad literature that accused him of cuckolding other members of the aristocracy,[14] and prompted a searching examination of his lifestyle by the radical press. The former Chartist W. E. Adams (1832–1906) remarked in the *Newcastle Weekly Chronicle*:

It is morally impossible that men can lounge through a lifetime without experiencing a great deal of misery and perhaps receiving a great deal of injury. A life of idleness is of all lives the most wretched and the most worthless. Without duties to discharge, without occupations to engage the time and attention, the lounger necessarily seeks relief in a succession of excitements. And the excitements that are sometimes relished the most are not always the most innocent or the most intellectual.[15]

Dorothy Thompson has questioned the centrality of such highly personalized lampoons. She sees them as having little validity in their own right and as merely reflective of the strong contemporary note of satire in Victorian politics.[16] Yet among rank-and-file Chartists, they were commonly held ideas that served to mark out a populist radical terrain. In many senses opposition to monarchy was part of an inherited belief system that was passed down through the generations. In later life Andrew Carnegie, who came from a strongly radical/Chartist family in Dunfermline, recalled the republican sentiments uttered by both his father and uncle in 1842:

As a child I could have slain king, duke or lord, and considered their deaths a service to the state and hence an heroic act [...] All this was inherited of course. I only echoed what I heard at home [...] I developed into a violent young republican whose motto was 'death to privilege'. I did not know what privilege meant, but my father did.[17]

Thompson's disregard for the central place of such anti-monarchist ideas within Chartism and her reduction of their exponents to a 'tendency' relegates republicanism to the margins of the movement. In many ways, however, she wilfully ignores the relevance of such sentiments to the large stock of memories of the English Civil War that came to occupy such an important place within movements of radical protest during the nineteenth century.[18] Such reliance upon a *remembered* Interregnum provided a means whereby a critique of the throne might be introduced into the myth of a popular constitution. Celebrations of the Commonwealth, in the same way as other radical themes such as the 'Norman Yoke' and the experience of 1688, provided a collective memory of the past that established a historical context for events in the present (by demonstrating the viability of non-monarchical government), while at the same time satisfying the desire for continuity that inspired conceptions of a mythic constitution under Alfred or Canute. The presence of such memories as a staple of anti-monarchist rhetoric therefore serves to rescue republican sentiment from the fringes of radical culture, and places it instead in the mainstream of radical arguments about the British past.

Memories of the Interregnum were never the exclusive preserve of any one political grouping. They were especially dear to the Dissenting community. Cromwell occupied a special place in the traditions of the Unitarian Church for his part in saving their founder, Pastor John Biddle, from the gallows.[19] In the North-East the Independents kept memories of a benign Cromwell alive during the eighteenth and early nineteenth century, when his public reputation had sunk to a low ebb. W. T. Stead wrote in later life: 'Oliver Cromwell is the hero-saint of the denomination, which kept his memory green during the dismal years that passed before Thomas Carlyle arose to disinter the Lord Protector from the rubbish heap under which his memory has been buried.'[20]

Several sects also celebrated an annual 'Cromwell's Day' on 3 September, the date of his death and of his victories against the Scots at the Battle of Dunbar in 1650, and against the royalists at Worcester in 1651.[21] It was overwhelmingly this Nonconformist vision of the Civil War as primarily a struggle to liberate Dissent that Dissenting radicals like Joseph Arch (1826–1919) and John Bright (1811–1889) articulated when they exalted the role of Milton or of Coke and Pym.[22] Nonconformist versions of the Cromwellian myth were, however, reluctant to disrupt the smooth flow of monarchical continuity in British history. Historians of Nonconformity saw the Commonwealth as a check to unrestrained kingship that purified tyrannical impulses within the constitution and provided a retrospective reproach to the immoral Restoration court.[23] At the same time these images held a particular fascination and provided a unique moral example for radicals. Lecturing at Bristol in 1850 on the Civil War period, Henry Vincent remarked:

He had selected this splendid passage in the life of our country because he felt that it not only brought them into contact with virtue of the noblest kind, with intelligence of the most useful order, but also into close relationship with some of those great principles of liberty in which the people of this country so justly boasted, the supremacy of just laws over anarchy and despotism, of freedom from the prerogative of princes and – what was of greater importance to all who felt the truths of Christianity – of the non-right of human powers to inflict pain and penalties upon a man because of his religious belief and, by inference, the necessity of the entire disseverance of the secular and religious power.[24]

This radical version of Cromwell's career was more robust than Nonconformity's memory of him as a founder of organized Dissent. Henry Vincent's speeches contained the clear message that the most virtuous forms of government were to be found outside the rule of princes. It was for this reason that the Interregnum period occupied such a central place in English radical thought, providing both inspiration and political example to a later generation of reformers.[25]

The package of notions taken from the Commonwealth period placed the constitutional idiom at the heart of the debate on government and made heroes of those who opposed the excesses of autocratic monarchs. Hampden and Sydney became crucial figures, but its main icon was Cromwell. Alan Smith has pointed to the demonization of Oliver Cromwell in folk traditions from the seventeenth century onwards. This feeling, however, was never universal, and in many areas, especially the radical West Riding, a more positive image of him persisted. There, as in other localities, he assumed the status of a Golden Age monarch, who had presided over a period of unparalleled justice and prosperity.[26] The treatment of Cromwell's body after his death and his lack of a final resting place also injected a strong note of martyrdom into his life that was celebrated in songs and biographical sketches.[27] In the 1840s such notions drew upon renewed interest in the Interregnum period following the bicentennial of the Civil War, and grew out of Cromwell's own rehabilitation in Carlyle's 1845 collection of his letters, published in the anniversary year of the battle of Naseby.[28] Carlyle's image of a Tory Cromwell, whose government was characterized by the values of decisiveness and firm leadership, demonstrates that he also had a contemporary incarnation for Conservatives.[29]

Among radicals Cromwell was chiefly exalted as a 'plain man who unmade kings', for his opposition to excessive executive power and, above all, for his refusal to don the crown.[30] In accordance with its central position, Cromwellian references saturated nineteenth-century radical rhetoric. In visual terms, the prevailing image of Cromwell was of an essentially radical figure. Engravings based on Benjamin West's late eighteenth-century portrait of Cromwell dispersing the Long Parliament in 1653 were particular favourites. The message projected was of Cromwell as parliamentary reformer and opponent of corruption within the executive (illus. 15). Henry Vincent was perhaps the chief custodian of his memory among the Chartists. His lectures on his career in the 1850s were so vividly evocative of his life and times that J. B. Leno recalled, 'you could hear the sound of the great man's jack-boots.'[31] In later years Vincent, rather than Carlyle, was credited by the radical community with popularizing the memory of Oliver Cromwell as reformer rather than despot.[32] This 'radical' Cromwell also featured strongly in the work of the Chartist poets. In 1854 W. J. Linton appealed for the sight and spirit of Cromwell's sword arm once more to revive flagging radical ardours, while at a reception for John Frost in 1856, Ernest Jones, reciting from his own poetry, asked for 'one glorious day of Cromwell's time' as an antidote to aristocratic misrule in the present.[33] For most radicals the name Cromwell became short-hand for a robust anti-monarchism. Watching the queen's procession to the state opening of Parliament in 1839, the Chartist Peter Murray McDouall delighted in shouts of 'the curse of Cromwell on every mother's son of them' from the spectators.[34]

15 An engraving of Benjamin West's *Cromwell Dissolving the Parliament* shows Cromwell as a pure, incorruptible politician ridding the nation of the venal Rump of the Long Parliament in 1653.

Such images of the Commonwealth were not necessarily irreconcilable with the ideas of the 'Golden Age' constitutions under Anglo-Saxon monarchs that featured elsewhere in radical thought. Despite the presence of agendas for monarchical and non-monarchical forms of government in such rhetoric, the two viewpoints were compatible and interchangeable. A reliance upon memories of the Commonwealth merely demonstrates the elasticity of the language of popular constitutionalism itself, and suggests that such discourses need not always be interpreted in excessively loyalist or patriotic ways.[35] The fractured continuity of the replacement of a monarchy by a republic that itself made way for a restoration was barely noted by commentators such as Ernest Jones, who represented the Puritan revolution as part of the same trajectory towards a corrective to the excesses of an unchecked, centralized executive. In this sense, Jones saw the Chartists of the 1850s operating in a tradition that dated back to the peasant revolt of 1381. Their battle he saw as:

That struggle which the men of Kent, Lincoln and Essex began [...] which the Puritans of Cromwell brought nearer to its issue, which the revolution which seated Orange on the throne developed in its middle-class aspect, and which the Chartists of today, if true to their mission, are destined to complete.[36]

Other radicals who adopted a strongly anti-monarchist stance teased out an alternative interpretation of the Anglo-Saxon constitution that emphasized the elective nature of Anglo-Saxon kingship, and the significance of the *folk-moot* as an integral part of the compact between the monarch and his subjects.[37] A radical squib in the *Poor Man's Guardian* from 1832 illustrates the infinite malleability of the imagery of the 'ancient constitution' by making its contempt for monarchical forms vividly felt in the present, while showering praise upon 'Just Monarchs' in the past:

Let knaves and fools in raptures sing
   Till they are hoarse 'God save the king!'
I pray – may heaven in mercy keep all
   From kings and priests, God save the people,
I'm not an advocate for kings
   – such haughty, empty, useless things,
The greater number, strange to tell –
   Their characters are black as hell!
I find but two without a blot
   Great Alfred and brave Castriot
But William Guelph, Britons caress him
   He is the perfect king, God bless him!

Disloyal people tell us that
  He is a – hush, I'll say not what
My gentle muse with truth in view,
  Must give to royalty its due!

Yet the same poem says of the historical King Alfred:

Illustrious sovereign! In thy reign
  No abject poverty was seen
No sluggish priests who fleece the fold
  No bishops wallowing in gold
No evil from which luxury springs
  No panders to the lusts of kings.[38]

It is therefore possible to discern a far greater degree of anti-monarchist sentiment than hitherto acknowledged amongst radicals of the
pre-1860 period, and even to detect a republican tinge among those
reformers not commonly acknowledged as such. Popular Cromwellianism bound the English radical community together and consolidated
its links with the Old Testament Nonconformist tradition. These
rhetorical forms remained a constant, acting as a political background
noise that underlined other reform activity, and came to the fore strongly
during later agitation.

Anti-monarchism was still an undercurrent in the reform agitation
of 1866–7. Malicious 'To Let' notices appeared on the gates of
Buckingham Palace in 1864 in the wake of the reform sentiment generated by Gladstone's 'Pale of the Constitution' speech. By using the
royal statutes governing public recreation in Hyde Park to prohibit
popular demonstrations in 1866, the Home Office placed the throne in
collision with the reform community at the height of the agitation. In
1866 and 1867 there were major confrontations in Hyde Park between
rioters, who demanded that such open ground be turned over to the
people, and the authorities, who enforced prohibitions on the rights of
public meeting in the royal parks (illus. 16). Unease about the throne's
custodianship of the public lands assumed by the Crown after the
Norman Conquest became a major popular issue in the 1860s.[39] Even
Victoria noticed the lack of public warmth towards her as she drove
through London in those years.[40]

In keeping with the style of previous reform agitation, the Reform
League couched much of its rhetoric in the accepted radical form of
the constitutional idiom. In August 1866 the Reform League activist
W. G. D'Gruyther responded to Victoria's refusal to receive a League
deputation by reminding her in an open letter of the flight of James II
in 1688, and suggesting that her own refusal to see her subjects

16 Crowds breaking down the railings round Hyde Park to gain admission during the riots of July 1866.

amounted to a similar abrogation of authority.[41] At branch level, the Reform League also resuscitated memories and the nomenclature of the Interregnum period. Cromwell and Hampden featured in the names of local branch associations, and addresses on the theme of the Commonwealth became staples of the lecture-circuit repertory.[42] Moreover, in 1868 the Reform League executive confirmed its republican sympathy by issuing statements welcoming the rebellion against Queen Isabella in Spain and the subsequent declaration of a republic.[43] Nevertheless, anti-monarchism did not achieve the status of a platform agitation in its own right until the 1870s, when radicals and reformers sought a new direction following the passage of the 1867 Reform Act. By this stage the main radical grievances concerning the franchise had been satisfied, leaving only the hitherto submerged discontent with monarchical power as the basis for a popular agitation.

The campaign against the queen of 1870–72 not only demonstrates the degree of support anti-monarchism could command at the height of its power, but also provides a useful indicator of the relative strengths of my own model of a non-Paineite *populist* republican form and Paineism proper. Throughout the campaign, its leaders described themselves as 'republicans'. Despite their frequent use of the term, however, they never put forward an effective model for a non-monarchical constitution, and their concerns were overwhelmingly those of an older generation of anti-monarchists.

The reasons for the emergence of a popular current of opposition to the throne in the 1870s are well known. Queen Victoria's withdrawal from public life and, in a marked break with parliamentary precedent, the government's application for donations from the Civil List to support the royal children and Princess Louise's new husband, the Marquis of Lorne, prompted a major debate about the nature of the state's financial commitments to the upkeep of royalty. During this period it was widely believed that Victoria added the money saved on public ceremonials to her personal wealth.[44] Even during her increasingly rare appearances on state occasions the suspicion remained that she was more interested in steering royal dowries for her children through parliament than fulfilling her public duties.[45]

Opponents of monarchy articulated the strong sense of public grievance against a wealthy and indolent royal family by emphasizing the comparisons between royalty and the beggars common in Britain's towns and cities. Cartoons in George Standring's *Republican* newspaper contained the clear inference that demands for royal dowries and other state handouts were fraudulent given the excessive wealth of the queen. In his cartoon 'Raising the Wind', which anticipated public disapproval of the expenses surrounding the marriage of Victoria's son Leopold, Duke of Albany, to Princess Helen of Waldeck in 1882, the royal couple are depicted as sham beggars, counterfeiting a state of poverty to defraud money from John Bull with the secret connivance of the head of the royal house (illus. 17).

The campaign against the Crown over public finances in 1870–71 precipitated a stronger popular response than any previous anti-royal agitation. Contemporaries compared it to the later Tichborne movement for the strength of public feeling it evoked.[46] It was certainly the largest popular campaign of the 1870s prior to the emergence of the Tichborne agitation, which by focusing attention on the claims of a pretender to the estates and title of the Tichborne family similarly highlighted issues of corruption within the state. It was also the first cause since the 1866–7 reform agitation to unite reformers in the metropolis with their counterparts in the provinces.

Significantly the geography of the campaign closely adhered to older areas of radical strength.[47] There were republican conferences in Newcastle, Sheffield and Birmingham, the first regional radical

Royalty " Raising the Wind."

17 The republican George Standring's attack on 'Guelphic gold-hunger' at the time of the
marriage of the Duke of Albany and Princess Helen of Waldeck.

assemblies held there since the 1840s, and active republican cells were
also established in Leicester and Nottingham. This strong organization
in the East and West Midlands was almost certainly connected with the
prominent part played by two Midlands MPs, Peter Alfred Taylor and
Auberon Herbert, in the republican campaign in Parliament.[48] In the
North-West, Bolton became the organizational focal point of the region
after the establishment of a republican club boasting three hundred
members in 1871. The trade unionist George Howell (1833–1910) also
noted the presence of republican clubs in Peterborough, Portsmouth,
Norwich, Cambridge and Exeter.[49] In addition, there was a strong
republican constituency in the North-East with clubs formed in
Newcastle, Bedlington and Sunderland.[50] In London republicans

mounted major demonstrations in all the capital's public spaces, particularly Hyde Park and Trafalgar Square, where they reasserted the right of metropolitan reformers to gather in open spaces that had been established by the reform campaign of 1866–7.[51]

The republican movement highlighted existing political divisions at the local level and proved so divisive that it provoked counterblasts which turned its meetings into battlegrounds. With the collusion of the local authorities, there was sustained disruption at Dilke's constituency meeting in Chelsea and at his addresses in Leeds and Derby. Moreover, George Odger (1813–77) was seriously injured by loyalists in an ambush at Reading railway station, while at Bolton a republican was killed by a Tory mob during a visit by Dilke to the town.[52] This event prompted stronger government interest in the movement than had been expressed in any agitation for reform since the Hyde Park riots of 1866.

This *popular* anti-monarchist belief was characterized by a hard acerbic edge that set it entirely apart from the well-reasoned prose of advocates of non-monarchical constitutions such as Thomas Paine. Disrespectful and insulting, it gloated over royal tragedies and the personal misfortunes of Britain's rulers. In this sense it conveyed a reactive, visceral opposition to the institution of monarchy. This spirit is captured by the tone of a debate at the Hole-in-the-Wall radical club, Clerkenwell Green, during the illness of the Prince of Wales, at which one veteran radical remarked: 'If it pleased the Lord to take him away from an earthly crown and give him a crown of glory, then it was one of those inscrutable decrees of providence at which we ought not to repine.'[53] It features again in the comments shouted from the audience when Sir Charles Dilke talked of his plans for trimming down court officials, including the royal undertaker, that on the contrary 'there should be more work for him'.[54] It remained a sentiment frequently expressed through the practice of disrespectful toastings, a phenomenon James Epstein has highlighted for the earlier period, but which persisted into the 1850s and beyond.[55] In the winter of 1871–2 there was a marked lack of respect among radicals for the Prince of Wales during a near fatal illness that transformed the monarchy's position in public esteem and created a sentimental drama surrounding his apparently impending death (illus. 18).

Like the commentators writing of the radicals of the 1790s, contemporaries were only too eager to ascribe this surge of anti-royal feeling to the direct importation of foreign and ultimately 'un-English' ideas and models of government into an inappropriate setting. The campaign was represented in the press as wholly derivative and slavishly Francophile.

18 The extravagant displays of public devotion during the prince's illness were epitomized by the Poet Laureate Arthur Austin: 'Over the wires the electric message came / He is no better, he is much the same.'

The *Saturday Review* wrote: 'The Commune only represents in a more practical form the doctrines of the Land and Labour League, the International Association and the other Jacobin Clubs of London.'[56] In contemporary satire the suggestion was made throughout the period that British republicans were simply mimicking events in France. Loyalist cartoonists feigned indifference to events on the Continent, while again hinting that radicals were impersonating their French counterparts. In a *Punch* cartoon by John Tenniel, Britannia admonishes a foolish and repentant-looking George Odger for his desire to emulate the French republican model, highlighted by a scene of disorder and revolt glimpsed in the background (illus. 19).

This sense of the republicanism of the 1870s as purely an imitative offshoot of events abroad has pervaded recent historical accounts of the events of these years and served to minimize, or even deny, those elements that placed it within the radical constitutional mainstream.[57] In reality, the campaign against the Crown was profoundly English in its reworking of the constitutional idiom, and in the uses it made of the images of 'Old Corruption'. As in the radical movement of the 1790s, the key text of the agitation was never solely Paine. Rather its

A FRENCH LESSON.

BRITANNIA. "IS *THAT* THE SORT OF THING YOU WANT, YOU LITTLE IDIOT?"

19 George Odger (distinguished by his shoemaker's hammer) takes 'A French Lesson' in politics and foreign policy from an irate Britannia: 'Is *that* the sort of thing you want, you little idiot?'

preoccupations serve to locate it more properly in the tradition of Edmund Burke's 1780 speech on 'economical' reform, which provided the inspiration and framework for Sir Charles Dilke's 'Cost of the Crown' speech in Newcastle in October 1871, and featured in his address in Leeds a few weeks later.[58] By choosing Burke's line of attack on executive power, it raised questions of excessive royal interference, the use of money to influence the complexion of government through placemen, and concentrated attention upon the unjustifiable state expenditure on the ornamental and excessive outward trappings of monarchy itself.

In its origins this was a debate purely about finance, but it rapidly assumed the proportions of a broader attack upon the power, privilege and prerogative of the queen herself. In many ways it bears the hall-marks of previous attacks upon the expense of monarchy at the time of the coronation of William IV and of Victoria's marriage to Prince Albert in 1840.[59]

As in these previous campaigns, the emphasis placed by reformers upon the Germanic origins of the House of Hanover allowed them to connect strongly with broader currents within English popular culture. Xenophobia has an established pedigree within the English radical tradition, and stigmatizing monarchs by association with 'alienness' was a long-standing populist tactic of all the major post–Napoleonic War movements of political protest. In this instance it also enabled opponents of monarchy to exonerate themselves from the charge that they harboured unpatriotic aims. In the 1870s such attitudes drew strongly upon the images and language employed by previous reform movements. In the 1830s William IV had been dubbed 'Mr Guelph' by the *Poor Man's Guardian*, and particular venom was reserved for his German-born wife, Queen Adelaide, who was booed at public meetings during the reform crisis.[60] In practice most of these chauvinistic assaults upon royalty tended to concentrate upon the German antecedents of the royal line. Even the Prince Consort was not immune to criticism on these grounds. In the *People's Paper* in the 1850s Ernest Jones, who was himself German by birth, strongly attacked the Coburgs for buying 'English land with English money', following Albert's purchase of the Osborne estate on the Isle of Wight.[61] By establishing the link in the popular mind between Prussianness, which carried strong undertones of continental despotism, and the marked German anti-liberal tradition, reformers were also able to damn the British monarchy by association. Such attitudes surfaced strongly during the 1866–7 reform crisis that acted as a bridge into the republican campaign of the 1870s. At a meeting in Trafalgar Square in June

1866, Osborne of the Clerkenwell branch of the Reform League vigorously attacked the Queen's new son-in-law, the Crown Prince Frederick William, husband of the Princess Royal, for his decision to take up a commission in the Prussian army in the impending war against Austria. In his remarks, and in Benjamin Lucraft's responses to them, radical rhetoric blended the themes of opposition to continental despotism, the Civil List pensions issue and memories of the Interregnum:

And as a sign of the times, let it be borne in mind that a certain Prince recently married to an English royal princess was according to the evening papers going this week to fight in the cause of despotism [groans]. That was one way of rewarding Englishmen for the willingness with which they saw a Royal Dower given, which was wrung out of the sweat of their brow.

The chairman, Lucraft, added: 'My friends, Charles the First was executed at Whitehall gardens. On Monday next we hold a meeting there. [tremendous and prolonged cheering].'[62]

In the 1870s Charles Bradlaugh, who was the republican leader most strongly influenced by the Paineite inheritance, omitted almost all references to Paine in his pamphlets and, embracing the mainstream radical tradition, concentrated his fire on the Germanic connections of the British throne. The very title of his pamphlet 'The Impeachment of the House of Brunswick' resonates with patriotic hostility to the alien bloodline of the royal house. As with William IV's wife, the widely disliked Queen Adelaide, royal trips to Germany to visit relatives in the 1870s continued to provoke outbursts of anti-German feeling reflected in Bradlaugh's comments on Victoria in his pamphlet:

When her Majesty travels in England great precautions are taken to prevent her from coming into contact with the common people who are her loyal and devoted subjects. When her Majesty is abroad, the natives of foreign parts being much superior to the ordinary type of Briton, are allowed greater indulgence. In England railway stations are cleared, piers and docks are carefully purged of the presence of the vulgar British subject. In Germany her Majesty is amongst those she loves, and there the same rigid exclusiveness is not maintained.[63]

Public sympathy for the infant French Republic during the Franco-Prussian War converted this anti-Prussian sentiment into a popular cause, and precipitated a wave of hostility towards the openly pro-Prussian faction at court, including the queen, that fed into, and in turn reinforced, the republican campaign.

In common with the radical movements of the earlier part of the century, the republican platform of the 1870s also held a strong appeal for a female audience. Recently Anna Clark has drawn attention to the language of domesticity used by Chartist orators in the 1840s to provide a point of contact within the movement for the National Charter Association's female following.[64] As Clark points out, such references were really about existing structures of sexuality and power that remained unchallenged by the movement, but metaphors of the hearth, the home and the domestic environment more generally served to augment the main Chartist message and made complicated political ideas explicable in purely household terms. A similar element is discernible in the republican campaign of the 1870s. *Reynolds's Newspaper* and the figureheads of the movement placed the marriage of Victoria's daughter, Princess Louise, to the Marquis of Lorne in 1871 at the heart of the debate on the monarchy. Her application for a Civil List donation for her husband and the government's decision to meet the cost of her dowry from the public purse spawned a wave of popular slogans, scurrilous songs and disrespectful alphabets on the Regency model. Thomas Wright recalled:

'The rattle of the royal begging boxes'; 'outdoor relief'; 'able-bodied paupers'; 'royal leeches'; 'royal spongers'; were the mildest terms of contempt employed in speaking of the subject. It became a stock workshop joke to speak of setting up the Marquis of Lorne as a greengrocer, or teaching him this or that handicraft to enable him to earn an honest living for himself and wife without coming upon the public.[65]

This image of the aristocratic Marquis of Lorne and his household provides a striking example of such domestic comparisons. By highlighting the Duke's lack of practical skills, and making the ironic comparison between the everyday privations of many poorer families and his own exalted status, it injected a note of outrage into the agitation inspired by the plight of poor working-class women living under the threat of the Poor Law. It also compromised his manhood by challenging his ability to provide for his family.

The *Newcastle Weekly Chronicle* detected in these issues a strong overlap with the contemporaneous agitation for a bill legalizing marriage between sisters-in-law and the husbands of deceased spouses.[66] This latter legislation was rejected by the House of Lords in the same sitting in which it approved a Civil List pension for Lorne, causing the *Chronicle* to remark:

Thus the Peers in a double sense insult the people. First by refusing their consent to a measure that is loudly called for, not only to make hundreds of homes happy by legalising morally lawful unions, and also to legitimize and make heirs-at-law thousands of children actually born in wedlock [...] Secondly by agreeing with an unseemly and defiant haste to an unnecessary increase of the public burdens.[67]

Such stark representations of the everyday inequalities afflicting women in Victorian society enabled republican agitators, like previous generations of reformers, to address the concerns of a female audience. Most republican associations accordingly had a mixed membership, although women were still often relegated to the support capacity of providing refreshments and stitching banners common in the political culture of the day.[68]

That such attitudes were in fact part of the radical constitutionalist mainstream is made apparent by the almost wholesale transfer of both branch associations and personnel from the earlier Reform League into the republican movement. The most fertile ground for the emergence of the new movement was thus in London's radical club circles, which had provided the bedrock for popular reform agitation since the 1820s and before. Charles Bradlaugh presided at the formal inauguration of the London Republican Club at the secularist Hall of Science, Old Street, in March 1871.[69] The hall was a long-standing radical meeting place and became the headquarters for all republican operations in the capital at the start of the campaign. Republican branches were never, however, simply updated secularist associations. Both the Eleusis Club in Chelsea and the Patriotic Club, Clerkenwell Green, which comprised survivors of the Reform League, also made the transition from League to republican branches during this period.[70]

In practice most branches of the kindred Land and Labour League were also interchangeable with republican organizations, and the Mile End branch, the Sir Robert Peel branch and the Hackney Road branch were all re-activated as republican associations.[71] This pattern was repeated in the provinces, and in Bolton the former secretary of the local Reform League, John Bramwell, occupied the same post for the republican club, which was based in the old Reform League premises at the Temperance Hall.[72] As in London, most of these regional clubs had little or no connection with secularism. In Wales and the North-East, for example, where secularism traditionally had few adherents, there was no significant freethought aspect to them. The Teeside Republican Club was political rather than secularist in origin and absorbed many Reform Leaguers.[73] Republicanism's role as the successor to the parliamentary reform cause meant that its style was conditioned by the cultural milieu in which a previous generation of radicals had operated. In many ways its success lay in its ability to breathe new life into this political culture. As with its predecessors, the club lay at the heart of the British republican experience. Like the Chartist and Reform League clubs, republican groups sought to erect a total radical environment that placed them outside Liberalism and perpetuated older radical styles and forms. The Birmingham republican and former Chartist C. C. Cattell wrote to the *Republican Chronicle* on this theme:

Republican should be the name to cover the whole ground of political and social reform. Public or concerted action no doubt would be somewhat limited at first because a majority must be obtained to assist any great principle effectively. But this would be more easily arrived at by people meeting each other and discussing things desirable and practicable. These clubs would then become National Schools and a power in stimulating the governing bodies of the country. Nothing is of more importance in a free country, than an intelligent public opinion outside the elected administrative powers. This is the safeguard of personal liberty and free institutions. If such institutions as these were established, the election of such persons as are now in our municipal and parliamentary councils would be impossible.[74]

Given the paucity of information relating to these clubs and the generally hostile environment in which they operated, it is difficult to chart the course of individual organizations. Nevertheless, it seems clear that they were intended to fulfil a basically convivial, yet at the same time educational role. The London Republican Club amassed a library of books and materials relating to past republican movements.[75] The Mile End branch enjoyed excursions to Rye House, Hertfordshire.[76] There were lectures on improving topics, such as land reform or aspects of the history of the British Commonwealth, and songs were composed and performed to honour particular leaders. There was no surly Cromwellian spirit prevailing in the clubs, rather the accent was on fun. The Reform League veteran Robert Coningsby commented on this frivolous aspect in a description of the Hole-in-the-Wall pub, headquarters for the Patriotic Club, Clerkenwell Green. He noted 'a funny plaster-of-Paris image of Garibaldi, which had been decorated with a sash of red ribbon by one artist and a cleverly executed black eye by another, possibly a rival'.[77]

A marked feature of these clubs was the use of republican paraphernalia and even separate styles of dress to create a distinct identity.[78] Meeting places were decorated with tricolours; members wore sashes and tricolour rosettes; a white, green and blue banner based upon W. J. Linton's designs for a republican flag was produced and used at republican conferences, while the 'Marseillaise' became the most popular song in the republican repertoire.[79] These outward trappings were more than just displays of arrant Francophilia and were intended to create the basis for a counter-culture that would make republicans recognizable to each other, as well as in society at large. Thomas Wright wrote of: 'The stagy, fanraronnading republicans who hoist red flags,

CHECK TO KING MOB.

20 *Punch* celebrating the crowd violence associated with the Reform League after the passing of the 1867 Reform Act.

address each other as "citizen" and indulge in high-sounding revolutionary talk'.[80] In many ways there are parallels with the Spenceans who also adopted different styles of dress and even speech to emphasize their 'apartness'. Such images of a republican style of dress were central to contemporary illustrations of radical activity. In 1867 a generic depiction of the Reform League in *Punch* showed the organization as a dangerous Jacobin dressed as a French *sansculottes*, with a republican sash and crowned with a mock coronet bearing the title 'King Mob' (illus. 20).

As with previous movements of reform, republicanism during the 1870s also sought to cement an alternative centre of loyalty through the creation of martyr figures who reflected the twin themes of dedication and self-sacrifice in the service of the cause. Attempts to turn the victim killed by a royalist mob during Dilke's visit to Bolton into a martyr were reminiscent of previous martyrdoms of the radical dead during the post-Napoleonic War reform movement and Chartism. William Scofield, a Bolton man with no previous history of attachment to radical causes, was, on the slenderest of evidence, elevated to the pantheon of those who had given their lives for reform. This process bears many of the characteristics of the martyrdom of Robert Lees, who died from wounds received at Peterloo, and of Samuel Holberry, the Sheffield Chartist who died in gaol in 1842. Like Lees and Holberry, Scofield was given a public funeral that attracted 5,000 participants and spectators, received radical accolades to his dedication and commitment, and was commemorated annually at a public soirée.[81] George Odger saw his death as linked to the same spirit that had inspired the mob attacks made on Joseph Priestly in 1792, but also drew the wider message from his life that:

Once more the old spirit of persecution has raized its hideous head and in so called free England men's lives are endangered by the expression of an honest conviction in favour of republicanism. In Bolton a victim has already fallen to this accursed spirit; at Reading I myself, by an almost imperceptible margin, escaped death from the hands of an infuriated host of savages, while Sir Charles Dilke has been subjected to no end of dangers.[82]

Allegations of partiality on the part of the coroner, and the subsequent acquittal of eight accused members of the mob, lent weight to Odger's remarks, and ensured that the affair attracted considerable press attention.[83]

Other features of an older radical culture also lingered in republicanism. The custom of naming children after prominent radical heroes was still strongly observed. In this case the anti-monarchist campaign of the 1870s threw up its own new generation of heroes that could be employed expressly for this purpose. The Bradlaughite coal merchant, William Chenery, for example, named his son Taylor Dilke Fawcett Chenery after the three middle-class radicals who voted for an inquiry into the Civil List in 1872. Subsequently he emblazoned the names on his coal-trucks and they became a well-known local landmark in the area of the Elephant and Castle in London.[84] In addition,

74

establishing republican pedigrees through genealogical research was an important part of reclaiming English history itself. The middle-class Leicester republican Peter Alfred Taylor was lauded for his descent from a republican haberdasher who was a Commonwealthman and a friend of the regicides.[85] At their margins such historical read-ings shaded into psuedo-sciences like phrenology that were characteristic of Victorian counter-cultural forms. To some republi-canism appeared as an inherited predisposition. Meeting Joseph Cowen Jr for the first time, the radical republican J. Morrison Davidson was struck by the fact that 'his features bore no trace what-ever of having been imported "at the Conquest"'.[86] Likewise he wrote of Sir Charles Dilke: '"That which is bred in the bone" says the proverb "will come out in the flesh". The anti-monarchical sympathies of the Dilkes, like those of the Taylors, are at least as much inherited as acquired. No fewer than three of the Dilke ancestry were among the judges of Charles I.' [87]

The radical cult of leadership was similarly well represented within the campaign against the throne. James Epstein has noted the impor-tance of the demagogic style of popular agitation in shaping the structure of British radicalism in the period between 1815 and 1848.[88] Central to this process, he argues, was the role of 'gentlemen leaders', men of a privileged position in life who forsook their natural alle-giances, posed as the representatives of the poor and dispossessed, and showed themselves prepared to sacrifice family, friends and influence as the price of their radical commitment. More recently historians have extended the significance of the gentleman leader into the post-Chartist period. They see the concept as influential in shaping the appeal of both John Bright and H. M. Hyndman, the two great plat-form orators of the post-1867 years.[89] Republicanism threw up a new generation of radical leaders cast in this mould, among them the charismatic John de Morgan, who fused the twin themes of republi-canism and defence of the open spaces to form the basis for a broad radical populism. In particular de Morgan's opposition to enclosure, his personal interventions in defence of threatened moorland and his willingness to break the law on behalf of the cause of public access echoed similar events in Oliver Cromwell's career and, appropriately for a republican agitation, allowed his followers to emphasize this connection.[90]

Nevertheless, the leader who most strongly captured the spirit of an earlier generation of radical leaders was the titular head of the move-ment, Sir Charles Dilke (1843–1911). A baronet, landowner and Cambridge-educated lawyer, Dilke's was the distillation of all previous radical leadership styles. In the 1860s he developed the first tentative contacts with the plebeian reform movement, and by 1868 was working actively with radical clubs in Chelsea to create a popular constituency organization that secured his successful return for the borough in 1874. He was a fine orator, a much-respected parliamentarian and a stern critic of unfair government who showed considerable courage in bringing the issue of the monarchy before the public.[91] On a number of occasions he risked serious injury at stormy meetings, but impressed his supporters by his nonchalant disregard for his own safety and his coolness under fire. At the Bolton meeting he refused to seek cover from missiles, or wear a hat to protect him from head injuries.[92]

Contemporaries also made much of his dedication, and portrayed him in true gentleman-leader fashion as both martyr and saint, unjustifiably reviled by an ungrateful press who ignored his work on behalf of the people. George Odger remarked on this theme at Bolton:

An attempt had been made in the press to create a feeling in the minds of the working-classes that would mitigate against one of the most able men in the country, who had travelled wide and gained experience of no ordinary kind. While other men were idle he was searching out information for the people of this country and every other country, and yet the man who had had the moral courage to do what he had done, had been calumniated and maligned. He did not attack the queen, but those who spent the money, and Sir Charles Dilke deserved the sympathy of every honest man in the world.[93]

In the event Dilke's contact with the republicans was short-lived, but in later years he remained a popular figure within the broader context of radicalism.

Republicanism's greatest contribution to nineteenth-century radicalism was, however, the degree to which it helped define a sphere of operations independent of, and outside, mainstream Liberalism. At a time when the forces of ultra-radicalism were contracting or becoming absorbed by the Liberal Party, it helped provide a focus for those unrepentant radical activists who remained stubbornly outside the Gladstonian consensus. During the 1870s republicanism and Liberalism were irreconcilably opposed. This rift was emphasized by the degree to which Liberalism had shed the strong association with republicanism and other Commonwealth values that had characterized eighteenth-century Whiggery.[94] As a consequence, under Gladstone's ministries the Liberal assault upon privilege stopped far short of outright abolition of monarchy and the hereditary principle. The dismay at royal interference expressed by Liberals as different in outlook as Palmerston and John Morley derived only from the frustrations of working with the cantankerous Victoria, and implied no broader programme of reforms in this direction.[95] Even Joseph Chamberlain, who did briefly advocate this course in the 1870s, sought to distance himself from such notions in later life, and by the 1890s, in his new Tory incarnation, had become one of the chief advocates of an imperial-style monarchy. Plebeian republicanism therefore acted as a conduit for the expression of disillusionment with Liberalism on the issues of the hereditary principle, inherited monarchy and aristocratic misgovernment. It gained its strongest support during the trough of the unpopularity of the Liberal government of 1868–74, and made particular targets of the great doyens of Liberalism, Gladstone and John Bright.

Its vehemence in targeting these former working-class icons of the 1866–7 reform campaign reflected a much broader groundswell of radical disapproval of the Liberal Party on trade union and social reform issues, which has conventionally been seen as transferring working-class radical support to Toryism, rather than channelling it back in the direction of an independent radical position. The person of Gladstone bore the brunt of these attacks. He was especially loathed for the part he played in drawing up the special bill, which he personally steered through the House, that allowed the Marquis of Lorne and the royal children to receive donations from the Civil List in 1871–2. In addition, he was strongly attacked for his role in devising the special service of thanksgiving to celebrate the recovery of the Prince of Wales from typhoid in 1872 that did much to restore the popularity of the Royal House.[96] Fierce criticism was also, however, levelled at John Bright and reflected a wider sense of disillusionment with middle-class radical politics following his transfer from the role of critic to that of pillar of the establishment. Radicals bemoaned his failure to satisfy the working-class expectations he had aroused in 1866–7 in his new position as President of the Board of Trade, or indeed to seek to ameliorate the lot of his former supporters in any way. In 1872 John de Morgan declared of him at a meeting at Middlesbrough: 'John Bright has turned flunkey and does not speak out for the people.'[97] Bright's own strongly affirmed support for the queen and his refusal to consider approaches from republicans to put his name forward for the presidency of the first British Republic[98] reinforced these radical doubts about him, and prompted particularly vicious criticism of his failure to oppose a special parliamentary grant awarded to the Prince of Wales to enable him to tour India in 1875. Scurrilous verses appeared in the radical press condemning Bright for his association with this measure:

His Royal Highness, Prince of Wales,
   To India would go,
To gratify some dream of life
   He held since long ago.
John Bright was by to sanction
   And support the royal grant,
Though many thousand people,
   Pine in poverty and want. [99]

The mid-1870s therefore marked the final fragmentation of the links between Bright and the broader working-class radical constituency that had formed the bedrock of his support in 1866–7.

The single most enduring legacy of the campaign against the throne of the 1870s was this association between republican ideas and a theatre of operations that was both independent of, and outside Liberalism. In later years British republicans continued to organize apart from the Liberal Party, and the anti-monarchist stance itself came to denote a stubborn refusal to compromise with the consensus of the existing party system. A thin republican strand therefore links together those movements which sought their rationale in opposition to the forces of Liberalism, and emerged particularly strongly in groups which worked towards independent working-class political representation. Republican sentiments were strongly represented within the Tichborne movement, which was the only mass working-class agitation to mobilize apart from, and in some senses in opposition to, Liberalism during the period of the late 1870s and early 1880s. For its leader, Edward Kenealy, Victoria's court was a thinly disguised Jesuit conspiracy presided over by the arch-Papist John Brown, which sought to deprive the Claimant and his honest Protestant champions of the natural rights of justice.[100] Pro-Claimant sentiment therefore fused ultra-Protestantism with established images of 'Old Corruption'. At the end of the century republicanism still routinely resurfaced in *Reynolds's Newspaper* and the new labour periodicals.[101]

In the nineteenth century British anti-monarchism offered a populist assessment of the evils of monarchy and of royal government in keeping with the British radical tradition of popular constitutionalism and the nature of British radicalism itself. It differs strongly, for example, from the contemporary French model. The British anti-monarchist tradition had its own lineage, its own martyrs and was strongly represented within the mainstream radical movement. It was certainly never simply Paine, although Paineism and 'everyday republicanism' have been confused. This confusion has misled scholars and allowed republicanism to be discounted as an effective force within radicalism itself. In the 1870s, however, it was able to organize a highly effective, popular campaign that drew attention to many of the weaknesses of the throne under Victoria. Subsequently it came to occupy a permanent place within the radical traditions of Labourism and helped in turn define a broader radical stance outside Liberalism.

3 'What Does She Do With It?': Radicalism, Republicanism and the 'Unrespectable' 1870–80

> These extensive premises to be let or sold, the late occupant having retired from business.
>
> (Handbill affixed to the gates of Buckingham Palace, 1864)

In late 1871 the slogan 'What Does She Do With It?' appeared chalked on walls in the East End of London. The phrase carries a unique resonance and is strongly associated with the 'republican' agitation of the autumn of that year. 'What Does She Do With It?' is the title of G. O. Trevelyan's anonymous pamphlet discussing tax and the expense of monarchy during the period of Queen Victoria's seclusion. At a popular level the phrase became transmuted;[1] in 1871 it became the cipher for a more broadly based populist discontent with monarchy and epitomized a new mood of popular disloyalty. Originally the product of the pen of a sedate civil servant, to a more popular audience the term implied the thrill of sexual immorality (or the absence of sexual fulfilment) and carried resonances from the world of low Victorian fiction and pornography.

It is now conjectured that stories of Queen Victoria's relationship with John Brown originated in obscene Parisian jokes that found their way to Britain in imported French pornography.[2] When released into the public domain the comment 'What does she do with it?' became not just a remark on royal finances but functioned as a *double-entendre* at a time when Victoria's affair with John Brown was well known and his name was frequently shouted from the crowd during Victoria's rare public appearances. Above all, the phrase captures the rambunctious populism of the campaign against the throne during this period and the salacious undertones that accompanied it. Wall-chalkings, Regency-style innuendoes, and satirical handbills suggestive of an older current of discontent with the monarchy were all very visible in this agitation, affirming the survival of a style of politics that is difficult to reconcile with the respectable face of a restrained popular Liberalism at the height of the Liberal meridian.[3]

The republicanism of the 1870s is familiar to most historians. It is most frequently discussed in descriptions of the 'republican riots' of November and December 1871. Older accounts often cite them, not to indicate a level of dissatisfaction with the crown, but rather to show the strength of a naïve monarchist Toryism fuelled by the politics of 'Beer and Britannia' that proved highly effective in disrupting the republican platform.[4] The image emerges here of an agitation that was unable to stand on its own terms and provided fodder for the shock troops of a robust Toryism. Most historians overlook the fact that the vast majority of republican meetings on Tyneside, Teeside and elsewhere passed off relatively peacefully. Nevertheless, Dorothy Thompson has quoted this 'republican moment' to show the weakness of a republican alternative in British radical culture, and the almost total absence of a real project for a non-monarchical constitution.[5] Other Historians such as David Cannadine and Linda Colley, whose preoccupation with royal ritual reflects their personal provenance in the 'New Elizabethan' age, have ignored the voices of the opponents of monarchy altogether.[6] The dismissive term 'crude republicanism' is sometimes used to describe the politics they articulated. It seems that while 'crude monarchism' is worthy of study, 'crude republicanism' is not. The 1870s provides the strongest evidence to date that the fortunes of the British monarchy have fluctuated markedly during the course of recent centuries. It was the campaign against the Crown of the 1870s that the Liberal MP and historian Justin McCarthy had in mind when he wrote that 'a more or less quiet level of republicanism is always afloat on the surface of English radicalism'.[7]

The greatest problems relating to English republicanism in the 1870s are questions of definition. It is far easier to dismiss this movement if it can be seen as nothing more than a straw man, or as a pale reflection of some other 'ideal type' of republicanism, like the French or Swiss models that Victorian historians such as E. A. Freeman frequently cited.[8] To describe it as a sect-like legacy of Bradlaughite secularism is to associate republicanism even more closely with 'marginality'. Traditionally, it has been caught in the slip-stream of the socialist revival. In some cases the activities of the Republican Land and Labour League are seen as an unsatisfactory interlude before the emergence of a recognizable Labourism and socialism in the 1880s. Royden Harrison has portrayed the former organization as severely wanting in comparison to the vibrancy of the later, overtly socialist, SDF.[9] This diminishes the relevance of 'republicanism' still further. Moreover, the waters are muddied by the fact that some republicans themselves despised this agitation, condemning it as insufficiently 'republican'. Mazzinian republicans like W. E. Adams who articulated a vigorous social reform programme embraced it at the time, but condemned it in later life. In his memoirs he wrote: 'What would be the value of a revolution that had for its root the accidental unpopularity of a Prince of the Blood?'[10] For Adams the republican agitation of 1871 was an ultimately sterile debate that raised no real issues of structural reform and led British constitutional reformers down a blind alley.

These conflicting readings leave questions unanswered about the relevance of the events of 1870–72 to the history of British republican thought and the problems it experienced in creating an agitation. The word 'republicanism' can be counterbalanced by the concept of anti-monarchism. At the heart of the nineteenth-century debate about royalty there stubbornly persisted the nexus of monarchy, aristocracy and their role in unreformed 'Old Corruption'.[11] The moral failings of the reigning monarch and heir to the throne, the royal fortune and the refusal of the queen to carry out her public functions stoked public disillusionment with monarchy still further. These issues must be taken on their own terms. It is possible to argue that the monarchy was becoming more exposed on the issue of public money and its deployment at a time when Gladstonian state reformism was stripping away and reforming layers of expensive bureaucracy within the civil service.[12] This left the monarchy vulnerable as the only high-spending element within the executive that was not subject to regular parliamentary and public scrutiny. Unlike other government bodies, monarchy was not perceived to be called to account either by government, public or press.

Throughout the nineteenth century it proved easier to mobilize opposition to the monarchy over the absence of the queen and royal authority than to do so around a platform of modifying, or even removing, its powers altogether. The satirical magazine *Tomahawk* captured the public mood in 1866 in a powerful appeal to Victoria to resume her public duties. Using the image of a vacant royal palace whose occupant had 'retired from business', it speculated about the condition of the royal residences of the future in the absence of a monarchical head of state. The dilapidated, overgrown Buckingham Palace overrun by rats and inhabited only by a stylized image of death symbolized the collapse of royal authority and the decay of the dignified element in the constitution (illus. 21). This suggests a submerged residue of pro-monarchist sentiment and a constituency of disillusioned royal supporters who were unlikely to desert the throne altogether.

For the regional press, both Liberal and Tory, it was often the Prince of Wales, rather than the monarchy proper, that was the real target.[13]

"UNDER ROYAL PATRONAGE."

21 The collapse of royal authority as imagined by *Tomahawk*. This public rebuke to Victoria was meant to advise her to resume her public duties.

Such responses were more than just the discontent of 'court milliners' and 'West End tradesmen', who saw their profit margins cut during the absence of the royal household from the London season, as intimated in the mainstream press. Liberal newspapers who represented contemporary opposition to the throne in these terms sought to minimize the degree of public hostility to Victoria and the extent of the problem.[14]

Even at their most basic, instincts of opposition to royal authority carried a real power. In 1864, for example, there were acrimonious meetings in the East End of London when the queen ignored appeals for clemency in the case of Samuel Wright. Wright, who was denied proper legal representation, killed his wife in a clear case of self-defence after she had attacked him with a knife. The case became a contemporary *cause célèbre* that channelled hostility to the police and inspired an angry campaign against the death penalty and public executions.[15] The verdict of death by hanging passed on the unfortunate Wright coincided with the birth of a male heir to the Prince and Princess of Wales, consolidating the royal succession. In the early modern period the reigning monarch had routinely marked the occasion of the birth of a royal heir, victories in battle or a coronation by exercising clemency for selected capital offences. Victoria and Albert's conscious crypto-medievalism at court and in the depictions of the royal family inspired a misguided faith that the condemned man would

83

22 'The Throne, Windsor Castle' In traditional royal iconography, a vacant throne suggested impending majesty, not dereliction of duty.

be reprieved in the traditional manner.[16] On this occasion, however, the decision was allowed to stand. This action provoked angry scenes in the East End. Loyalists accused the queen of failing in her traditional duties and of flouting immemorial royal tradition. For disgruntled monarchists, justice was still seen to reside within royal authority. As in the debate about the royal seclusion, which provided the background to the campaign, it was her absence, and not her presence, that was at issue. At a series of sullen public meetings crowds refused to cheer the birth of the child.[17] At the height of the reform crisis in 1866 the queen was again criticized for ignoring public opinion when she allowed Lord Derby to form a Conservative ministry in preference to a Liberal one under Gladstone, despite clear indications that public opinion favoured a Liberal government committed to reform. Liberal newspapers accused her of ignoring the feelings of 'the mere hewers of wood and drawers of water' on this issue.[18]

The Wright case and the anti-royal hostility generated during the reform debates of 1866–7 were classic instances in which the throne was seen as failing in its responsibilities and public duties, but it was unlikely that the crowd that refused to cheer the birth of the Duke of Clarence or who booed the queen in 1866 would support a broader campaign for the abolition of the throne. The Wright case in particular demonstrates that the disillusionment with the monarchy transcended the political divide. The 1860s and 1870s were marked by dissatisfaction with royalty amongst former monarchists and radicals alike. It is the socially conservative *Tomahawk*, not radicalism, that has bequeathed us some of the most powerful anti-monarchist images of the period. The magazine skilfully played with images of an absent queen. Absence was central to many of the medieval and early-modern representations of monarchy. As Ernest Kantorowicz has demonstrated, it was a feature of Christian kingship that the monarch was a fusion of the corporeal and the divine.[19] The office itself was always present though invisible, in the judiciary, as lawmaker; in places of worship, as religious leader; and in the affairs of state, as ruler of the kingdom. In such representations the vacant throne stood as an emblem of impending majesty (illus. 22). *Tomahawk*, however, showed a throne not only empty, but with the orb, sceptre, crown, and robes of office discarded. Embellishing these images of absence, *Tomahawk* featured illustrations of a vacant throne that, through the dejected lion beneath and the apparently sad features appearing in the folds of the royal robes, expressed mourning for a queen shunning her duties to the nation and to her subjects. Here the ruler's public body has all but died (illus. 23). These visions, however, were projected to point up deficiencies that needed remedying, and there was little of genuine republicanism about them.[20]

Nevertheless, issues of 'sleaze' carried a particular resonance for radicals, and within much overt 'republicanism' were encoded echoes of the popular politics of the period 1830–67. Corruption within the state and the morality of the throne had always dominated radical thinking, and there remained a significant amount of implicit, if not actually explicit, criticism of the monarchy in the politics of Chartism and post-Napoleonic War radicalism. When Ernest Jones lectured on

WHERE IS BRITANNIA ?

23 The vacant and abandoned throne under Victoria.

the 'Hereditary Aristocracy' in 1856, before an audience that included some courtiers, it was inevitable that his comments would stray into the broader issues of criticizing the hereditary principle within monarchy, the throne's relationship with the Church of England, and the expense involved in the construction of Buckingham Palace.[21] Much routine dislike of the Church of England and its monarchical links surfaced within the Chartist movement, and Ernest Jones, not untypically, referred to it as 'Cranmer's bastard'.[22] The potential impact of such criticism was not lost on the governing parties. Gladstonian Liberals and Tories were united in their belief that the hereditary structures of the royal state were so intertwined that to criticize one component element within the equation was to open the door to further indictment of the foundations of the succession within monarchy.[23] Furthermore, there was nothing new about criticism of the expense of monarchy during royal weddings and at the time of opulent public ceremonial. The Chartists were past masters at this. Indeed the 'republican' outburst of 1871 was preceded by an almost unnoticed year-long radical campaign against the cost of the royal wedding between the Marquis of Lorne and Princess Louise.[24] Before the context of politics changed with the advent of the Paris Commune, this attracted little, if any, comment in the respectable press, and only scorn in the conservative satirical magazine *Fun* (illus. 24). It is important to remember that this campaign was not unique to Britain. In Wilhelmine Germany in the 1890s the issue of court corruption and intrigue was widely used by Social Democratic Party (SPD) journalists to show the moral failings of monarchy and to predict the imminent collapse of the Old Order.[25]

1871, however, was an exceptional year. The declaration of the Paris Commune and the subsequent blood martyrdom of the Communards raised the spectre of red revolution throughout Europe. The Commune in turn renewed anxiety about the other recent republican experiment in Spain, where the Bourbon Queen Isabella had been deposed in 1868 in an episode that was also widely discussed in both radical and conservative circles in Britain.[26] In 1874–5 Spain embarked on a second republican experiment. As a consequence it remained the preferred destination for British republican tourists like Charles Bradlaugh and James Thomson.[27] The Spanish rising revived memories of Spain's reactionary role as the linchpin of the Holy Alliance after 1815. Such upheavals therefore reinforced the view that the overthrow of monarchy was something that happened in despotic Catholic countries, where traditional English liberties were absent, and which created favourable conditions for the transmission of republican beliefs that undermined monarchy elsewhere. In 1871 there were strong fears that republicanism seemed to be spreading. In Australia proposals for an Australian federation promoted by the Irish (former Young Ireland) premier of Victoria, Gavan Duffy, seemed to presage an Australian republic and the break-up of the empire.[28] This caused consternation in the popular press.[29] These considerations engendered a panic of prodigious proportions about the presence of red and republican agitators in the beer halls and on the open ground of the capital. Such sentiments fed into the anti-French hostility that was widespread at court and in polite society during the Franco-Prussian War. In her conversations with Gladstone, Victoria directly attributed

THE DARLING'S DOWRY.

Britannia :—"DON'T MIND THEM! THE *REAL* WORKING-MEN DIDN'T GRUDGE IT!"

24 Britannia comforts Princess Louise with the words 'Don't mind them! The *real* working-men didn't grudge it!' *Fun* saw the campaign against royal dowries as unpatriotic and disloyal.

the spread of republicanism to French experiments in non-monarchical government.[30] Moreover, the French republic under Napoleon III had produced excesses that tarnished the reputation of republics as upholders of democratic freedoms.[31] This view was echoed in the anti-republican literature of the early 1870s where it was routinely suggested that the French defeat in the Franco–Prussian war could be laid at the door of the National Assembly's decision to embrace a degenerate republican system of government.[32] Such discussion made the British monarchy appear respectable as an institution, and altered perceptions of the campaign against the royal dowry, which was now portrayed as a breeding ground for violent activists. Against this background any opposition to monarchy at all seemed 'un-English', 'Jacobin' or an intrusion by alien continental forces. In the popular press of the 1870s, much as in the 1790s, France again fulfilled the role of an 'anti-Britain', and outbreaks of republicanism in England were blamed almost entirely on French émigrés. In popular satire republicans were depicted dressed in foreign garb and affecting continental styles of beards and side-whiskers. The conservative satirical magazine *Judy* portrayed republicans as anarchists and demons, luring the British working man away from his true loyalties (illus. 25). Commune refugees also frequently appear in the sensationalist stories and temperance literature of the early 1870s, in which they are portrayed as vile spreaders of sedition in drink-sodden halls.[33] In the metropolitan temperance tract *The Trial of Sir Jasper*, the central character can only be redeemed when he turns his back on the culture of the radical debating halls to which he is addicted nearly as much as to drink:

> Halls where hoarse sedition-mongers spout,
>   And Bacchus revels with his rabble rout,
> The fetid dens where rules and triumphs vice,
>   Where 'Commune' outcasts cog the mental dice,
> Reeking with blood from as yet unwashed hands –
>   The blood of good men boasting they have spilt,
> Proud of their shame and glorying in their guilt,
>   They bear their filthy froth to many lands.[34]

In some cases, refugee elements were blamed for the increasing and vocal criticism of the throne in the period 1871–2.[35] Radical contemporaries were aware of these comparisons and rejected them out of hand. At the unveiling of a monument to the former Chartist leader Ernest Jones in Ardwick Cemetery, Manchester, in 1871, his disciple the Rev. S. A. Steinthal disavowed all connections between the native tradition of radicalism and the French example and excesses of the Republic:

In the name of republicanism they saw a neighbouring nation divided and struggling, party against party, and they might be sure that those who liked to see the power of the privileged class, under whatever name, sustained would not be slow to charge upon those principles of republicanism and radicalism the errors of which some of their friends were guilty.[36]

A WARNING.

25 A Mephistophelian republican seated on a barrel of gunpowder seeks to mislead a radical, whilst the prone figure of a dead Communard implies the prospect of violence on the Parisian model.

Nevertheless, this association between 'Frenchness' and radicalism lingered. In the 1880s Dilke's exposure to 'French Vices' during his visits to Paris was used as an argument to further discredit him during the Mrs Crawford divorce scandal.[37] Such crude caricature, however, has masked and distorted perceptions of an agitation that was actually in a very English style of politics, with its roots deep in the traditions of the radical platform. Sir Charles Dilke barely mentioned contemporary events in France in his 'Cost of the Crown' speech, referring instead to English radical precedent and specifically to Edmund Burke on 'economical' reform. Others cited Cromwell, Hampden and Pym, or precedents established in the white settler colonies.[38]

Ultimately, the movement that emerged in Britain in the period 1870–71 was an agitation that might best be described as anti-monarchism or 'crude republicanism'. It is not alien to the English radical tradition but, on the contrary, integral to it. This set of ideas is distinct from the experience of contemporary European counterparts; it was never characterized by a declaration of rights of citizenship nor did its adherents espouse a republican project rooted in classical precedent as happened on the continent in 1848 or at the time of the declaration of the French Republic in 1870.[39] Anti-monarchism was none the less real for all that. In many ways it is typical of a long-established style of radical politics in Britain in which definitive declarations of principle and programmes for action are less significant than the tone and feel of the platform experience.

This is not to discount the existence of a network of republicans proper who, inspired by foreign precedent, imbibed the cerebral republicanism of Sir Charles Dilke, George Odger and Charles Bradlaugh. Charles Booth noted that the republican *Reynolds's Newspaper* was much in evidence on the London radical club circuit he explored in the 1890s. He wrote: 'The tone is not so much Liberal, or even radical, as republican, outside of the lines, authorized or unauthorized, of English party politics, and thus very uncertain at the ballot box.'[40] In debates held at the republican clubs like the Hole-in-the-Wall at Clerkenwell Green in the 1870s, speakers who could offer no reasoned arguments against the institution of monarchy and merely abused the royal family were berated by the chairman during debates.[41] Reformers who proposed a fundamental restructuring of the royal state distinguished between the powers of 'the throne' and those of 'the Crown' and challenged the influence wielded by the monarch on such issues as the prerogative. In contrast, those who merely opposed the accession of the Prince of Wales or expressed unease about an absent Victoria are more properly anti-monarchists. Their support for 'republican'-style rhetoric was conditional and could be won back to the values of altar, throne and cottage. This is the substance of W. E. Adams's criticisms of the watered-down republicanism of 1870–71. The case was made even more strongly by the former republican W. T. Stead when he commented about Dilke's 'Cost of the Crown' speech of November 1871:

I remember leaving the meeting with a bitter sense of humiliation. To this depth of insane trifling then had sunk the republican enthusiasm that had flamed heaven high in 1848! Elaborate arithmetical calculations that we might possibly, by dispensing with the monarchy, save ourselves the cost of an extra pot of beer. Twopence halfpenny per head all round as the inducement to rouse the British nation to an attack upon the monarchy of Alfred, of the Edwards, of Elizabeth and Victoria – the inducement was too ridiculous.[42]

Conscious of the obstacles to forming a platform for their ideas and the limitations of complaints of the anti-monarchist variety, republicans proper used periods of excessive royal unpopularity, like the 1870s, to reach out and manipulate an anti-monarchist constituency (both inside and outside radicalism) disgruntled by heavy tax burdens and the vacuum left by an absent head of state. Against the background of a strong royal state, a triumphant Gladstonianism and a bickering and divided radicalism, there was, however, little room for a movement geared to the abolition of the throne. Despite that, the radical campaign against the crown of 1871–2 was the one moment when these three elements of republicanism, disgruntled loyalism and crude anti-monarchism were momentarily united. The 'carnivalesque' outbursts of both defenders and opponents of monarchy that surrounded Dilke's public meetings and his speeches on royalty in the commons allowed him to straddle the boundaries between a polite and an 'unrespectable' critique of monarchy.[43] Indeed the vicious barracking of the three critics of monarchy, Dilke, Henry Fawcett and P. A. Taylor, in the parliamentary debates on the Civil List of 1872, aroused public sympathy for their cause, especially as one of their number, Fawcett, was physically disabled. Radicals and non-radicals alike were outraged by the way in which their opponents 'heartlessly and brutally derided, hooted and jeered a blind man'.[44]

Republicans nevertheless felt the odds stacked against them. Some modified their republicanism, lowering their sights to campaign against the most exposed excesses of royal privilege and the mythologies supporting them. In some ways this was displacement. At a conference at Birmingham that included the veteran Birmingham Political Union radical P. H. Muntz, it was the House of Lords, not the monarchy proper, that was the object of attack.[45] Such strategies drew upon popular resentment against the Lords' attempt to block the measure to disestablish the Irish Church in 1869, and to impede the Army Regulation Bill in 1871, which abolished the purchase of commissions by the sons of aristocratic families. Perversely, this latter bill only escaped mutilation after Gladstone's use of a royal warrant to force its passage through the second chamber.[46] By the end of 1871 Sir Charles Dilke had switched the focus of his campaign from the monarchy to the peers and the House of Lords.[47] Individual republicans followed different paths in this regard. Daniel Chatterton, who described Queen Victoria as a 'blood-stained old woman', went on to campaign fiercely for easily available birth-control in the 1880s. For him the right of women to reclaim their bodies from the moralizing of a 'scoundrelly kingcraft and priestcraft' was inextricably linked with the preaching of a state church endorsed by a female ruler in her role as 'Defender of the Faith'.[48] For some radicals, like the secularist Aurelis B. Wakefield of Hipperholme in West Yorkshire, 'republicanism' was merely one of a whole series of radical causes jostling for position within a broader political and social milieu. In an article on his life he is described as 'a prominent Anti-vaccinist, a Cremationist, a Republican, Malthusian and Liberationist, also an advocate of Co-operation'.[49]

As part of this retreat from full theoretical republicanism, the 1870s witnessed a very significant upsurge in the number of struggles over rights of way and other more general issues of land-ownership.[50] Landholding in Britain was buttressed by a legal framework built around the monarchy. Moreover, under the terms of an agreement between Crown and Commons at the time of Victoria's accession, administration of the largest of the Crown estates was turned over to Parliament as a concession to defray the cost of Civil List payments. Victoria was always deeply upset by radical attacks on the role of the Crown in landholding and maintained that the throne divested itself of its hereditary lands and revenues at the accession of each new reigning monarch. There was a note of special pleading on this score in her correspondence on the Crown lands with Gladstone. On occasion she tried to portray herself as a 'pauper queen':

Another great mistake made by the radicals is *not* distinguishing the difference which exists between the very rich landed proprietors and the royal family. The former inherit large fortunes – many far larger – *not only* than the royal family but than the sovereign himself and yet have no *status* or court to maintain. Whereas *we* have no property – nothing of our own and must maintain this status, and are expected to give largely to charities etc.[51]

Nevertheless, the radicals who took part in these campaigns contested the throne's disclaimers and referred quite specifically to the royal insistence that restrictions impeding popular recreations and festivities on Crown lands be upheld.[52] Royal relatives, such as the Duke of Cambridge and the Duke of Connaught, who were rangers of the royal forests, were also particularly targeted.[53] In addition, the administration of the Prince of Wales's personal estates in the Duchy of Cornwall was a frequent point of contention.[54] W. E. Adams and John de Morgan, among others, articulated these ideas strongly in the radical press, while in the countryside the Agricultural Labourers' Union viciously criticized the heir to the throne during its campaign against enclosures by the Duchy of Cornwall.[55] Myths of the 'Norman Yoke' and of the king and his nobles as descendants of the robber barons and 'the bastard William' fed such disaffection. Here the monarch was portrayed as a supporter of privilege, who inspired the defenders of the old order and conspired with them to deny the people their civic freedoms and basic rights of citizenship.[56]

The republican campaign of the 1870s also raises fundamental issues about radical continuities, which are central to any understanding of later developments in the mass platform after mid-century. Republicanism's significance in this regard can only be understood by examining the agitation's precise relationship to Liberalism. After 1867, with the demand for parliamentary reform temporarily satisfied, these older elements within radicalism, which had always been present, resurfaced. In the 1850s, in similar circumstances, they had also come to the fore during a period of radical retreat after the failure of the petitioning campaign of 1848. In 1872, following the attempt by Feargus O'Connor's nephew, Arthur, to assassinate Queen Victoria, memories of the movement were revived, and battles over the traditions of Chartism were refought in the radical press (illus. 26).[57] As with traditional radicalism, anti-monarchism in the 1870s was even-handed in its rejection of both existing political parties. Republicanism thrived at a time of considerable radical disillusionment with orthodox political structures. The decline of mass-platform radicalism on the Chartist model and the failure of Liberalism to fully represent working-class interests left a vacuum barely filled by the competing political parties that promised much, but offered little. Dislike of political parties was a common radical characteristic during these years;[58] for republicans both Toryism and Liberalism were perceived as props of the royal state. Republicanism was especially hostile to a Liberalism that under Gladstone's guiding hand was inventive in the use it made of royal ritual to buttress the position of the throne during the tide of 'typhoid loyalism' of 1872 that surrounded the near fatal illness of the Prince of Wales. There is indeed little evidence of a radical continuity

26 Arthur O'Connor's attempted assassination of Victoria in March 1872. John Brown apprehended the assailant.

infusing and abetting Liberalism. Rather, many radicals remained defiantly outside existing party-political structures.[59]

Radical 'republicans' were condemned by both Tories and Liberals as unacceptable outsiders in British politics. They in turn castigated Gladstonian Liberalism for its toleration of a corrupt monarchy and a dissolute and unpredictable heir to the throne. Much, of course, has been made of the Liberal 'modernizers'. Figures like Dilke, Joseph Chamberlain and Goldwin Smith are sometimes seen as instrumental in forging a radical Liberalism, attached to the coat tails of the Liberal Party, and part of a shared current of politics that demonstrates the convergence, rather than the disjuncture, between radicalism and Liberalism.[60] Republicanism has been portrayed as part of this creed. This mirrors contemporary Tory criticism that the Liberals were a party of unenthusiastic patriots whose Nonconformist and temperance wing made them spiritless in the celebration of important and usually alcohol-sodden moments like the royal jubilees. Some regional Tory newspapers sought to smear the Liberals by suggesting direct links between Liberals, republicans, Communards and Fenians, and implying that Gladstone was reluctant to distance himself from such company.[61] It now seems, however, that the role of the Liberal modernizers has been exaggerated. All deserted their early republicanism in the wake of the Commune. An astute municipal manager like Chamberlain realized the importance of royal patronage to the success of the new

HE STOOPS TO CONQUER.

The Right Hon. J— C— (a Red Republican—kissing hands) : Let us dissemble.   No matter.   The time will come !

27 The Birmingham satirical magazine *Dart* lampooned Joseph Chamberlain as a repentant, untrustworthy republican whose relations with royalty were characterized by excessive displays of loyalism.

borough councils, and the degree to which a royal boycott of a local authority could endanger the new experiments in municipal government. It is unsurprising then that he effusively welcomed the heir to the throne on a visit to Birmingham in 1874.[62] Moreover, rather than meeting the cost of the visit from the local rates, he paid for it himself from his own personal fortune.[63] The journalist Richard Whiteing recalled in his memoirs: 'The whole kingdom breathed a sigh of relief when it heard that he had been "nice" from first to last. His manners were perfect; his decoration of the town was a model [...] He knew what he was about: it was his first step into notice as a governing man.'[64] Subsequently other members of the royal family, including the queen, received a warm welcome in Birmingham (illus. 27). After his death, local legend, encouraged by the city's Liberals, rehabilitated Chamberlain and represented his 'republicanism' as a slur deliberately manufactured by his enemies. As the Birmingham city fathers realized, too great a reputation for republicanism could badly damage the civic culture of a town council. Manchester discovered this to its cost when Queen Victoria refused to open the city's new town hall in 1877. Contemporaries construed this as a deliberate rebuff to the newly-elected mayor, Abel Heywood, a former Chartist who had been imprisoned for his role in the war of the unstamped. The local press, however, saw it as an implied criticism of the erection of a statue of Oliver Cromwell on the site of the first skirmish and casualties of the English Civil War by Heywood's wife, Elizabeth Salisbury Heywood, in 1875 (illus. 28).[65] The taint stayed with the city, and the view that Queen Victoria disliked the capital of the cotton industry and its belated homage to Cromwell became an entrenched part of local folklore,

28 Cromwell's statue in Manchester, *c.* 1940, in its original position outside the Cathedral.

surviving Victoria's visit to Manchester to open the Manchester-Liverpool Ship Canal in 1894 (illus. 29).[66]

In contrast to radicalism, which attracted support from civic leaders, republicanism as a movement suffered from its inability to win the adherence of any national politicians of stature. The campaign against the Crown of 1871 would have looked very different had it not been for the intervention of Sir Charles Dilke. Nevertheless, figures like Dilke and Goldwin Smith, who knew the heir to the throne well and moved in the same social circles, found it difficult to sustain a campaign against someone they were on good personal terms with and met regularly at society functions. By the mid-1870s Dilke was seeking to conceal his republicanism. His republican novel, *The Fall of Prince Florestan of Monaco*, was published anonymously to avoid ridicule and public hostility.[67] At the end of his life, when he had distanced himself from his former republican ideals and was on good terms with Edward VII, he faced radical accusations of betrayal.[68] The biographies that appeared after his death tried, however, to exonerate him, insisting that he was a theoretical, rather than a practical republican. They claimed that he had mistakenly blundered into an agitation not of his own devising and that his comments about the throne had been misunderstood.[69]

Once it became a liability to profess anti-monarchist views, politicians disavowed their former republicanism. In the general election of 1874 republican associations made Liberal/radical MPs who had

29 Queen Victoria as civic goddess officiating at the opening of the Manchester-Liverpool Ship Canal.

supported curbs against the Crown vulnerable to attack from the Tories and, on occasion, from their own side. Against the background of attempts to unseat him for disloyalty to the Liberal Party over issues of foreign policy, Joseph Cowen Jr ascribed the label of 'republican' to Tory smears and denied all involvement in the Tyneside republican clubs of the early 1870s. He commented: '[My] enemies wanted to convey the impression that I was some desperate hobgoblin, who was going to swallow all the institutions of the state; to drive the Queen into exile, to turn the Chancellor out of the House of Lords, and, in fact, to bring about some extraordinary social or political upheaval to the land.'[70] Moreover, republicanism suffered severely from the lack of a publicly recognized intelligentsia identifiable with its ideas. Contemporaries made much of the debates about republicanism at Cambridge University, where a marked anti-establishment tendency cohered around Henry Fawcett in the early 1870s. Through these discussions a Cambridge Republican Club was established in 1870 dedicated to sexual equality and 'hostility to the hereditary principle as exemplified in monarchical and aristocratic institutions'.[71] Nevertheless, republicanism in the older established universities never really progressed beyond undergraduate high-jinks and the subversion of College toasts to Church and King at high table.[72]

In the final analysis, the anti-monarchist campaign was a pariah. It existed almost entirely outside the political mainstream, despising Liberals and Tories equally for their collusion with monarchical structures. The radical convenor of a republican meeting in Derby in December 1871, J. Charles Cox, wrote: 'The very name of Liberal will shortly become a term of reproach on the lips of the people, as Tory and Whig have been treated before it.'[73] Most important of all, republicanism resolutely eschewed new political forms and stubbornly adhered to the mass platform tradition of political radicalism. From his exile in Canada Goldwin Smith urged the formation of a formalized Republican Party in Parliament, but his advice was ignored.[74] In some ways the agitation most closely resembles the populist 'anti-party' politics of the US, Australia and the Continent during this same period. This view is supported by a growing body of evidence showing that traditional radical opposition to 'political parties' remained a fixed and continuous part of the political landscape into the middle years of the nineteenth century and beyond.[75]

Republicans refused to compromise with party forms altogether. They attacked partisan local magistrates, both Liberal and Tory, who failed to police republican meetings adequately, and in Derby, Bolton and elsewhere exposed local politicians who colluded with the loyalist mobs to disrupt their proceedings.[76] In Northampton, following a campaign by local radicals, the chief constable of the county was ironically admonished by the House of Lords for his part in removing posters advertising a meeting critical of royalty.[77] Republicans also made heroes of those who opposed the excesses of 'party', mob violence and electoral corruption. George Odger became the best known of these figures. In later years his death in 1877 was attributed to injuries inflicted during the disturbances at Reading in 1871 'by a gang of roughs, hired by the local aristocracy to defend the sacred interests of royalty'.[78] The unlikeliest of these martyrs for free speech was the Protestant demagogue William Murphy, who died of wounds incurred at a riot orchestrated by his Liberal opponents in Whitehaven in late 1871.[79] Given these circumstances, it seemed appropriate for satirists to measure the extent of Chamberlain's renunciation of his republican past by representations of him, not only as the friend of the Prince of Wales, but also as a 'King of the Caucus' in Birmingham, where his manipulation of the machinery of local politics cemented Liberal ascendancy in the borough (illus. 30).[80] In addition, the anti-monarchist campaign sought to wrench back the trappings and outward forms of radicalism that the Liberal Party had drawn on in the 1850s and 1860s to buttress its position in areas like the North-West

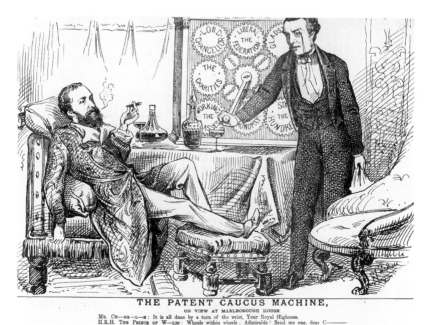

THE PATENT CAUCUS MACHINE,
ON VIEW AT MARLBOROUGH HOUSE.
Mr. Ch—mb—l—n : It is all done by a turn of the wrist, Your Royal Highness.
H.R.H. The Prince of W—les : Wheels within wheels ; Admirable ! Send me one, dear C——

30 Chamberlain as 'King of the Caucus' and friend of the Prince of Wales activating a 'political caucus machine'.

and the Midlands. At Bolton there was a literal, as well as metaphorical, battle over the corpse of William Scofield, the by-stander at Sir Charles Dilke's republican speech in the town who was killed by a Tory mob in December 1871. Liberals, after initially disowning the meeting, hoped to make him a martyr for Liberalism in the North-West. In sharp contrast, radical anti-monarchists wanted him to be remembered as a victim of political persecution by the state in the manner of Robert Lees fifty years earlier.[81] There was even a brief radical campaign to generate support for the term 'Bolton-loo' to wrest the memory of Peterloo back from the Liberals, but the term never inspired the same demonstrations of feeling as the original.[82] Elsewhere at Derby and Reading, anti-monarchists attacked the innovative and sophisticated techniques for disrupting and breaking up meetings implemented by the new party structures.[83]

This sense of 'apartness' had profound implications for the way in which British republicans viewed the world. They saw themselves as marginal, even as 'cranks', and frequently used this word to describe themselves. Such images were reflected back at them. Satirical cartoons in *Judy* showed Dilke as a vile object, plucked from the hearth by Judy as a housewife with a pair of fire tongs (illus. 31). Significantly, the republican platform was omitted altogether from contemporary Liberal accounts of the role of popular protest in overturning the barriers to political reform in the nineteenth-century British state.[84] This constituted a form of internal exile from the Whig constitutional tradition. The vocabulary of separation that characterized English republicanism has been invoked to illustrate the marginal nature of the republican position, but is more properly viewed as a statement of non-compliance with the existing order. An obituary of Joseph Cowen by the republican J. Morrison Davidson described him as losing himself and his republican bite when he deserted the mass platform and entered Parliament as an MP.[85] In fact, this sense of being outside and looking in is something radicals have always expressed very strongly during periods of hostility to party. Exclusion, both figurative and literal, was a long-standing part of the radical tradition. Rohan McWilliam has noted the way in which radicals turned insults intended to marginalize their position to their own advantage. Outraged supporters of the Tichborne Claimant, described as 'fools and fanatics' by the Lord Chief Justice, took to describing themselves as such on their banners.[86] In this way, the language of their opponents was reclaimed and became an emblem of pride. Like the Chartists before them, there was an element of anti-statism about the republican agitators of the 1870s and a feeling of excommunication from the

WHAT SHALL WE DO WITH HIM?

31 Sir Charles Dilke as an unpleasant object examined at arm's length.

respectable political nation. The activities of republicans were monitored and republican meeting houses and premises closely watched by the police. Obituaries of the West Riding radical Leonard Robinson, first president of the Bradford Republican Club, recalled pitched battles in the club when police spies were discovered on the premises.[87] Republican anti-statist rhetoric was simply an extension of traditional radical culture, and republican 'cranks' sought to reclaim the 'cranks' of an older political lineage to place themselves within the historical ancestry of radicalism. Andrew Carnegie wrote: 'I honour these cranks very much – all real reformers are cranks in their day; Pym, Hampden, Cromwell were, and John Bright himself was a very pronounced one, till he brought the nation up to his level.'[88]

The republican agenda provoked a battle for the soul of the English nation itself. As in the days of Richard Carlile, republicans looked for 'an unmediated and ahistorical present' far removed from the linear traditions of monarchism and national pageantry.[89] Accordingly anti-monarchists installed the Commonwealth and John Milton in their pantheon of truly British moments;[90] in return loyalists extolled the tradition of Nelson and military victories during George III's reign. These issues were contested in the early months of 1872 at meetings convened by George Odger to condemn the violence used by the riot-ers responsible for the death of William Scofield at Bolton. In a hostile account of a republican demonstration in Trafalgar Square, the image of radical banners obscuring the friezes around the base of Nelson's column and covering the Landseer lions conveyed the vision of a thou-sand years of British history whose eradication by a rootless and imported agitation appeared imminent. The National Gallery, where the pictorial treasures of the nation were personally safeguarded by the queen in her role as custodian of the national past, was given a central place in this vignette:

The illumination came from the gallery immediately in front of the National Gallery, and shining over the heads of the countless mob it showed brilliantly on that part of the monument where one of Nelson's victories is depicted in metal [...] This historic picture was in part hidden by a banner bearing the motto 'Liberty, Equality, Fraternity'.[91]

Contemporary engravings of the scene show the republican crowd surging around Northumberland House, the last of the great eigh-teenth-century aristocratic mansions on the Strand, and characterized by the distinctive neo-feudal lion rampant on its battlements (illus. 32). In this depiction there are distinct echoes of the dark and insurgent cityscape portrayed in Gustave Doré's engravings of London in circu-lation at the time, which were themselves inspired by the public executions he had witnessed in Paris during the Commune.[92] The influence of Doré is very apparent in the graphic black-and-white representations of figures in the crowd. The republicans are lit menac-ingly from behind by the artificial lights used at the demonstration and appear poised to swallow Northumberland House. As Peter Mandler has shown, a perceived threat to Britain's national heritage of castles

32 A republican meeting in Trafalgar Square in February 1872.

and stately houses was an important part of the moral panic surrounding the 'red' agitation of 1871.[93] The destruction of Warwick Castle by
fire at the beginning of December conveyed a sense of crisis in which
the very fabric of the national past seemed under threat from the disorder and chaos that had engulfed Paris. Regional newspapers
manipulated the associations between the destruction of a historic
monument established by King Alfred's daughter, Ethelfreda, that
contemporaries saw as expressive of Anglo-Saxon liberties more
widely, and the new threat posed by the 'revolution mongers'. There

was an implied danger here of a new and tyrannical 'Normanism' in republican form that sought to undermine the traditional monarchical liberties of the 'freeborn Englishman'.[94] Many provincial newspapers accordingly reported the fire in the same edition in which they covered the Dilkite riot in Derby; in some cases they are described on the same page.[95] More extreme reports in the local press carried accounts of looting during the blaze that intimated the collapse of existing structures of power and authority.[96] Engravings of the scene reaffirmed the existing feudal hierarchy of lords and commoners against foreign influences, showing servants, family members and the local community working together to save treasures, works of art and historical relics from the fire (illus. 33).

In many places regional traditions of patriotism to altar and throne were also invoked by loyalists. At Derby it was popular memories of the role of the local regiment the 'Derby Blues' in turning back the Jacobites at Clifton Moor in 1745 that inspired disruption of a republican meeting, and allowed the local Conservative paper to write: 'The loyalty of Derby has hitherto been above suspicion [...] The corporation is behind no other municipal body in its possession of that virtue.'[97] The Jacobite risings of both 1715 and 1745, when the Stuart armies were forced to retreat through Lancashire by Hanoverian forces, were also recalled to enthuse local royalists during public debates at the

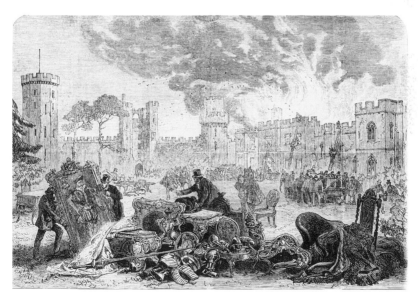

33 The fire at Warwick Castle in December 1871. For a modern audience, this event raises inevitable comparisons with the 1992 fire at Windsor Castle, which also had implications for the monarchy.

Republican Club in Preston in 1872.[98] In addition, there were significant clashes with the Tory-aligned Orange lodges of the North-West, in which naïve monarchist Orangeism and a reversed contempt for royalism came into open conflict. In 1870 Pope Pius IX's Doctrine of Papal Infallibility caused Orange Lodges in both England and Ireland to place themselves on a war footing. During the royal crisis of 1870–72 they rushed to reaffirm their loyalty to throne and altar.[99] At Bolton such declarations fuelled the Orange involvement in the attacks on Sir Charles Dilke's meeting in the town.[100] Subsequently the men arrested on suspicion of orchestrating the attack became popular loyalist heroes who were cheered during their court appearances in Manchester. The *Bolton Guardian* remarked ironically: 'They could not have been more lustily cheered had they each been a recipient of a Humane Society medal.'[101] Here again it was overwhelmingly issues of history and national memory that were in contention. Orange broadsides of the 1860s cast the Order as upholders of constitutional freedoms and spoke of the threat posed by reformers to the traditional English religious liberties connected with the Crown and the Reformation:

> The spirits of your fathers must rise at every sound,
>   That strikes at knavish traitors, wherever they are found,
> To where Cranmer and good Ridley fell your thoughts must ever go,
>   And picture to yourself, how well superstition they laid low.
>
> Protestants awake, the crisis is at hand,
>   When Pope and Priests would dominate o'er this our favoured land,
> But we will rally round our Queen and fight for her good cause,
>   Our Protestant religion, our freedom and our laws.[102]

Close analysis of the republican campaign of 1871–2 provides the strongest evidence to date of the survival of an older strand of radical politics, however naïvely expressed, that existed outside Liberalism into the 1870s and beyond. This was a body of ideas that, although diffuse, could never be amalgamated into Liberalism or Toryism and clung tenaciously to the memories of an older radical tradition. Republicanism's exclusion from Liberalism seems especially pronounced in the light of recent research that places Gladstone, rather than Disraeli, at the heart of the rehabilitation of monarchy following the illness of the Prince of Wales in 1871–2.[103]

It is still surprising to consider how many radicals warmed their hands at the fires of the agitation against the throne during this period. Among the unlikely figures who became involved are George Howell, who expressed enthusiasm for a temperate republican platform in private. The image of Howell that emerges from his private correspondence during this period is very different from the public face he presented in negotiations with the wealthy Liberal backers of the Reform League. Writing to Goldwin Smith in 1873, he showed that he was a cautious republican who looked forward to the advent of a future republic 'in the hands of good men and true'.[104] In 1889 he was also active in campaigns to demand curbs on Civil List grants to royal offspring.[105] This residue of an older radical tradition overturns conventional views of Howell as a devout and willing Gladstonian. Similarly Robert Applegarth and W. R. Cremer were named by Sir Charles Dilke in an interview in the *New York Times* as closet theoretical republicans who shared the movement's aims, but felt constrained by their association with respectable Liberalism.[106] In 1876 Thomas Burt and William MacDonald, the first working-men Lib–Lab MPs, represented the interests of radicals by championing petitions in the House of Commons for curbs on Civil List payments to the Royal Family. None of the aforementioned are personalities that one would normally associate with such an extreme body of ideas. Noticeably, neither Applegarth nor Cremer objected to being described as 'republicans' in an American newspaper that the wealthy backers of the Liberal Party were unlikely to read. They were more wary of being known openly as such in Britain, where they had a lot to lose by being identified too closely with the 'republican' cause. This says quite a lot about the temporary, strategic nature of the mid-century radical alliance with Liberalism. The activities of those figures who expressed sympathy with the republican platform suggests that many of the accords pioneered with Liberalism during this period were short-term tactical expedients that required compromise with existing beliefs still vigorously articulated in private.

Ultimately, however, the Commune irrevocably altered respectable perceptions of nineteenth-century anti-monarchism. Opposition to monarchy, in either its republican or its anti-monarchist variants, could now no longer be seen as 'English' or indeed 'respectable' in any sense. W. T. Stead recalled:

For a little while it was possible that the French Republic might, by raising again the old flag of the revolution, evoke the potent passions which in 1848 shook Europe to its centre. The expectation was disappointed. All hope from that quarter was dashed to the ground by the mad outbreak of the Commune. Paris, after 1871, was no longer the storm centre of Europe. The Republic was only a Republic in name. It was controlled by men who detested every idea that had made Republicanism the ideal of our youth. The glamour was gone. Judged by the supreme test of wager of battle, the ideas of our modern democrats had been found woefully wanting.[107]

As Stead suggests, the Commune reflected a broader groundswell of disillusionment with foreign republican examples within the Victorian public. This was less significant for self-professed republicans than for the disgruntled monarchists and the anti-monarchist constituency within radicalism who had swelled the ranks of the opponents of the throne in 1870–71. To hardened republicans, the word 'Commune' was less a manifestation of bloodthirsty revolution than an expression of an Arcadian vision of peasant life, strongly evocative of the natural landscape and village culture. Romantic republicans such as William Morris or Eliza Lynn Linton still portrayed the Communard spirit in these terms in novels and commemorations into the 1880s.[108] Stead, however, expressed the disillusionment of republican fellow-travellers. On these grounds the Commune discredited for a decade or more the basis of any overt republican references whatsoever, particularly where they were rooted in continental precedent or drawn from 'non-monarchical' histories written abroad. At a broader level, it emphasized the poverty of republican examples for those seeking an alternative to a monarchical constitution in the mid-Victorian period.

In the 1860s slavery, caucus politics and the rule of unbridled 'money lords' had also irreversibly tarnished the reputation of American democracy. Before Abraham Lincoln's Emancipation Proclamation freed the slaves in northern-held territory in 1863, the United States presented a basic contradiction: an 'unfree' people in a 'free' state. In contrast, the colonial example of Canada seemed to demonstrate the stability and prosperity brought by dominion status under the Crown.[109] In 1871–2 disillusionment with the United States remained very apparent amongst both radicals and Liberals, divided over whether Washington's plans for international arbitration in the *Alabama* dispute reflected American concerns of fair-play in international diplomacy, or merely the acquisitive interests of a 'Yankeedom' intent upon boosting unjust claims for compensation. Accusations that American democratic values were entirely bogus and hypocritical were rife amongst English radicals during this period.[110]

Moreover, in South America and Mexico, where the collapse of the Bourbon monarchy at the beginning of the century had been embraced by the Chartists and led to the adulation of Simon Bolívar in radical circles, absence of kingly rule now seemed to herald a gradual slide into chaos that encouraged fresh adventurism by the imperial powers. British radicals were particularly outraged by Napoleon III's attempt to install the Austrian Archduke Maximilian as Emperor of Mexico in the 1860s.[111] After the restoration of the Spanish Bourbons in 1874 and the revival of royalism in France, only the Swiss republic survived as the sole untarnished republican project in Europe and the New World.[112]

The republican campaign of 1871 brought together a conflicting array of allies during a difficult and contentious 'republican moment'. These various elements were strange bed-fellows. There was considerable disharmony between the tones of disgruntled monarchists, anti-monarchists and committed ideological republicans. The collapse of the campaign did not, however, mean the end of opposition to the throne. After the 1880s criticism of the anti-monarchist and republican variety concentrated on the increasing spectacle of royalty during the jubilees and the imperial display of the *fin de siècle* period. This perpetuated the domestic tradition of an 'unrespectable' view of monarchy. During these years it was increasingly the Crown's royal extravagance that was at issue, evoking a response that focused on the spectacle of monarchy, rather than on the legitimacy of the existence of the Crown itself.

4 The Crown, the Radical Press and the Popular Anti-jubilee 1876–98

> Lord help our precious Queen,
>   Noble, but rather mean,
> Lord help the Queen.
>   Keep Queen Vic*Toryous*,
> From work laborious,
>   Let snobs uproarious,
> Slaver the Queen.
>
> ('A Jubilee Version of "God Save the Queen"', the *Bulletin*,
> quoted in *Reynolds's Newspaper*, 19 June 1881, p. 1)

Queen Victoria's Golden and Diamond Jubilees provide important markers in the course of nineteenth-century British history. Occurring at a time when economic competition, imperial rivalry and the spectre of separatism in South Africa and Ireland threatened the unity of empire, the lavish military displays and imperial pageants that so impressed contemporaries now appear hollow. In recent research the jubilees are frequently invoked as part of a broader historical concern to chart the course of empire and to pinpoint the exact moment at which the possibility of British national and imperial decline became imminent. As part of this process, the dissident voices of imperial zealots like Kipling have been re-examined to find evidence for contemporary realization that the imperial meridian had passed.[1] In the work of Dennis Judd and Asa Briggs, the imperial spectacle of the 1897 jubilee has been represented as a moment of extreme poignancy; those who celebrated the perceived zenith of empire were not experiencing the highpoint of Britain's influence in the world but rather the beginning of its decline.[2] In that sense the jubilees have become a nostalgic point of reference, saturated in maudlin patriotic sentiment and dressed up with the pious self-congratulation of empire. In addition, the jubilees are frequently seen as lulling the senses of the Victorian public and creating the framework for the twentieth-century cult of monarchy rooted in pageantry, theatre and kitsch popular display more suited to the context of an imperial experience, but providing consolation in a post-colonial Britain that refused to acknowledge the reality of its own decline (illus. 34).

Historians of popular politics have never fully addressed the issues raised by radical opposition to the jubilees. On the contrary, they have portrayed the jubilees as a truce between radicalism and the state during which all potential for opposition had been removed. From this perspective, the jubilees emerge as displays of community acclamation for monarchy in which all strands of the British political tradition were represented. In part, such views draw upon the attitudes of contemporaries who celebrated unanimity, not dissent. When the repentant physical-force Chartist Benjamin Wilson collapsed and died at Halifax while delivering a homily to Queen Victoria during the jubilee of 1897, his death provided a satisfactory punctuation mark for the local press, drawing a line under the Chartist militancy of the 1840s and demonstrating the stability that had been achieved under Victoria's beneficent rule.[3] For former opponents of the Victorian state like Wilson, the jubilees were a yardstick of personal and political progress, demonstrating how far even former advocates of physical force had become

34 Queen Victoria leaving St Paul's Cathedral on jubilee day 1887 after the service celebrating her 60 years on the throne. This particular jubilee is usually represented as the apogee of royal ceremonial.

reconciled to the economic and social consensus of the 'Age of Equipoise'.[4]

Close scrutiny of the radical press, however, reveals that the public spectacle of the late-Victorian monarchy was not unopposed. Victoria's jubilees provided a fresh opportunity for radicals hostile to the throne to castigate the excesses of the royal state. Whereas in the 1870s it had been the absence of the monarch that provided the basis for criticism of Victoria, now it was the drain on the public purse resulting from the lavish royal display surrounding the queen's public appearances that incited the ire of reformers. Moreover, for every Chartist veteran like Benjamin Wilson who made restitution for his former radicalism and died honoured and respected by his community, there was another like James West of Macclesfield who died penniless and alone in internal exile in the town of his birth in the jubilee year of 1887. The irony of West's lonely death in poverty in a year designed to celebrate the progress achieved under Victoria's reign was not lost on the contemporaries who wrote his obituaries.[5]

Historians have traditionally proved dismissive of the vocabulary of republicanism in the later years of Victoria's reign. While conceding that monarchy did attract criticism from reform movements, they have nevertheless dismissed such agendas as marginal to the radical mainstream, on the grounds that after 1870 anti-monarchists never managed to generate a political agitation devoted exclusively to the abolition of the Crown or to a modification of its powers.[6] The attention this opposition has commanded has therefore tended to concentrate on those moments in which anti-monarchist sentiments crystallized around an active campaign, particularly at the time of Queen Victoria's withdrawal from public life in the period 1870–72. Such work overlooks opposition to the throne as an impulse underlying the assumptions that promoted other forms of radical activity and that resurfaced within the broader context of attacks upon aristocracy, landed wealth and the hereditary principle. For the post-1880 period such responses are almost entirely ignored in favour of a view that stresses the socialist and anti-Liberal credentials of the early Labour pioneers. The failure to examine this stratum of belief within the radical agitation of the 1880s has reinforced existing impressions of British movements of political protest as overwhelmingly compliant, loyal, and uncritical of the institution of monarchy.

The radical upsurge of the 1880s that laid the foundations for the emergence of organized labour after 1900 was once seen as a unique phenomenon that signalled a major shift away from older, established political forms and provided the springboard for independent action outside the framework of the two main political parties.[7] Recent work, however, has stressed the continuities with earlier movements rather than the departures evident in this stage of political development. Older images of these agitations as socialist or Marxist inspired are now giving way to interpretations that stress the similarities with, rather than the shift away from, an earlier radicalism.[8] Viewed in these terms the campaigns launched by the Democratic Federation and its successor the SDF can best be understood as expressions of a revival in already existing political forms, rather than a sharp break with their agitational predecessors.[9] These organizations also demonstrate the degree to which older preoccupations of opposition to privilege and anti-monarchism continued to set the tone for most of the major radical movements of this period, long after such narratives are usually assumed to have faded.

The vocabulary of anti-monarchism remained an important element in the popular perceptions of royalty in the late-Victorian period. The salacious, voyeuristic element within popular culture persisted in mainstream radical discourses and continued as the stock-in-trade of the new socialist and ultra-radical agitators. In the wake of the continental influences of the aesthetic movement and the trial of Oscar Wilde in 1895, the lampoons traditionally used to de-mystify monarchy and ridicule its pretensions to the political and moral leadership of the nation took on a new lease of life. The Wilde affair both heightened fears about the moral and sexual decadence in society circles frequented by the Prince of Wales, and also drew attention to the apparent decay of British manhood and the physical degeneration of the national blood-stock.[10] Images of such decadence and traditional anti-monarchism fused in contemporary depictions of Edward VII.

Rather than fading, such images came to preoccupy a whole new generation of reformers in the *fin de siècle* period. The Prince of Wales was the republicans' trump card;[11] even the court feared that the public would reject him as king after Victoria's death. Imported anti-monarchist literature like Max Nordau's *Conventional Lies*, which compared the British royal family to the ailing Habsburgs in Austria-Hungary, compounded this sense of crisis by raising the spectre of a Europe-wide collapse of monarchy.[12] Particularly evident in literature of this sort was a further recycling and updating of historical memories of the Regency. Queen Victoria was acutely aware of this controversial legacy in the royal blood-line, and remained sensitive about christening any of her grandchildren with the traditional Hanoverian name of George. Like the propagandists Richard Carlile or William Hone earlier in the century, radicals still concentrated their fire on the heir to the throne and sought to undermine the long-term stability of the Crown by dismissing him as too incompetent and immoral to rule. In the case of the future Edward VII, the parallels with George IV were readily apparent.[13]

Contemporary French illustrations at the time of his coronation showed him as a reincarnation of the Prince Regent grasping a handful of ill-gotten gains and a balance sheet for his creditors (illus. 35). Such images dogged him particularly at the time of the Tranby Croft scandal in 1891, when the revelation that the illegal card game baccarat was played for money in court circles fused with end-of-the-century angst to reinforce popular perceptions of the corruption of royal life. The criticism of Edward that emerged from the radical press following his court appearance in connection with the scandal evoked memories of the worst aspects of the Stuarts, and was couched in similar terms to the scurrilous broadsides directed against the Hanoverian princes in the previous century. *Reynolds's Newspaper* wrote:

It may be doubted whether the adulterous Charles and George were, allowing for the period in which they lived, much greater offenders against law and morality than the gentleman who on Tuesday was compelled to testify in the witness box as to the fashion in which his time is spent and the degrading associations with which he is connected.[14]

The scandal reinforced the argument of radical critics of the throne that the recent £36,000 grant to the royal children would be swallowed up by the prince's gambling debts.[15] There remained a strong populist dimension to such protests. The suspicion of existing power structures manifested in them, the distrust for the corrupt and venal system of the court they expressed, and their sense that monarchy was a system that needed to be broken to preserve the political health of the nation place them in a long radical tradition of populist politics.[16] Often they relied upon burlesque, inversion imagery and carnivalesque, 'world turned upside down' signs to convey the inequalities of wealth and power they satirized. The image of royalty as 'beggars' and 'drones' battening on the industry and enterprise of other men was a favoured one that juxtaposed the indolent and unproductive world of the court alongside the thrift and vitality of commercial urban culture. A correspondent wrote of the royal family in Richard Carlile's *Gauntlet* in the 1830s:

The man who does nothing in society for his own support is a tax, an encumbrance and a nuisance upon him who does something; and in a civilized community such a man has no right and no claim to be tolerated. He is a pest, a beggar and a filcher of other men's substance.[17]

Nº 326. 7ᵉ année. 2 Février 1901.

15 centimes.

Le Rire

JOURNAL HUMORISTIQUE PARAISSANT LE SAMEDI

Un an : Paris, 8 fr.
départements, 9 fr. Étranger, 12 fr.
mois : France, 5 fr. Étranger, 6.50

M. Félix JUVEN, Directeur. — Partie artistique : M. Arsène ALEXANDRE

La reproduction des dessins du RIRE est absolument interdite aux publications, françaises ou étrangères, sans autorisation

122, rue Réaumur, 122
PARIS
Vente et Abonnement
9, rue Saint-Joseph, 9

LE GOTHA DU « RIRE ». — Nº XXXIII

ÉDOUARD VII, roi d'Angleterre, empereur des Indes

(Air connu.)
Edouard-Albert,
Tu succéd' à ta mère.

Et ta mère à son oncle,
Qu'était roi d'Angleterre !

35 A scurrilous French image of Edward VII before his coronation shows him as a financial reprobate dogged by bad debt.

115

That such attitudes remained part of the radical mainstream is made apparent by the manner in which the anti-monarchist generation of the 1880s sought to position themselves in relation to British historical memory. Like previous radical opponents of monarchy, they worked with the grain of the constitutional tradition, and sought legitimization for their views by reference to accepted high points of inherited constitutional liberties. It was precisely these traditions that the queen was seen as renouncing. In 1876 Benjamin Disraeli's Royal Titles Act, which elevated Victoria's title from Queen to that of Empress of India, was seen as flouting constitutional precepts, violating Anglo-Saxon freedoms and the Revolution Settlement of 1689, as well as presaging a slide into Bonapartist-style Caesarism.[18] In popular parody Disraeli was represented as a vile tempter, seducing Victoria into an un-British and un-democratic ruling style (illus. 36). This reflected long-standing radical disquiet about Victoria's meetings with Napoleon III in the 1850s, and his subsequent period of residence in the royal palaces after his exile from France.[19] Such intimacy led to accusations that Victoria was colluding in his autocratic ambitions and seeking to imitate them in Britain.[20] At a protest meeting in Newcastle Town Hall the radical R. S. Watson commented that the title of 'emperor' had been tarnished by its associations with Napoleon III 'enough to make the name of emperor stink in the nostrils of every honest man';[21] the *Newcastle Weekly Chronicle* also ran a series of scurrilous verses on the issue recalling the traditional liberties of the 'freeborn Englishman' that were bill-posted around Newcastle:

> I remember, I remember,
>   How Britons used to boast
> That they were ruled by law, not might,
>   Nor strength of armed host.
> Was it a childish ignorance,
>   Or do we slavish grow?
> We never had an empress yet,
>   We will not have her now.[22]

The events of the Interregnum continued to provide the cardinal reference point for such sentiments. *Justice* portrayed SDF critics of the throne as heirs to this Commonwealth tradition and compared the rhetoric of Chartists like Ernest Jones and Bronterre O'Brien on monarchy to Henry Vane's defiance of the establishment during the Long Parliament.[23] Like radicals in the 1830s and 1840s, they also found inspiration for their opposition to the throne in the career of Oliver Cromwell.[24] During the 1880s Cromwell remained a major icon

"Empress! the way is ready and not long;—
if thou accept
My conduct, I can bring thee thither soon."

Milton.

"A subtle traitor needs no sophister."

Henry vi, *Part* ii.

36 This image of Disraeli as the snake in the Garden of Eden, from an 1880 pamphlet, mirrored popular distrust of both Victoria's imperial title and Disraeli himself.

for the pioneer socialist organizations; as in earlier decades anonymous correspondents who wrote to radical newspapers used his name as a *nom de plume*; socialist clubs like that at Plaistow in London were named after him; and his career served as a point of reference for the radical press.[25] In the countryside Joseph Arch's commemorations of the battle of Naseby provided agricultural labourers with the opportunity to criticize the Prince of Wales for poor wages and conditions on the royal estate at Sandringham.[26] These allusions to the 1640s became especially widespread at the time of the Irish Coercion Bill of 1881.

The *Radical* highlighted the failure of progressive opinion in the house to challenge Irish coercion by recalling parliament's defiance of Charles I in 1642 at the time of the arrest of his parliamentary opponents. It remarked:

Then the speaker was the creature of the king, as today he is the creature of the prime minister; but when his majesty came down in person to demand the surrender of the five obnoxious members, the house was true to its trust and sent the king about his business, our lot, we are afraid, has fallen on degenerate days.[27]

In the 1880s the chief vehicle for anti-monarchism became the radical Sunday weekly, *Reynolds's Newspaper*. A major survival from the Chartist era reaching an annual readership of 350,000 (including the Prince of Wales who kept up with the latest scandal about himself in its columns), *Reynolds's* provided an anchor and a focus for radical activity at a time when the reform movement outside Liberalism was in decay.[28] It was therefore natural that most ultra-radical and reform opinion should cohere around the stance of the paper, and for socialist organizations in London, where it had a large circulation, to gravitate in its direction. In the early 1880s it supported the Democratic Federation and the SDF. *Reynolds's* had a long anti-monarchist pedigree that served to position the paper outside mainstream Liberalism and made it the natural beacon for such organizations.[29] In the 1860s it broke the story of Victoria's dereliction of her public duties following Albert's death, and was the first newspaper to campaign actively on this issue.[30] In 1875 its founder, the former Chartist G. M. W. Reynolds (1814–1876), re-affirmed his own deeply held opposition to the throne, remarking at a banquet for employees of the newspaper at Alexandra Palace that his popular weeklies were 'written to show up aristocracy and monarchy in their true light'.[31] In the closing decades of the century this outlook continued to define the stance of the paper under the editorship of his brother, Edward Reynolds, and after 1894, of William Thompson.[32] Such sentiments were not, however, confined exclusively to *Reynolds's*. The paper set the tone for other radical weeklies, and strong opposition to the monarchy was also articulated in Henry Labouchère's journal *Truth*, George Standring's the *Republican*, Samuel Bennett's the *Radical*, the secularist *National Reformer*, and the SDF organ *Justice*.

Inspired by this sympathetic press, anti-monarchist attitudes resurfaced in all the major political campaigns of the latter part of the nineteenth century. As with earlier agitations, the most vociferous criticism of monarchy in the 1880s was generated by debate about the national finances. Continuing themes first raised in the eighteenth century, this sentiment was frequently an expression of opposition to financial profligacy within government.[33] It thus occurred particularly where treasury money was used to fund civil list pensions, create dowries for the royal children, or underwrite public ceremonial. In the 1870s this critique of government was aided by the revelations of 'whistle blowers' from within the civil service who anonymously released a trickle of information outlining the expense to the nation of the royal family's financial privileges.[34] Such exposés put flesh on the bare bones of earlier, more impressionistic accounts of royal wealth and aristocratic state pensioners.[35] As George Jacob Holyoake pointed out in 1876, these attitudes had a long pedigree and were an accepted part of the radical mainstream; the public outcry surrounding Sir Charles Dilke's speeches on this issue in 1871 thus took many reformers by surprise:

It is not long since a lecture was delivered by Charles Dilke at Newcastle-upon-Tyne, in which, among other considerations of state economy, he mentioned incidentally the expenses of royalty. The chairman on that occasion was Mr Cowen. It did not occur to him, nor to the audience, that there was anything extraordinary in the economical criticism made by the member for Chelsea. More than a week elapsed after its publication in the *Newcastle Weekly Chronicle* without its attracting any attention. Then a writer in the *Times* – from some motive, presumed to be personal – discovered that the financial address was an avowed revolutionary oration.[36]

Given the centrality of such ideas within radicalism, the government's decision to grant a pension to Victoria's third son, the Duke of Connaught, and to his wife in 1878 opened the way to much the same accusations of financial impropriety and condemnations of the expense of monarchy that had accompanied the grant to the Prince of Wales in 1871. Discontent with this arrangement manifested itself strongly even amongst the moderate agricultural labourers' unions; at a meeting in Warwickshire, Joseph Arch expressed opposition to this measure in almost identical terms to those used in the early 1870s:

They had had another little bill before parliament just lately, namely £10,000 per annum for the Duke of Connaught and £6,000 per annum for his wife should she out-live her husband, and this the country was giving to a man who had never done a tithe for the people of England what he, Joseph Arch, had done. They were told that this money must be paid for the purpose of maintaining royalty. (A voice: 'Bother royalty'). He did not wish to interfere with royalty, as long as it did not interfere with him and rob him.[37]

Taking up this theme in 1890, the former Chartist Andrew Carnegie returned from the United States and toured Scotland to draw attention to the Crown's privileged financial position. At Dundee he contrasted the wealth of royal pensioners supported from the taxpayer's purse with the poverty of former soldiers (survivors of the Light Brigade among them) left to fend for themselves in old age: 'The Prince of Wales got £105,000 per annum or the gross earnings of 30,000 people and the men who fought their country's battles died in the workhouse.'[38] At a popular level such sentiments connected strongly with the long-running radical opposition to income tax. In the 1880s they fed off a profound sense of frustration with increased tax burdens, reaching new depths in 1882 when the marriage of Victoria's son, Prince Leopold, to Princess Helen of Waldeck, coincided with the stringent budget of that year. *Reynolds's Newspaper* commented: 'We might usefully inquire how much royal and aristocratic personages take out of the present budget and how much comparatively royalty and aristocracy contribute to taxation.'[39]

By this period the burden to the taxpayer of new methods of royal transport, particularly the queen's yacht and train, had caused radical attitudes on this subject to harden. Although the press sought to justify the expense of the queen's steel-reinforced railway carriage on the grounds of security at a time of increased Fenian activity, for radicals it rapidly became a symbol of unnecessary opulence and privilege. Radical newspapers highlighted the expense of these measures and the inconvenience caused to the travelling public by the closure of stations, and tight security on the line when the train passed.[40] The various royal yachts came under heavy fire for similar reasons, but were also criticized as a hazard to navigation and for their role as pleasure steamers for visiting foreign princes. In 1875 an accident in the Solent in which the royal yacht *Alberta* capsized a smaller vessel, the *Mistletoe*, with the loss of two crew-members, resulted in a public outcry and generated a wave of scurrilous songs that highlighted the popular resentment of such privileged methods of transport.[41] Above all, attempts by the captain of the *Alberta*, the queen's cousin, Prince Leiningen, to use his royal connections to influence the inquest jury to exonerate him of blame in the accident led to radical criticism of courtiers who tried to 'override English law'.[42]

The targeting of individuals and familial groupings at court, whose indiscretions were repeatedly exposed in the radical press, brings anti-monarchist rhetoric within the populist frame of reference outlined by Patrick Joyce.[43] Often these courtiers were the self-same royal children and scions of high-ranking aristocratic houses ridiculed by an earlier generation of anti-monarchists. In the 1840s the *Northern Star* had published a series of attacks on the Duke of Cambridge, criticizing his inclusion on the Civil List.[44] In the 1880s the duke remained a widely disliked figure. His promotion to Commander-in-Chief of the army on the grounds of connection alone provoked strong radical hostility and precipitated a long-running campaign that highlighted his unsuitability for the role.[45] *Reynolds's* also continued the vilification of junior branches of the royal family like the Albanys, the Edinburghs and the Connaughts, who had all attained high rank in the army, the admiralty and the civil service.[46] Moreover, radicals subjected the pedigrees of court dynasties like the St Albans or the Buccleuchs to a searching examination that highlighted their illegitimate origins and aimed to discredit their connection to the royal bloodline and concomitant right to state pensions. Unearthing memories of Stuart dissoluteness, *Reynolds's* described the presence of such families on the civil list as 'the wages of prostitution'.[47] The country's great military families were also included in these attacks. At a lecture at the Lambeth Democratic Association in 1881 entitled 'Royal Bastards and Court Favourites', the radical Woods criticized the favoured position of the Marlboroughs at the Hanoverian court and accused them of embezzling the cost of the construction of Blenheim Palace from the nation.[48]

For many radicals this issue of a corrupt court raised the spectre of the monarchy as the screen for hidden forces that were able to manipulate its central role within the constitution. Such attitudes were a variant of the long-standing radical conspiracy-theory view of the state's relationship to its citizenry that emerged strongly in contemporary agitations like the Tichborne movement.[49] Invariably these forces were both foreign and sinister; most radicals projected their fears onto these shadowy presences behind the Crown. *Reynolds's*, for example, drew upon popular memory of the German anti-democratic tradition to suggest that a cabal of German advisers close to the throne were importing continental despotism into Britain. Such attacks were a continuation of the belief that Prince Albert had exercised unwarranted control over the queen during his lifetime. Writing of his posthumous influence over Victoria, *Reynolds's* commented:

We well know that since the queen married Prince Albert she has interfered incessantly in political matters. This is shown in publication of leaves from her own diary when also the reason for so doing is stated. Prince Albert did not like constitutionalism: a thorough German at heart he was a warm adherent of German institutions, of which absolutism is the principal.[50]

In 1876 suspicion of Disraeli's Jewishness and a misunderstanding of the references to political conspiracies in his novel *Lothair* fuelled a strident radical opposition to the Royal Titles Bill that was rooted in anti-Semitic sentiment and fear of eastern-style potentates. The *Newcastle Weekly Chronicle* wrote:

He is among us, but he is not of us. Our common sense he seems to hold in contempt. It does not suit his Oriental tastes which would have had ampler and more appropriate scope if fate had made him the Grand Vizier of the Sultan or the First Minister of the Shah.[51]

During the Eastern Question crisis of 1877–8 radical opponents of Disraeli's support for Turkey against Russia accused him of ensnaring Victoria in his mysterious schemes to extend Jewish influence and control in the Middle East at the expense of the other European powers.[52] Victoria herself was the target of attacks that accused her of concealing her Jewish blood and harbouring racially determined avaricious designs on English money. A correspondent in *Reynolds's Newspaper* commented:

It is by no means the first time that it has been asserted that the Queen has Semitic blood in her veins. In fact her family name, Wettin, is borne by many Jewish families abroad. But whether that be so or not, she would not discredit the most typical Hebrew in her capacity for the exercize of those very un-queenlike traits of the accumulating and hoarding of money.[53]

In a similar vein, radical criticism of the central place of John Brown in the royal household echoed the anti-Scottishness and anti-Catholicism that had provoked attacks on the Scottish presence at court in the eighteenth century.[54]

In radical discussion of the German influences behind the throne, there was a strong sense of the dangers posed by the monarchy's appropriation of constitutional functions under the existing system. In 1886 the split in the Liberal ranks over Irish Home Rule and Victoria's decision to promote a Tory–Unionist government highlighted contemporary fears about her willingness to intervene directly in politics. There was still, however, no formulation of a vocabulary of natural rights of justice or of citizenship on the part of radicals to express the freedoms contravened by centralized royal power. Instead, the radicals of the 1880s took their cue from the anti-monarchist rhetoric of the Chartist era. The Teutonic origins of the royal dynasty continued to provide an easy target for reformers and enabled them to draw upon the same images and language of German despotism employed by previous radical movements. As in the past, they highlighted the 'Germanness' of the royal family, their alien, continental connections, and the large number of German relatives who received subsidies, places and honours from the British state. Radicals hoped that such revelations would offend the chauvinistic sensibilities of the British public, while at the same time exonerating the radical camp from the charge that they harboured unpatriotic attitudes. These sentiments surfaced in most of the adverse commentary on monarchy during this period. A much quoted popular rhyme spoke of 'the very dogs in England's court [that] bark and howl in German'.[55] In 1890 *Reynolds's Newspaper* stated with reference to the royal household that: 'We should not be sorry to see the whole brood sent back to Germany',[56] and in 1882 the paper remarked of the wedding of Victoria's son, the Duke of Albany (Prince Leopold), to Princess Helen of Waldeck:

There is much in the royal marriage that is both ghastly and grotesque. On Tuesday last a flight of locusts descended upon our shores. This appearance, according to scriptural records, has always brought devastation upon the unhappy lands whose produce the vermin devoured. Germany is the country that has most frequently invaded us with these mischievous and much dreaded visitors, and on Tuesday last a ship-load of them was disembarked at Queensborough. No more appropriate vessel than 'The Locust' could have been selected by the admiral at the Nore to perform, if required, this duty.[57]

For most radical opinion the genuine essence of Englishness resided in the critics of monarchy, rather than in its defenders. Radicals cited Milton, Paine and Thackeray as examples of the true spirit of the nation, while *Reynolds's* noted the irony of a country 'past masters in the art of crawling' that could not 'produce the much prized royal commodity at home'.[58]

The image of the court as a sybaritic institution that corrupted all those exposed to it was an essential ingredient of the anti-monarchist rhetoric of the 1880s and 1890s. In particular this image informed the perspective of radicals who felt betrayed by the Lib–Lab MPs elected to the House during this period. Such charges recall those directed against reformers like William Cobbett and Francis Burdett in the 1830s, who were also accused of succumbing to the lure of royal favour and the aristocratic embrace of government once they entered parliament. In the 1880s this mood reflected the frustrations of reformers and socialists who felt that the Lib–Labs had failed to satisfy the radical expectations they had aroused. *Reynolds's Newspaper* was highly critical of Henry Broadhurst in the early 1880s when 'he first rubbed clothes with the sons of dukes and millionaires'.[59] The radical press was also dismayed by erstwhile radical champions, such as Sir Charles Dilke and John Bright, whose radicalism, their followers believed, had been tempered by exposure to public office. Morrison Davidson wrote of former republicans who once in government hastened 'to Windsor to beslobber the royal fist'.[60] In 1883 the socialist journal *Liberty* published a critical profile of Dilke that bitterly attacked his new-found friendship with the Prince of Wales on these grounds and accused him of forgetting his own republican principles of 1870–71:

In place of the stern, unbending, uncompromising denouncer of royalty, robbery and public jobbery of every kind, we have the sleek, pliant, gratified, smirking courtier, who is ready to swallow all his former life to retain his comfortable position, and catch occasionally a condescending smile of recognition from royalty. In the littleness of his soul he basks in the sunshine of the great, and will continue to do so while he forms a factor in the governmental machine.[61]

Similar charges were levelled against John Bright when he became President of the Board of Trade in 1880. *Reynolds's Newspaper* remarked: 'His great blunder was to allow himself to be dragged into the malarial circle of the court. True he made that fatal plunge with sad forebodings. He would rather, he said, "have remained amongst his own people" [...] No honest man can serve two masters – a queen and a people. Monarchy and democracy are wide as the poles asunder.'[62] For the SDF, entry into court circles was an act of collaboration with the establishment, little short of treachery. George Lansbury remembered that Harry Quelch was ostracized when he joined a deputation from the London Trades Council to meet the Prince of Wales: 'Quelch appeared in what is known as morning dress, a high hat, white waist-coat etc. One would have imagined from the indignation all this caused that he had deserted and gone over to the enemy.'[63] Such attitudes breathed new life into the theme of Cobbett's 'Thing' as a corrupting agent of the 'people's champions'.

Anti-monarchism in the 1880s also drew upon the utopian vision of a younger generation of radicals. In particular it reflected an emerging current of concern for the plight of animals expressed strongly in such circles.[64] In this theme images of German barbarism and the heartlessness of the royal court fused. Prince Albert had been strongly criticized for his love of hunting earlier in the century. Through the depiction of his wholesale slaughter of English wildlife, contemporary engravings managed to suggest that the Prince Consort was introducing barbaric Teutonic hunting customs into England.[65] Moreover, the image of an aloof, unconcerned royal family that had only disdain for the existing order of the natural world confirmed older stereotypes of a dissolute and drunken aristocracy obsessed with hedonism and the gratification of its own pleasures. After Albert's death these images were projected onto the Prince of Wales who remained a keen hunts-man throughout his life and was publicly criticized for tiger hunting during royal visits to India and for his advocacy of vivisection.[66] In 1869 the radical E. A. Freeman mounted a noisy campaign against the prince's involvement in field sports that attacked the 'contemptible hypocrisy' of those who acted as 'patrons of societies for the prevention of cruelty to costermongers' donkeys' whilst 'delighting in the cruel and unmanly massacre of tame pigeons'.[67] Taking up this theme, *Liberty* commented on Queen Victoria's condemnation of the consumption of lamb in 1883:

If Her Majesty would be good enough to turn her attention to the question of 'sport', her pigeon-shooting son and others might possibly have their minds opened to the fact that to prick out the eyes of birds to make them an easier mark for slaughter is a degraded and brutal pastime, in which no man of honour and courage could take part.[68]

In the 1890s the *Clarion* also waged a major campaign against court patronage of the deer-hunting meets at Hurlingham. The first public petition against hunting in Britain was organized by the Humanitarian League against the hunting of royal stags in 1900.[69] The issue was again one of the sordid spectacle of such events, particularly where the presence of visiting German dignitaries enabled radicals to make the connection with a callous 'Germanness'.[70] In 1891 the paper upbraided Victoria for her attendance at Hurlingham following her publicly stated opposition to hare-coursing on Tyneside:

I wonder whether Her Majesty ever heard of Hurlingham or of the performances of her own buckhounds on the tame deer; and if so whether she sees any difference between the 'sport' of the rough colliers and that of the noble pigeon-shooters and buck-hunters who might reasonably be expected to know better.[71]

In addition the *Clarion* ran a gloating feature listing the names of aristocrats who had been injured as a result of hunting accidents.[72]

In 1887 and 1897 these various criticisms of monarchy crystallized around campaigns launched by *Reynolds's Newspaper* against the public ceremonial of Queen Victoria's Golden and Diamond jubilees. Most existing work in this area has stressed the manifestations of chauvinistic and patriotic fervour produced by the jubilees or their increasing commercialization.[73] This has meant that opposition to these royal festivals has been overlooked or marginalized. David Cannadine and Linda Colley detect in these rituals a celebration of 'altar, throne and cottage' rooted in past royal ceremonial that successfully laid the foundations for the vibrant and assertive sense of Victorian English identity.[74] According to this reading royal celebrations that were also

37 Life Guards leading the Naval Contingent across London Bridge on jubilee day 1887. The centrality of military images in that celebration was intended to remind the public of Britain's military prowess.

reaffirmations of 'nationhood' reached a height of perfectibility in the jubilees, which were essentially 'national' rejoicings in the tradition of the victory celebrations that accompanied the end of the Napoleonic and Crimean Wars (illus. 37). Unsurprisingly, the 1887 jubilee was accompanied by a new monarchist consensus in parliamentary politics that, against the background of the Home Rule Crisis, led Joseph Chamberlain to speculate about the formation of a 'centrist' party that would unite the best of the Tory and Liberal parties and render the extremes impotent (illus. 38). The Liberal R. B. Haldane saw the ceremonial of the 1887 jubilee as a vulgar symbol of the weakness rather than the strength of monarchy, and hoped a National Party project might rejuvenate it.[75]

Cannadine and Colley are right to highlight the increased sophistication of British royal ritual and ceremony after the 1870s. When Victoria succeeded to the throne in 1838 the British court was dowdy and impoverished. By the 1830s much of the ritual surrounding George III as a 'patriot king' that had characterized the Napoleonic War period had been allowed to lapse. Rites of royal passage, including birth, death and coronation, were greeted with apathy, or even downright hostility. At the time of George IV's death, monarchy had lost control of the streets and his coffin was pelted with excrement during the state funeral. In the 1840s the *Northern Star* frequently derided the rare appearances of the young Victoria or the royal dukes in the

LIGHT AND SHADE.

38 Gladstone as an owl, the bird that fouls its own nest, roosting in the rubbish tip of his divisive Home Rule policies for Ireland. Behind him the British Lion expresses the splendour of the 1887 jubilee.

regions and in Scotland.[76] Leaving the Chartist convention of 1839 early to watch Victoria open Parliament, Peter Murray McDouall recorded booing from the spectators and mocked 'the state carriage like a great big candlestick in the centre of which was stuck our young queen as yellow as a penny candle and about equally as attractive'.[77]

During these years civic ritual and pageants connected with royal events in the industrial towns and cities were sufficiently unusual and poorly organized to face regular invasion by the Chartists. In 1840 meetings in London and Carlisle convened to congratulate Queen Victoria on her escape from an assassination attempt were badly disrupted by Chartists demanding social justice for the poor, the release of Feargus O'Connor from gaol and the impeachment of the government.[78] The Staffordshire Chartist William Ellis was transported for orchestrating one such intervention during a meeting in the Potteries to celebrate the birth of the Prince of Wales.[79]

Even before the end of Victoria's seclusion, however, there are signs of an increased formalization to the pageantry and spectacle surrounding her rare public appearances.[80] By the 1880s the British monarchy had an enviable reputation for staging some of the most elaborate and imaginative royal festivals in Europe, with the 1887 jubilee a case in point. Moreover, by the late-Victorian period royal ritual had become strongly intertwined with the civic pageant and fêtes of the new provincial town councils. This created new agendas for radicals who opposed the cult of monarchy and limited still further the rhetoric previously deployed in opposition to the throne. Radicals now became exclusively concerned to discredit the window-dressing of the royal state and the expense that lay behind it, to the exclusion of broader arguments about social justice and equality before the law. This added a new element to anti-monarchist rhetoric that sometimes found a popular appeal, but did little to broaden the prevailing critique of the throne or incorporate humanist and secularist objections to it.

Radicals recognized the need to break the self-confident assertion of power and tradition that came to characterize the late Victorian monarchy. Both jubilees were about the celebration of an unchanging and timeless royal order. Accounts by revellers reveal that some of those who were old enough dressed in the same clothes they had worn in 1838 at the time of Victoria's coronation, as if the intervening years had left society completely unaltered (illus. 39). At Chipping Sodbury, one elderly woman who had been present at George III's jubilee celebrated again in 1887 wearing the same 'Leghorn [bonnet] of coal-scuttle shape' she had worn in 1809.[81] Those who had no original clothes dressed up in the style of 1838. The jubilee bonfires were similarly timeless, recalling the beacons lit to signal the approach of the Armada, and evocative of the long-standing traditional liberties of Protestant England (illus. 40).[82] In the cities of the north a spurious crypto-medievalism was very apparent in much of the jubilee ceremonial. Here

39 An invitation to elderly residents of Saddleworth near Oldham to attend a celebratory dinner in commemoration of Victoria's accession. These events projected an image of timeless royal rule.

40 Jubilee bonfire on Oldham Edge in 1897. Such events were portrayed as bringing the entire community together.

the construction of links with an imagined medieval past was important to restore ancestral memories of a pre-industrial golden age under sage royal rule, and to deny the social dislocation created by urbanization and industrialization.[83]

In Manchester the corporation constructed a heritage theme-park of early nineteenth-century buildings, complete with blacksmith's forge, to reflect the flavour of British life at the time of Victoria's accession.[84] Similarly in Coventry in 1897 the first Lady Godiva pageant for a number of years was held to reinforce Victoria's associations with traditional civic freedoms conferred under the monarchy's pre-Norman ancestors.[85] Historians have consistently underestimated the ability of radicals to construct alternative narratives in opposition to royalty's command of this highground of British history. Nevertheless, radicals too had living historical lineages and, as with the defenders of the throne, always appreciated the importance of grounding their hostility to the jubilees in past precedent. At a meeting of an alternative parliament at the Charing Cross Hotel during the 1887 jubilee, radicals used the formalized language and procedures of Parliament in a satirical Queen's Speech to highlight the defects of government policy during Victoria's reign (illus. 41).[86] There was more than mere irony at work here; such observations also showed a profound awareness of the alternative historical memories apparent within the institution and precedent of Parliament and signalled a broader search for a purer, non-monarchical constitution.[87]

The failure to mark formally the bicentennial of 1688 the year after the 1887 jubilee left the way open for radicals to reclaim the undercurrents of freedom from unrestrained royal rule encoded within the

41 'Some Rough Sketches at a "Sitting" of the Charing Cross Parliament', which first assembled to express disquiet at Victoria's jubilee celebrations in 1887. Annie Besant is 'Home Secretary'.

events of the Glorious Revolution.[88] In 1898 the Chartist jubilee convened by *Reynolds's Newspaper* to celebrate the fiftieth anniversary of the last Chartist petition was staged as a self-conscious antidote to recent royal rejoicings, and set out to undermine the queen's jubilee by invoking Britain's hidden history of opposition to the Crown in the 1680s. The paper remarked that the venue for the commemoration at Rye House in Hertfordshire was carefully chosen to mark the Rye House plot of 1683: 'This place was once the resort where some of the greatest nobles of England plotted the murder of Charles II, king, blackguard, would-be tyrant, traitor to his country, and born religious hypocrite.'[89] For the organizers of this event the attempt to assassinate the king was a 'republican' moment. Above all, the involvement of Commonwealthmen like Algernon Sydney in the conspiracy demonstrated to radicals that Chartism, anti-tyranny and republican virtues were synonymous.[90]

Cannadine and Colley's explanation of the role of monarchy addresses the rituals surrounding the throne during the jubilees primarily as pageant, and less as confident and aggressive displays of state power. In this sense they have overlooked an essential ingredient in the composition of the Victorian military state. There were strong military undertones to both events (illus. 42); the climax of the 1897 celebrations in London was a parade of military forces from throughout the empire, and there was a review by the queen of the fleet at Spithead. These elements were very apparent to contemporaries and were widely noted in the radical press.

42 'Defenders of the Empire': imperial soldiers in London for the 1887 jubilee, including units from Borneo, Sierra Leone and Australia and a Hausa regiment from West Africa.

The jubilees were never truly inclusive events, open to all sections of the community; some were always excluded, particularly the poor, radicals, opponents of militarism and, in 1897, opponents of colonialism. *Reynolds's Newspaper* was the main mouthpiece for those who felt dispossessed by such ceremonial. An exhibition of the queen's jubilee presents in the poorer districts of London's East End in 1887 provoked comments on the disparities of wealth and power revealed by the festivities.[91] In 1897 it drew attention to preferential seating arrangements that favoured 'the swells' and made little concession to the poor who wished to see the procession – 'do not imagine that they were missed!'[92] Above all the jubilees were about the regulation of public ritual. Both jubilees were rigorously policed to prevent the assassination of the queen. In 1897 there were rumours that Scotland Yard intended to intern all foreign radicals resident in the capital, and the police mounted round-the-clock surveillance of anarchist clubs in Soho and Fitzroy Square.[93] In the aftermath of the 'Bloody Sunday' riots in Trafalgar Square in November 1887, there were bitter ruminations in the radical press on the hidden powers of the monarchical state once the veneer of royal ritual was scraped away, and the apparent lack of concern on the part of the queen for her subjects injured or sleeping rough in the square.[94]

The public ceremonials of the jubilee therefore provided radicals with the opportunity to dissect the rituals of the royal state, and opened the way for discussion of the feudal and anachronistic survivals present in the stage-sets of monarchy. It was no longer the queen's absence that was the target of the reform community, but her presence. For radicals the traditional display surrounding monarchy merely sanctified centralized power. Given the recent emphasis on the continuing importance of the aristocracy throughout the nineteenth century, anti-monarchist critiques might well be seen as displaying a far shrewder understanding of the realities of the Victorian state than hitherto appreciated.[95] *Reynolds's* had long campaigned against chivalric and heraldic elements at court and in public life. In discussions of this theme it attempted to alert the radical community to the dangers they posed to constitutional liberties.[96] Nevertheless, following the established pattern of previous criticism of royal coronations, weddings and christenings, it used the weapon of derision to highlight the excesses of jubilee ceremonial (illus. 43). There are echoes of Jack Wade's *Black Book* in the tone employed by such ridicule. His attacks on 'the parade of crowns and coronets, of gold keys, sticks and wands and black rods'[97] are repeated in *Reynolds's* description of the 'flummery' surrounding the presentation of Parliament's jubilee oath of

43 'Oh! the jubilee!!' A republican parody of jubilee ceremonial. The caption notes that the artist 'has been shot'.

loyalty to the queen in 1897. Speaking of rituals 'direct from the lumber room', it commented:

Fancy a number of fat, middle-aged gentlemen squeezing themselves into braided coats, and wearing swords and cocked hats then crawling up and kneeling to kiss the hand of the diminutive woman who is on the throne. And what a sight to see all these legislative doodles leaving the royal presence by retreating backwards like crabs.[98]

For the secularist J. M. Robertson, writing in the *National Reformer*, the main lesson to emerge from the emphasis on empty spectacle during the jubilees was 'the intellectual destitution of the case for monarchy'.[99]

Radicals defined themselves in terms of their non-participation in such ceremonial. It was opposed by mainstream radical opinion almost from the start. Such non-compliance with royal ceremonial could be either individual or collective. It ranged from discussions about releasing balloons over London packed with republican pamphlets in 1887, to simply staying at home and reading a good book.[100] During both jubilees radical clubs in London provided havens of tranquillity where royal events might be ignored in comfort. Particular contempt was reserved for radicals who broke ranks and took an active part in the rejoicing. Such strength of feeling on this issue recalls the acrimonious divisions within plebeian radicalism at the time of the public ceremonial to celebrate the recovery of the Prince of Wales from typhoid in the 1870s.[101] As in 1872, radicals who led the deputations of working-men intended to reaffirm the loyalty of the lower orders to the person of the monarch were vilified by the radical press. In 1887 George Potter and G. J. Holyoake were especially criticized on this basis. *Reynolds's* remarked of the presence of Potter at a London Trades Council deputation to Sandringham:

Sycophants of royalty are the worst enemies of the working-orders, and those who parade themselves as their friends frequently do so for their own aggrandizement and glorification and nothing else. This we believe to be the case as regards Mr Potter who represents number one and perhaps half a dozen others.[102]

Holyoake was also criticized for his participation in a working-men's jubilee extravaganza at the Crystal Palace, and was sufficiently stung by these attacks to justify his attendance in his autobiography.[103] In 1897 the Fabians were the targets of similar criticism in *Reynolds's Newspaper*. Under the headline 'Socialist Royalists', the Webbs were attacked for taking the initiative in proposing an oath of loyalty to the throne. It concluded: 'After this we must expect to find them making friends with landed gentry, clergy and capitalists.'[104]

The radical press also attempted to subvert the royal and patriotic meanings of the jubilees by discrediting their loyalist associations. Seeking to recapture the language and trappings of radical 'jubileeism' from its pro-monarchist accretions in 1887, *Reynolds's* appealed directly for a return to the true principles of the biblical jubilee of Leviticus which occupied a central place within the language and imagery of radical culture.[105] In so doing, it caricatured the injustice of a festival that redistributed honours and titles amongst the rich, rather than wealth or land amongst the poor and deserving:

A year of jubilee ought to bring great comfort and relief to the people at large. Once in every fifty years the land had to be redistributed amongst the people [...] The modern notion of a jubilee seems to be to contrive a state of things which shall produce a distribution of peerages, baronetcies, knighthoods and ribands in society.[106]

In 1897 the *Labour Leader* adopted a similar position and accused loyalists of devising a pretext for 'the counterfeit' of the egalitarian principles contained within the model of the Hebrew jubilee.[107] *Reynolds's* publicized a more private sense of unease among members of the public who were dissatisfied with the opulent ceremonial of the jubilees. Its letters page acted as a forum for numerous complaints on this topic. The radical press more generally also gave special prominence to personal testimonies of the pressures brought to bear on those who sought to stay apart from the rejoicing. Radical columnists like W. E. Adams recorded that they found the exhortations to 'jubilate' in 1887 unbearable and expressed the hope that there would be no more jubilees.[108] Such sentiments offer a snapshot of individual acts of defiance and provide a unique insight into an unspoken underground attitude of opposition to monarchy that has left little record elsewhere in Victorian culture.

In 1887 *Reynolds's Newspaper* highlighted the reluctance of many members of the armed forces to contribute to the Prince of Wales's proposals for an Imperial Institute in London funded by the public, as evidence of disillusionment with royalty amongst even the most patriotic sections of society.[109] A private writing under the pseudonym of

'Tommy Atkins' confessed that he had been coerced into contributing to the Institute and attacked a subscription system that 'enables company and commanding officers to know and keep a list of the names of the men who do not subscribe'.[110] In 1897 a correspondent gave a personal account of his own experience of 'jubilee bullies' that recalled the excesses of the Jingo rioters of 1878:

> 'Take off your hat' was the remark addressed to me by the well dressed bully in the stalls during the performance of the Royal Aquarium on the afternoon of Jubilee Day, and, as I refused to do so, this loyal defender of the queen forced me to defend myself by first knocking off the article in question and afterwards striking me fiercely with his fist. He closed and my opponent's head opened from the effects of it coming in contact with something a little harder.[111]

Throughout the jubilee summers of 1887 and 1897 *Reynolds's* sought to counterbalance the staged public protestations of loyalty by drawing attention to such popular opposition to the celebrations. Other reform newspapers like the *Radical* hoped that in the aftermath of the festivities the populace would come to realize the folly of such royalist rejoicing: 'We can but hope that, in a few days or weeks, John Bull may wake up with a splitting headache, and reflect that he has acted like a consummate ass.'[112]

For radicals the example of Australian resistance to the jubilee was crucial in heightening awareness of the defects of the royal state in both its domestic and colonial settings. In 1887 Australia alone among the white dominions furnished evidence of opposition to the celebrations. Australia had a long history of non-compliance with staged royal ceremonial. Contempt for the monarchy was also frequently expressed in journals like the *Bulletin* that campaigned for a loosening of the colony's ties to the Mother Country and which savagely satirized an 'unmanly' British democracy, 'where caricatures of manhood such as Cambridge, Battenberg, Leiningen, Sax-Weimar and the rest of the noble unemployed are forced as pensioners upon the nation'.[113] The tone of such papers harmonized well with that of *Reynolds's Newspaper*. Like *Reynolds's*, the main targets of the *Bulletin* were the wealthy and over-privileged aristocratic elite ruling society from Sydney, whose presence as colonial administrators was especially resented in the freer setting of the New World.

For these Australian journals the true traditions of the seventeenth-century English revolution were to be found, not in England, but rather in the colonies, where Australians were portrayed as the direct heirs to the authors of the American Declaration of Independence. In July 1887 the *Bulletin* pushed this line vigorously when Independence Day celebrations in the United States coincided with the jubilee festivities in Australia.[114] In both Australia and the United Kingdom images of the mythic freedoms of the Australian bush helped underpin such ideas. These attitudes fed back strongly into the British radical press. Writing from Australia at the height of the jubilee of 1887, the transplanted British secularist Joseph Symes emphasized this theme:

This is a new land; once the peaceful, bloodless revolution becomes dominant we shall go further than the old lands can yet proceed. In spite of the toadyism and the petty tyranny so prevalent here, there is a strong undercurrent of genuine freedom, above which the hoary institutions of tyranny float, as yet buoyed up by social corks and bladders filled with old-world sentiments and pious vapours. But their fate is neither doubtful, nor distant.[115]

In June 1887 radicals in Sydney invaded a meeting of the jubilee committee in the Town Hall, overturned a vote of loyalty to the sovereign, and passed a motion in favour of a separate Australian republic. Later meetings of the committee were packed with loyalists by the organizers to prevent a recurrence of this event.[116] This episode received maximum exposure in the radical press in Britain.[117] The campaign in the radical weeklies also gained impetus from the example of Australian opposition to fund-raising events for the Imperial Institute in the dominions.[118] There was a lively exchange of views between British and Australian radicals over this issue, and the *Bulletin* was frequently quoted by *Reynolds's News* on the subject.[119]

At the height of the 1887 celebrations *Reynolds's News* devoted many column inches to anti-jubilee sentiment in the United Kingdom, reporting both formally orchestrated opposition to the ceremonies, and individual acts of non-compliance. At the beginning of that year it had opened its columns to a committee chaired by H. H. Champion that sought to raise subscriptions for a 'people's memorial' satirizing the celebrations.[120] In addition, it was instrumental in co-ordinating a campaign by metropolitan radical clubs in protest against the expense of the staged royal events. This attracted some support from ratepayers. In smaller, newly incorporated boroughs, expensive jubilee ceremonial stretched local budgets. As a consequence there were frequent wrangles in many council chambers between those who belived that the jubilees should by marked by civic architecture that celebrated the dignified part of the constitution and those who wanted to see a commemorative outlay of funds to local orphanages, hospitals and charitable trusts. On occasion such factionalization could tip over into anti-monarchist display.

At Congleton in Cheshire the burden placed on local finances by the cost of a new park, a commemorative drinking fountain and public baths strained goodwill in the town, provoking a rebellion by rate-payers in 1887. At a meeting of the town council to plan the celebrations, the national anthem was booed and rebels turned 'their backs to the plat-form [...] put on their hats and rushed from the room, causing the otherwise agreeable meeting to break up in some confusion'.[121] *Reynolds's* similarly highlighted a protest by councillors in St-George's-in-the-Martyr vestry, east London, against parish support for the Imperial Institute.[122] During the Diamond Jubilee the paper publicized the discontent with expensive public ceremonial expressed by some local councils, particularly those in Brierley Hill in the West Midlands and Audenshaw in Manchester. It gained particular satisfaction from Audenshaw council's decision to spend money earmarked for the jubilee celebrations on extending its municipal cemetery.[123]

More subversive acts of opposition, some of which involved breaking the law, were also recorded in the paper's columns. In 1887 it reported the smashing of windows in Norwich town centre following a meeting at which SDF speakers criticized the expense of royalty.[124] In 1897 it gave prominence to accounts of the premature ignition of jubilee bonfires at Frinton-on-Sea on the south coast, at Walton-on-Naze, Essex, and Cleeve Cloud in the Cotswolds.[125] It denied that these were random acts of arson, indicating anti-jubilee verses from the paper that had been left at the site of the attacks and which 'pointed to good old *Reynolds's* as the schoolmaster'.[126] Contemporary photographs of the Oldham jubilee bonfire at Oldham Edge in 1897 show the presence of a police guard, suggesting that such acts of arson were not isolated incidents (illus. 44).

The public places chosen for such ceremonies were themselves contested spaces; Oldham Edge was a traditional meeting place for reformers and had strong Chartist and radical associations.[127] In some rural communities radicals prevented the planting of jubilee trees on common land by invoking long-standing rights of access and physi-cally impeding local dignitaries from carrying out the task. Such events went unrecorded by the loyalist provincial press at the time, but emerged from the later reminiscences of those who had taken part.[128] Furthermore *Reynolds's* drew attention to mock 'Diamond Jubilee Processions', describing that at Walton-on-Naze in detail. It was:

Formed of an old cart made up as a state coach and drawn by eight donkeys. In this was seated an old man, faked up as the queen, accompanied by her imme-diate relatives, guarded by young fellows dressed in court and military uniforms and mounted on donkeys [...] The crowd received the procession with joviality and mirth.[129]

44 Another photograph of the jubilee bonfire on Oldham Edge in 1897 clearly shows the presence of a police guard.

In these events, carnivalesque images of inversion were again very apparent. Irreverent burlesque was also present in popular literature. In his account of the 1887 jubilee in Lancashire, dialect writer Ben Brierley conveyed a similar desire for social levelling in a dream sequence in which the Prince of Wales lives the life of a weaver for a day and is set to work on a loom.[130] In this description there is a strong sense of the high brought low and the low elevated to a higher station.

Using *Reynolds's* it is possible to map the incidence of opposition to jubilee events. The most overt opposition occurred in the Celtic fringe. Here the celebration of royalty and 'Englishness' that underpinned the jubilee festivities in England frequently caused offence, and high-lighted the dependent nature of these regions on a centralized bureaucratic structure in Westminster. In both Scotland and Wales, emergent Home Rule tendencies expressed through the Scottish Land and Labour League and Cymru Fydd compounded resentment at the expense of the celebrations and resulted in the boycotting of some patriotic displays.[131] In Scotland, as elsewhere in 1887, subscriptions to the Imperial Institute were opposed, and Glasgow Trades Council refused to contribute to a jubilee memorial in the city on the grounds of expense at a time of trade depression.[132] Such views were articulated

strongly by the plebeian radical weeklies on the fringes of the Liberal
Party in Scotland. The *Radical Times* came close to advocating outright
independence in its remarks on the 1887 jubilee:

The money proposed to be squandered in impotent vanity, let it be appor-
tioned in the spirit of a purer patriotism which loves mercy before sacrifice
[...] Is there any wonder that the shout for Home Rule is echoing through
Scotland, Ireland and Wales? In what other way than Home Rule are the intol-
erable sufferings and inequitable restraints of the toiling poor in those
countries to have relief and human justice done to them?"[133]

In parts of Wales there was a similar pattern of non-compliance
during the jubilees. Royal ceremonial was routinely disregarded in Wales
to a degree unthinkable in England both during and after the Victorian
era. Victoria was often snubbed during her infrequent visits to Wales for
her role as Defender of the Church of England in a period of religious
revivalism in which Welsh Nonconformity was asserting itself.[134] When
she died in 1901 the only fox-hunt in the kingdom to continue its meets
throughout the period of national mourning was the Tivyside Hunt in
Dyfed.[135] Moreover, the 1887 jubilee coincided with the Welsh Tithe War
which provoked rioting against church commissioners in Mont-
gomeryshire in June and July.[136] In London H. H. Champion pointed to
the large number of financial contributions to the 'people's memorial'
from Wales in that year.[137] In 1887 loyalists were also booed at a public
meeting in Llanelly and there were refusals to co-operate with the festivities by Neath Corporation and Cardiff Trades Council.[138]

In Ireland the jubilees reinforced the sectarian divisions present
within Irish society; Protestant loyalists in the north celebrated them
rapturously and used them as a pretext for attacks on Catholics, while in
the Catholic south they were bitterly opposed.[139] In southern rural
Ireland the jubilees reaffirmed the expulsion of the Irish from the wider
Anglo-Celtic community of the British Isles and exacerbated tensions
caused by the Land War. Opposition to them was thus systematic and
sustained. The jubilees coincided with a period of resistance by the
republican nationalist community to royal visits and ceremonial, beginning in 1885 with hostile demonstrations against the visit of the Prince
and Princess of Wales.[140] In addition, the 1897 jubilee occurred during
preparations for the commemoration of the 1798 rising. As part of
this process disruption of the jubilee ceremonies became a wider expression of anger against British rule that highlighted the subservient and
colonial status of Ireland. In 1897 nationalist intellectuals used the
jubilee as the occasion for counter-demonstrations at which James
Connolly consigned a coffin marked 'The British Empire' into the river

Liffey at Dublin, and black flags were flown in Cork and Skibbereen. In Derry a Union Jack was hoisted symbolically over a slaughterhouse.[141] Elsewhere the '98 committees and clubs set up their own commemorative statuary and architecture honouring the heroes of 1798 that sought to subvert and reclaim the 'loyalist' landscape of Ireland's towns and villages.[142] These demonstrations were noted sympathetically by the radical press in England; protests against the subscription to the Imperial Institute in 1887 and actual outbreaks of disorder in 1897 outside Trinity College, Dublin were given prominence by *Reynolds's Newspaper*.[143]

Such disruption frequently spilled over into the Irish migrant communities on the mainland. In 1897 the national conference of the Irish National League in Manchester voted to ignore all public events connected with the jubilee, and a correspondent in *Reynolds's* suggested that effigies of the Fenian martyrs, Allen, Larkin and O'Brien, should be suspended across the route of the jubilee procession in the Strand.[144] Prominent in all the Irish opposition to the jubilees was a profoundly different vision of Victoria to the commonplaces that characterized royal rejoicing throughout the rest of the British Isles. In Ireland folk memories of her as the queen who presided over the diaspora of the 1840s and, who, according to legend, had offered a derisory £5 for famine relief provided a powerful resonance into the 1890s and beyond. In addition, the 1887 jubilee coincided with Lord Salisbury's Coercion Bill restricting rights of public assembly which was subsequently christened the 'Jubilee Coercion Bill' by the supporters of Home Rule.[145] In Irish historical memory Victoria's reputation was always tarnished by these associations with Ireland's sufferings. As a result 'The Famine Queen' jibe remained a powerful element in nationalist propaganda up to the turn of the century, and was recalled during her state visit to Dublin in 1900:

She comes as she came in '49 to cozen Ireland. She will fail as she failed then, when a million of Irish corpses lay at her feet. Since she ascended the throne of England not ruthless Elizabeth wrought more havoc on our nation. Five million of our people she has banished – three million more she has banished to famine graves. But the nation lives and will survive her smile, as it will survive her scowl.[146]

Contemporary nationalist cartoons during the jubilees were strongly influenced by these elements. A vitriolic image of 1887 shows Queen Victoria as a smirking tyrant, enjoying the manhandling of 'Miss Erin' on her way to incarceration under the Conservative Coercion Measure. Before her ejection 'Erin' points at a list of grievances deposited before

Victoria's 'shrine of loyalty' including 'evictions', 'closure' and 'poverty' (illus. 45).

The opposition of the popular radical weeklies to the royal jubilees highlights the vigorous anti-monarchist feeling that existed amongst radicals in the 1880s. In both tone and content such sentiments were almost entirely unchanged from the views articulated by reformers at

45 'Miss Erin' as a victim of the 1887 jubilee Irish Coercion Bill implemented by Lord Salisbury (in a gaoler's uniform) and a smirking Queen Victoria.

the beginning of the nineteenth century. This attitude towards the monarchy remained a marked feature of the labourism of the 1890s. Queen Victoria's death in 1901 was thus the occasion for critical retrospectives on her reign in the radical press; *Justice's* verdict was typical: 'Her late majesty was a very selfish and self-regarding old lady. From the date of her accession to the day of her demise she never took a single step towards improving the lot of the mass of her people.'[147] Keir Hardie's *Labour Leader* was more magnanimous but nevertheless mounted a traditional radical campaign against the extravagances of Edward's court after the coronation.[148] Yet despite such sentiments, suspicion of the court and kingship was not reflected in the legislative programme of the Labour Representation Committee. Regardless of the private opinions of many labour politicians, the anti-monarchist rhetoric of the 1880s failed to translate into practical political terms once British labour entered into partnership with the Liberals and moderate trade unions to become a contender for power. The tensions this created within labourism surfaced during acrimonious debates in the 1920s. There were always voices within the Labour Party that objected to the 'courtier' pretensions of leaders such as Ramsay MacDonald.[149] Here there was a marked area of conflict where the shade of the old populist radical tradition and the advocates of pragmatic entryism into the establishment clashed (see chapter 7).

Anti-monarchism within nineteenth-century radical thought represented an ultra-radical state of mind, rather than a coherent programme for action. Its inchoate nature meant that it never arrived at a systematized model for non-monarchical forms or a doctrine that might translate into practical political terms. In this sense anti-monarchism was a manifestation of an excluded populist style of political activism that could not survive radicalism's transition from a crusade of the dispossessed into a contender for power, still less as a participant in active government. This is not to invalidate the role of anti-monarchism in mobilizing criticism of the establishment by those operating outside the networks of power and government. Above all, anti-monarchism served as a conduit for the voices of the excluded, and furnished a ready platform for condemnations of privilege, the hereditary system and the injustices of the royal state. In this form anti-monarchism had an immediacy of impact that contributed substantially to the success of a radical platform populism throughout much of the nineteenth century.

5 Anti-monarchism in the Colonies: Anglo-Australian Dimensions 1870–1901

> Where Britain's flag flies wide unfurled,
>   All tyrant woes dispelling,
> God makes this world a better world,
>   For man's brief earthly dwelling.
> (Children's Diamond Jubilee Song, 1897)

> Sixty years she's reigning a holding up the sky,
> And bringing round the seasons, hot and cold, and wet and dry.
> And in all that time she's never done a deed deserving jail.
> So let joybells ring out madly and delirium prevail.
> Oh the poor will blessings pour on the Queen whom they adore.
> When she blinks with puffy eyes at them, they'll hunger never
>   more.
> (The Australian poet VICTOR DALEY on Queen Victoria's
> sexagenary procession in London, 1897)

Recent controversy in Australia surrounding the link with the Crown and an indigenous head of state has opened up a public debate that reflects changing perceptions of the British throne in a wider Commonwealth setting. This is a theme that has received relatively little consideration by the historical profession. Until recent years modern British historians did not regard monarchy, either in a domestic or in a colonial context, as a subject worthy of study. Instead, scholarship in this area has traditionally been confined to biographies of influential royal figures or to histories of the role of monarchy within the constitution.[1] These attempts to explain the power of monarchy in terms of its constitutional and ceremonial function have failed to recognize or analyze the voices of the opponents of the royal state, especially in an imperial context. One can scarcely avoid such voices both in Britain and in the empire in the period after 1850, which was, at times, dominated by opposition to royal rule. Moreover, there was significant interaction between the currents of opposition to the throne in Britain and in an imperial setting.

By the 1880s British radicals were looking increasingly to the British white-settler colonies in the Southern Hemisphere for examples of non-monarchical forms. An excessive focus on the mechanics and trappings of an establishment monarchism dominating the public sphere barely allows for the possibility of opposition to the throne in the broader empire. Key events of the period for conventional imperial history are the Royal Titles Act of 1876 and the 1887 and 1897 jubilees, which are read as popular ceremonial exercises that entrenched the concept of the imperial Crown at the heart of British politics. The repercussions of this ceremonial for the wider context of the empire and the opposition it sometimes provoked are only now beginning to be researched.[2] The standard accounts also fail to engage with attempts to undermine the notion of Victoria's position as head of a successful imperial family that underpinned the royal jubilees, the pageantry surrounding the Imperial Institute in London, and the Colonial and India Exhibitions of 1886. Consideration of the wider imperial context of the jubilees forces a modification of their emphasis on the success of the ceremonies surrounding the British monarchy in the nineteenth century and reassesses the form opposition to monarchy could take in the colonies during periods of royal rejoicing.

The monarchy allied itself to empire at the moment when it seemed to be the nation's greatest priority. Monarchist claims for the existence of an imperial family under royal stewardship deserve, however, further consideration. Empire undermined, as well as buttressed, the throne. In reality, the movements of political protest that mounted some of the strongest challenges to the Crown in the nineteenth century did not originate at home but in the empire. An imperial monarchy that refused to acknowledge diversity and difference within the empire, or saw it as suborned to a wider imperial mission, created problems not only for the non-white nations of the empire, but also for those white-settler colonies, where limited political autonomy was possible.

The British monarchy of the nineteenth century is unthinkable without the backdrop of empire. The lavish scale, gorgeous stage-sets and immense expense of the Victorian monarchy were designed for imperial, as well as domestic, consumption.[3] After 1858, when India was brought directly under British rule from Westminster for the first time, Indian representatives and the trappings of the Mughal emperors were incorporated into the domestic ceremonial of the Crown. Disraeli's decision to elevate Victoria's title to Empress of India in 1876 strengthened the Indian connection and represented an attempt to create a truly imperial throne, where the presence and magnificence of the British court and imperial stage-sets were combined. The imperial Indian connection thus established a new highpoint in state pageantry. Thereafter the importance of India to the broader empire ensured that the country occupied a central stage for royal rites of passage, particularly coronations, deaths and christenings. Victoria herself always had Indian servants in attendance, amongst them the loyal Munshi, who replaced John Brown as the queen's confidant and friend after the latter's death in 1883.

The splendour of an imperial monarchy was conveyed by the elaborate throning rituals of the Durbars at the Indian imperial capital of Delhi. The first Durbar was held in 1876 and marked the proclamation of Victoria as Empress of India. Thereafter they recurred at regular intervals to celebrate the imperial coronations of Edward VII in 1903 and of George V in 1911. The Durbars framed the power and authority of British rule in India. After the divisive events of the Indian Mutiny of 1857, they reaffirmed British power and provided a point of unity and abasement for the local landowners and notables whose loyalty had been brought into question by the events of thirty years earlier.[4] It was thus important that the grammar of the royal rituals held at Delhi should mirror the magnificence of those of the Mughal court. An attempt was made here to create a genuinely indigenous monarchy that reflected the authentic traditions of pre-British India.

The success of the Durbar in India is undoubted. It healed wounds and appealed to the hierarchical values within Hindu society that underpinned the caste system.[5] For domestic critics of the throne, however, it reaffirmed the connection between power, imperial plunder and the enormous expense of British adventurism abroad. Royal visits to India were frequently shown as re-enactments of previous acts of conquest and aggression fought under the banner of 'Queen and Empire'. The visit to India by the Prince of Wales in 1875 provides one such example of apparent imperial opportunism. When Edward arrived at the height of the cholera epidemic of 1875–6, the visit was much criticized, even by British officials. Subsequently his itinerary had to be re-drawn to avoid the areas worst affected by the epidemic. At home, radicals condemned the expense of the visit, attacked his slaughter of local wildlife and repeated scurrilous rumours about his intimacies with Indian dancing girls. Above all, they portrayed the visit as an opportunity for Edward to line his pockets and repay his gambling debts:

The presents [received] were an important feature, especially to a young man who is head-over-heels in debt. The Prince of Wales took out about £60,000 [in presents] and is reported to have received in exchange others amounting to ten times that value. These he will keep and the country will have to make up the difference to the Indians. Albert Edward is his mother's son. He may be a little addled upon things in general, but upon the main chance he is all there.[6]

Such charges were repeated throughout the empire. At the time of Victoria's 1897 Diamond Jubilee, the Australian radical journal the *Liberator* recalled:

Over twenty years ago when the Prince of Wales had overwhelmed himself with disreputable debts – debts which even Beaconsfield had not the cheek to ask the Commons to pay – that mountebank sent him to India to sponge upon the people there. The fellow went through the country, taking up contributions from the Indian princes, who, in turn, put the screw on their wretched subjects. In this way he liquidated his debts.[7]

The strong connection between Crown and empire cemented by the spectacle surrounding the Durbars meant that the monarchy often attracted criticism for its role as an imperial figurehead during the colonial wars of the late nineteenth century. Towards the end of Victoria's reign strong ethical objections were voiced to autocratic rule in distant lands, both domestically and externally. Radicals at home were vocal in their opposition to an unbridled militarism that imperilled the country's imperial position and raised concerns about the health and stability of democracy at home.[8] For many advanced reformers the sabre-rattling jingoism and uncritical nationalism of the 1890s posed a serious challenge to the liberal idea of rational politics by public discussion. In the closing decade of the century anti-imperialists like Henry Labouchère questioned the use of force in the suppression of the Matebele Revolt in Rhodesia in 1896–7, and in expansionist attempts to coerce the Boer Republics between 1899 and 1902. The Boer War in particular was seen as throwing the hitherto wise course of empire off track by an arrogant display of imperial adventurism.[9] The Boer position was a strong one that gained the support of the organ of advanced radical opinion, *Reynolds's Newspaper*. Radical newspapers like *Reynolds's* had a long-standing interest in colonial and British dominion affairs. In the 1850s it had campaigned to rectify abuses in colonial administration in both India and Australasia and to abolish slavery in the wider empire.[10] During the Boer War it took a provocatively anti-war line and condemned the lack of restraint on the part of the British military in their treatment of the Boers. Domestic criticism was joined by a chorus of international condemnation. After the use of concentration camps and anti-insurgency techniques by the military, Victoria was depicted in the

European press as a tyrant, whose hands dripped with the blood of the innocent.[11]

By the end of the nineteenth century reform opinion in Britain and the wider empire felt that the Boer War demonstrated the impoverishment of the imperial mission; for many radicals and some Liberals it seemed that empire no longer represented civilization and enlightenment. In contrast to the majority of British colonial wars, the Boer War was fought between peoples of European descent with strong historical bonds and a close monarchical connection through the House of Orange and the joint experience of the Glorious Revolution of 1688. This had serious repercussions for the image of the empire in the white-settler colonies as a racial union of the 'English folk' with a shared history and identity. It was now less easy to maintain, as did coronation manuals for children in 1902 at the time of Edward VII's accession, that 'though the British Empire is widely scattered, it is in heart and mind closely united. As a symbol of that unity we have one king, one flag. The king, indeed, is more than a symbol of unity, he is a link, a living link, that actually binds the parts together.'[12]

The term 'Britishness' used with reference to nineteenth-century Australia is a contentious one, both in its academic and popular usages. It marginalizes the minority populations and, still more, the Aboriginal people, who were probably the majority of the population for much of the century. To assert 'Britishness', it seems, is to challenge Australian nationalism. Nevertheless, the three following points might be made: First, the population of Australia and New Zealand, 2.5 m. in 1881 and 3.5 m. in 1891 (excluding both Aboriginal people and Maori), was by that time overwhelmingly Anglo-Celtic in origin, with, in 1891, perhaps a quarter born in Britain. The number of non-Aboriginal native-born Australians ranged from a little over half in Queensland to more than three-quarters in Tasmania;[13] second, urbanization in Australia was even more advanced than in Britain, and Melbourne and Sydney were regarded by visitors as very like the major British provincial centres; Asa Briggs quite rightly included Melbourne in his study, *Victorian Cities*[14]; third, these cities were characterized by a common cultural heritage from Europe. Australians read British books and newspapers in major civic libraries, listened to British music, looked at British art, and went to British-inspired theatre. Melbourne claimed the largest Shakespeare society in the world. Australian newspapers, partly as a product of the improved cable communications at this time, were full of British news.

For these and other reasons, it is intelligible that the phrase 'Liegeman of the Queen' was not simply a constitutional truism.

Monarchism was woven into the life of Australia as a group of colonies. But so, too, was anti-monarchism. The anti-monarchist tradition was drawn from 'Home', but was also home-grown. The issue emerges repeatedly in the familiar resting-points of Australian history. From an Aboriginal perspective, Wendy Brady points to the basic historical fact that Australia was a republic prior to colonization.[15] This tradition was fully apparent to Australian radicals and reformers. Moreover the role of penal servitude and forced migration in the foundation of the Australian colonies fostered a historical memory of dispossession that represented Australians as the 'bondsmen' and outcasts of empire, driven abroad by 'the cruel laws of Our Gracious Queen'.[16] In later years the trappings of an infant nationalism were assembled from these fragments of memory and experience.

In the 1840s and 1850s the Anti-Transportation Movement, opposed to any further transportation of convicts to the colonies, adopted the first indigenous flag. Subsequently, it was used by miners seeking the franchise and other goals when they took on British troops at the Eureka Stockade in 1854. These radicals were in part influenced by migrants from the United States. The American model was, and remains, important for the republican tradition in Australia. It influenced one of the most famous publicists of the cause, the Reverend John Dunmore Lang, author of *Freedom and Independence for the Golden Lands of Australia*, published in 1852. In Australia the American model was unambiguously embraced, rather than rejected as was often the case in Britain. For organs of the radical/nationalist press like the *Bulletin*, the true traditions of seventeenth-century liberties of minimal government and a purified politics were to be found not at 'Home', but in the colonies, where Australians were the heirs to the ideas of the American rebels of the War of Independence. In Britain, in contrast, John Bright and other reformers routinely referred to the United States in their oratory, but as an emblem of meritocratic egalitarianism, rather than as a model for an alternative form of government.[17]

Lang represents a Scottish link to Australian nationalism; the Irish is more familiar in the person of Peter Lalor, a leader of Eureka, whose father was a prominent Irish nationalist. The Australian loyalist press tended to attribute anti-royal outbursts to the Irish presence in the colonies. In so doing they were able to play down the element of anti-monarchism that underlies Australian culture, hint at unpatriotic attitudes and minimize the importance of the changes likely to flow from the dissolution of Australia's links with the empire. In reality the Irish involvement in Australian republicanism was limited. Recent research has demonstrated that only the wealthiest and most respectable class of migrants were in a position to make the long voyage south.[18] Images of a displaced Fenian nationalism transported to the Australian colonies by penniless migrants are therefore over-drawn and misread the careers of a few key individuals.[19] Moreover, the public outrage that followed the attempt by a deranged Irishman on the life of the Duke of Edinburgh in 1868 during the first royal tour of Australia produced anti-sedition legislation too extreme even for the British Colonial Office and converted many people of Irish descent to the virtues of keeping their heads down.[20]

For many Australian observers, the distinctive feature of the 'new imperialism' of the late nineteenth century was the manifest British attempt to draw the Australian colonies closer to Britain by bonds of defence and finance. By the end of the century anxieties about competition from rival European powers led imperialists to place an excessive reliance on the connections with the white-settler colonies, especially Australia and New Zealand, which were perceived as an important part of an imperial defence axis within a larger Anglo–Saxon power bloc.[21] This frequently created unease among Australians and on occasion fostered an answering Australian nationalism. The movement for closer links – an Imperial Federation League was formed in London in 1884 – offered permanent status as part of the British empire underpinned by a loyalist vision of Australia's future direction.[22] This flatly contradicted the popular expectation that colonial status would, at some unspecified time, lead to independence and hence a republic. Conflict had already arisen between these two alternative visions by 1890. This debate ran concurrent with, and was in part shaped by, a dominant political issue of parliamentary politics in Britain – Irish Home Rule. For the architects of empire the prosperous Australian colonies had to be kept tied to Britain for the sake of the unity of the United Kingdom itself and to maintain the joint benefits of trade, a common defence bond and a popular empire at home delivering prosperity and a convincing economic lead over its European competitors.[23]

The central strut in the 'new imperialism' of the *fin de siècle* was a venerated monarchy. As Balfour remarked when he was Conservative prime minister, the colonists had no unlimited loyalty to Britain, but they 'could be much more effectively stirred by royalty's emphasis on a shared attachment to the old Queen and her family'.[24] Colonial literature featured numerous references to juvenile loyalism, seeing the future of the empire as rooted in a new generation of white imperial subjects (illus. 46). The problems for nineteenth-century monarchism more generally arose from the absence of the queen, rather than from

46 'A Little Colonial Girl' as icon and embodiment of the future of the white settler colonies in the empire.

her presence. Gladstone had warned her about this in a domestic setting, when in 1870–71 critics were putting 'To Let' signs on the railings of Buckingham Palace. This was even more true of Australia after 1870, when there was only one royal tour, despite colonial government pressure for more. The teenaged sons of the Prince of Wales visited in

1881, but usually the various colonies made do with their governors, although they could prove to be an unsatisfactory substitute. Governors lacked the presence and appeal of the royals, and the exercise of the residual constitutional powers they enjoyed could be divisive. The *Bulletin*, the Australian radical weekly, argued that viceroys like the governors of Victoria and New South Wales, Henry Loch and Lord Carrington, had a secret agenda and were the instruments of British policy, whereas some local advocates of Australian federation were liable to be branded as traitors on the grounds that they proposed the vision of a different, independent Australia. Nor was the governors' social role acceptable to all the community. Government House functions were seen as socially exclusive. The queen's birthday was celebrated each year and royal events marked, but the associated church services were often a cause of friction in a community without a state church, where the role of Anglicanism was bitterly contested. Conflict arose not simply between Nonconformists, Catholics and Anglicans, but also between believers and freethinkers. It was characteristic of the mounting support for freethought that the *Bulletin* carried its own London interview with Charles Bradlaugh in 1886, indicating the zeal both shared for republicanism.[25]

A feature of Australian republicanism was its link to nationalism and independence. In contrast, anti-monarchism in Britain did not take issue with the territorial integrity of the British Isles. Although there was a greater degree of hostility to the throne in the Celtic Fringe, anti-monarchism itself offered no clear vision of a decentralized United Kingdom; still less did it embrace a federal agenda. In the Australian case, however, the assumption of eventual separation and independence was widespread. Talk of ripe fruit falling from the tree and children growing up was a long-standing part of colonial discourse.[26] In some ways, it was intended to subvert patriotic representations of the loyal colonial young as future citizens of empire and willing subjects of the queen.[27]

Historians have tended to dismiss the claims of the Australian Natives' Association, formed in 1871, to the laurels of Australia's first nationalist organization appealing to the growing majority of 'native born' Australians. Its chronicler suggests that its members only became susceptible to republican utterances under the influence of drink.[28] Nevertheless, the broader political ferment of the 1880s and the continuing debate about empire fostered a cultural nationalism that provided the bedrock for republican ideas. The rejection of the Old World with its monarchy, which seemed to symbolize and embody the values of that hierarchical society, was a feature of the period.

Moreover, Australians represented themselves as everything Britain was not. From the 1890s Australia's self-image was of a population of 'plain outspoken men' and 'natural democrats', speaking a vernacular language of republicanism that provided an antidote to British political and cultural elitism.[29] As part of this feeling, a literature evolved in nineteenth-century Australia that exalted the role of native flora and fauna and which portrayed the bush as a great leveller, stripping away the ranks, privileges and status of the Old World. The words of a popular Australian ballad spoke of an Australia in which 'every man is king, each home a monarchy'. Russel Ward's classic work *The Australian Legend* shows that the myth of 'the bushman' contributed to a vigorous Australian nationalism, which, in the aftermath of the First World War, began the process of distancing the former Australian colonies from the empire and the mother country.[30] Such notions rehabilitated the outlaws and robbers who ranged through the Australian outback (illus. 47). By the end of the nineteenth century Geoffrey Boxall was able to write that 'to their influence is due some of the sturdy republicanism of the modern Australians'.[31] An influx of non-British and Asian migrants after the 1890s subsequently reinforced a continuing drift away from the country's European origins.

There is a strong familial resemblance between anti-monarchism in Britain and Australia in the later part of the nineteenth century. Three areas of debate emerge very strongly and find echoes in both contexts.

47 The Australian legend of the 1890s brought the country's landscape and outlaw history together. Here lookouts from Ned Kelly's gang keep watch in the Strathbogie Ranges, New South Wales.

They can be called in contemporary terms immorality, extravagance and militarism. Opposition to the monarchy on these grounds, both in Britain and Australia, directly challenged domestic and imperial hierarchies and the monarchical order they sustained. In Britain, a variety of themes crystallized around these attitudes. Above all, the royal family, having attempted to establish itself as a moral exemplar for the nation, ran the risk of criticism when its behaviour fell short of the standards it espoused.

The Australian nationalist newspapers borrowed some of the anti-monarchist ammunition of their British counterparts. Morality was an essential component in this transfer.[32] Disrespectful articles and gibes presented a mirror image of the arguments for monarchy and adapted them to a local setting. The idea of hereditary rule was unsuitable, it was argued, for a democratic community with a strong commitment to freedom. Persistent rumours of illegitimate Hanoverian children resident in Australia also projected an image of the Southern Hemisphere as an unloved dumping-ground for unwanted royal issue. Personal loyalty and reverence to such morally flawed individuals was deemed inappropriate, and the radical press lost no opportunity to ridicule the royal family on the grounds of their behaviour or personal appearance: Victoria was an ease-loving, whisky-swilling woman of eighteen stone and the Prince of Wales was usually referred to as 'Tum'. During the 1890s William Lane's socialist paper the *Boomerang* christened Victoria 'the premier stout woman'. In addition John Norton, proprietor of the irreverent organ *Truth*, was tried for seditious libel after describing Queen Victoria as 'flabby, fat and flatulent' and the Prince of Wales as a 'turf-swindling, card-sharping, wife-debauching, boozing rowdy'.[33] Although Norton escaped imprisonment, the case was widely publicized and undermined the gravitas of the royal family in the colonies. Such insubordination was more than just the desire to prick the pomposity of remote and unappealing social superiors; it undercut the moral leadership of the crown by heavy-handed implications of moral failings. A cartoon linking the Prince of Wales and Sir Charles Dilke made this point well; both, it was suggested, were to visit Australia and both were involved in sex scandals. Indeed, one Victoria politician put the issue of the appropriateness of a royal visit to his constituents. The proposal to invite the prince, despite his alleged failings, was narrowly supported with the elderly and respectable supporting the motion, while the young and noisy opposed it.[34] Again, the generational imperative seemed to be towards disloyalty.

In previous chapters I have argued that anti-monarchism was much stronger than hitherto suspected within plebeian radicalism in Britain in the 1880s and 1890s. It was sustained by scurrilous attacks on royalty in the radical press and in contemporary pamphlets. Nevertheless, despite the fact that British anti-monarchism drew together much the same elements that prompted opposition to royalty in the Australian popular press, opponents of monarchy were incapable of mounting a coherent challenge to the throne on these terms alone. Australian visitors to Britain, like the émigré radical John Norton, were struck by the limitations of this kind of rhetoric which seldom rose above the level of mere abuse.[35] In his Australian radical journal *Truth*, Norton combined a heady mix of Paineism, Bonapartism, and William Cobbett-style journalism.[36] Themes such as radical nationalism, chauvinism and opposition to the establishment featured in the British radical press as they did in Australian journals like the *Bulletin*, but failed to touch an equivalent popular nerve or reach a wider audience outside radicalism. The circulation of Britain's leading radical weekly, *Reynolds's Newspaper*, which stayed at the 350,000-mark for the last three decades of the century, suggests that the paper was failing to find a new readership.

In Australia, in contrast, irreverent gibes at Victoria's expense reached a wide audience through an expanding radical print culture. The flowering of republican advocacy in the newspapers belongs predominantly to the late 1880s and early 1890s. The *Bulletin* was by then a 'power in the land',[37] and there was a marked increase in the number of radical journals in circulation, including the *Radical*, published in Newcastle, New South Wales, which attracted a number of crusading journalists to its staff. Anti-monarchism was a part of the received opinions of these radical and working-class organs; it lent itself well to the irreverent humorous style which was the stock in trade of the *Bulletin*. The large circulation dailies were generally more conservative, but at this time the hint of separation, independence and republicanism was a stand-by of leader writers fulminating against the British Colonial Office or the general failure of the British government to meet Australian demands. Correspondence in *Reynolds's* also shows that the paper had a large circulation in Australia. It was much imitated, especially in John Norton's *Truth* – 'the Australian *Reynolds's* – which lifted whole stories from its parent paper.[38]

In Britain Sir Charles Dilke was the only liberal politician of note to advocate reform of the monarchy in the 'republican' agitation of 1870–71. Dilke's career as a British 'republican' provides a link with the anti-monarchism of Australia. He toured Australia and New Zealand in the 1860s and campaigned for closer ties of imperial unity between Britain and the white-settler colonies. Dilke's criticism of the monarchy placed him outside mainstream politics in Britain for many years, to the extent that he was semi-criminalized in the popular imagination; the November 1871 edition of the *Illustrated Police News* featured a picture of him on its front cover next to images of a stabbing at Leeds and a murder committed by two young boys (illus. 48). In contrast, thinkers who questioned monarchy were revered and admired in the Australian colonies. John Dunmore Lang's indigenous republican tradition persisted after his death and remained a staple of those who debated the prospect of eventual Australian separation from the empire. In 1888, during the centenary celebrations of European settlement on the Australian mainland, a statue of Lang was erected in Sydney before an admiring crowd, whilst the plinth for an unfinished jubilee statue of Queen Victoria was colonized by republican and freethinking orators who harangued the Crown on unemployment and the evils of empire.[39]

Against this background, anti-monarchism was more frequently a feature of Australian rather than of British politics, but the issue presented problems. The future development of the Australian colonies could be conceived as following one of two paths: permanent attachment to the empire through some form of imperial federation or full independence on the United States model. An Australian republic, however, presented the problems of how, and in what form, the colonies might separate from the empire. These difficulties may be summarized as follows. First, there were legal obstacles to advocating a republic; urging the overthrow of the monarchy was dangerous in the face of sedition laws. Moreover, Australian high society thrived on the imperial connection and the trappings of empire. In popular opinion, expressed by J. F. Archibald, Sydney in the 1880s 'limped in apish imitation after London ideas, habits and manners'.[40] As late as 1886 the *Bulletin* claimed that Britain was more advanced in its republicanism than New South Wales, and that a residual monarchism lingered among Australian workers inclined to say 'God Save the Queen'.[41] Second, one colony would not be able to declare itself independent without the others, given the fact of their intimate connection. Hence the federation of Australia seemed a necessary preliminary to independence. A federated republic was part of the programme of the Australian Republican League in 1888, but that too was problematic. Not all the colonies adhered to the frail Australian Federal Council established in 1885. There was a debate as to whether or not New Zealand should be included, and the legislation establishing the Council, or any properly funded and constituted successor, would have to receive the royal assent in the British Parliament. Third, the military

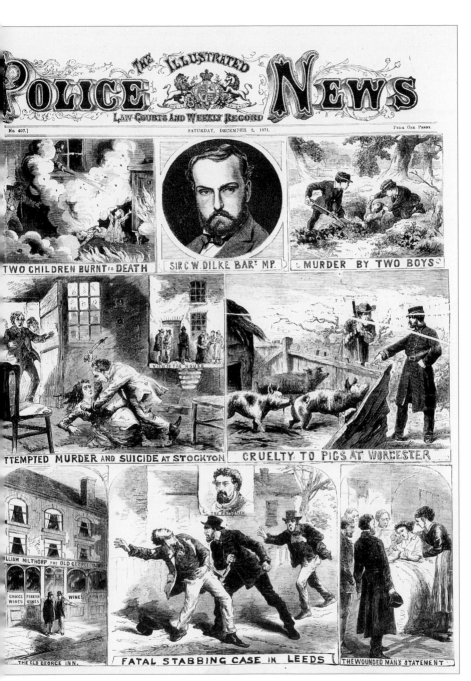

48 Sir Charles Dilke (top centre) surrounded by images of chaos and disorder.

and naval force of the colonies was subordinate to, and integrated with, the command structure of the British armed forces. An outright American-style revolt against imperial rule was also difficult to imagine. Finally, the 1880s was a period of dependency upon British capital, and the tie to the empire, although not essential, was considered an element in the availability and cost of the funds raised. Thus, an affirmation of loyalty was considered beneficial in financial circles.

Nevertheless, republicanism gained momentum in Australia. To understand this process is to understand the course of progressive democracy in the white-settler colonies. The adult male franchise became well established in the middle years of the century. Thereafter, political debate centred around how best to remove the remaining obstacles to a fairer, more equitable voting system and a written constitution. Republicanism fitted in under this last heading, but the word was also used to include the thrust towards a broadening civic inclusion, which was in its turn integral to the whole labourist outlook. The years 1887–8 presented a peak of republican activity in Australia, which made it, for some years, a feature of radical programmes.[42] In Sydney there were 'republican riots', as they were termed by contemporaries, in response to the attempts to arrange celebrations for the queen's jubilee of 1887 (illus. 49). In August 1887 an Australian Republican Union was also formed. Its launch presented many features familiar in the overlapping advocacy of the cause in Britain and Australia: nationalism and independence through the formation of an Australian Federal Republic, the proposition of the United States as a model, and the opposition to hereditary rulers and their vice-regal representatives, as well as to the expense and the imperial honours, which were seen as attempts to cultivate the Australian sympathizers of monarchy.[43] Underlying this Australian hostility to the Crown was the dislike of the imperial splendour that was a substitute for the physical presence of the monarch. An imported Empire Day, which was first celebrated in Australia on 24 May 1905 (Queen Victoria's birthday), was bitterly resented and lampooned as 'Vampire Day' by the *Bulletin*.[44] On other occasions the colonial governors were targeted. The *Bulletin* showed colonial officials like James Service, premier of Victoria, as eager dogs fighting over the scraps of imperial titles delivered by a footman from the backdoor of the Colonial Office (illus. 50). Here colonial authority was depicted as craven and servile to the throne.

A number of other contemporary events gave a particular edge to Australian republicanism in these years. They raised, in their different ways, the disadvantages of the British connection and made the formation of an Australian republic seem attractive. The jubilee, with its talk of

THE ILLUSTRATED AUSTRALIAN NEWS

No. 385.   MELBOURNE, SATURDAY, JUNE 25, 1887.   PRICE { WITH TWO SUPPLEMENTS } 1s.

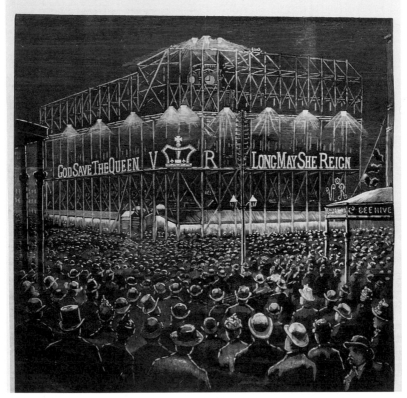

49 Jubilee illuminations in Melbourne during the celebrations of 1887.

monarchism and imperial federation, was twinned in the public mind with the centennial in January 1888 of European colonization. Both helped foster republican discourses. Moreover, some Australians were concerned that the Crown had failed to provide sufficient support for Australian interests in relation to the South Pacific and China. The British appeared to be appeasing German expansionism in New Guinea,

159

50 'His Tail: A Natural Conclusion'. The Cockney 'Hupper Servant' asks: 'Don't want no bone? Then wot 'ave ye been wagging yer tail about? Hevery body on *these premises* thought yer was 'ungry!' Service is shown at the extreme right.

and French involvement in New Caledonia and the New Hebrides, as well as controlling an influx of cheap labour from the Pacific Islands destined for the Queensland sugar plantations.[45] This last was part of the larger concern of nationalists and labourites with what was termed 'coloured labour'. The issue of Chinese migration dominated the newspapers in 1887–8 and trade union-based Anti-Chinese Leagues were widely established.[46] The British government appeared reluctant to apply to China the degree of pressure necessary, in the view of critics, to terminate the inflow. A crude racist rhetoric accompanied this campaign, in which the Chinese were denigrated as 'menial' workers and whites were celebrated as destined 'to fill the high places of the earth'.[47] An editorial in the *Bulletin* during the jubilee celebrations read:

The Jubilee Chinaman of 1887 will blossom under the fostering influence of Imperial Union. Imperial Union will throw Australia open as a country to be exploited by every unwashed tribe in the British dominions; it will drag the white man down to the level of the Chinaman and the coolie.[48]

In this regard, Australian republicanism was strengthened as a consequence of the insufficiently racist and xenophobic attitude of the British government. A *Bulletin* cartoon anticipating the 1888 centenary of white settlement on the Australian mainland illustrates the theme. John Bull is shown expelling William Lanny, the recently deceased last male Tasmanian aborigine, from Australia and confirming the literal extinction of the aboriginal threat in Tasmania. Behind him a group of grotesque racial stereotypes (Chinese, German, French, etc.) seem to be enjoying the spectacle but shelter under Bull's power and patronage (illus. 51). The message is clear that Australia had been made safe for foreign colonization by Britain.

Among the extensive legal powers of the governors was the exercise of the prerogative of mercy, which always had the potential to mobilize

51 Racist images were a feature of the Australian satirical press. Here the elimination of the Tasmanians is alluded to in comic vein.

popular opinion when it was used to commute the sentences of, for example, bushrangers, rapists, or Pacific Island traders guilty of kidnapping and murder. To take the last case, a Queensland governor, Sir Anthony Musgrave, became involved in 1887–8 in a major dispute with his premier, Thomas McIlwraith, on the grounds that Musgrave insisted on exercising the prerogative at his own discretion, and not at that of his ministers. This constitutional debate was fuelled by dislike of the labour recruiters and the racism never far from the surface in contemporary Australian nationalism. The issue was taken up in other Australian colonies. There was ample room for conflict with governors, and the demand was made in Queensland and elsewhere for consultation before governors were selected. In this way they might be made accountable to the local governments, rather than to the British Colonial Office. A particular dimension of the Queensland concern was that the proposed appointee was Sir Henry Blake, a man associated with the coercion policy in Ireland.[49] Thus simple constitutional points had dimensions that reached deep into contemporary society and inspired demands for republicanism. McIlwraith advocated a national separatist policy, and similar nationalist movements briefly became popular throughout the colonies. In New South Wales the debate in the Legislative Assembly on the appointment of governors revealed a general tendency to look upon separation as inevitable, causing some prominent politicians to declare for a republic.[50]

The imperial ceremonial of the end of the nineteenth century accelerated the move towards a mainstream republicanism. Australians now commonly articulated the disadvantages, rather than advantages, of the imperial connection. Severe famines and outbreaks of cholera and bubonic plague on the Indian sub-continent in 1876 and 1897 suggested that the imperial system might be breaking down altogether, and provided an abiding image of the starving and neglected citizens of empire (illus. 52). In 1897 John Norton questioned the worth of philanthropic famine relief appeals to wealthy society in Sydney during an outbreak of bubonic plague in India, and called for the queen to celebrate her jubilee by the magnanimous gesture of using part of her fortune to alleviate distress there. He wrote:

Why not present a truly loyal address to her majesty asking her to be graciously pleased to surrender a fair proportion of her millions she has hoarded up during her long and glorious record reign for the relief of her starving, plague-stricken, loyal Indian subjects.[51]

This image of a starving, deprived empire carried over into representations of the 1887 jubilee, showing malnourished Australian

52 Starving famine victims at Madras, India in 1876, the year in which Victoria assumed the title of Empress of India. The Victorian public were unused to such images, which caused considerable controversy.

citizens queuing up to provide revenues for the Crown personified by an obese and greedy Victoria (illus. 53). In contrast, colonial governors and officials were scorned for the eagerness with which they took up invitations to attend the royal jubilees in London in 1887 and 1897. Royal favour and preference could thus divide, as well as unite, Australians.[52]

For most Australian radicals it was impossible to disentangle monarchy from other expressions of Victorian state power. In part this was a natural consequence of the role of the Crown as the embodiment of the military/naval establishment. In the nineteenth century Victoria and the royal heirs and relatives held a large number of military pensions and offices. Throughout her life Victoria boasted of her background as a soldier's child and took a close interest in the design of military uniforms and medals. In recognition of her close connections with the army and navy, her funeral in 1901 was conducted with full military honours. By the later part of the century the tradition of depicting members of the royal family in uniform was already well established. In the 1880s uniform-wearing princes on ceremonial and state occasions became the butt of jokes in the British radical press. Victoria as Commander-in-Chief of the armed forces caused mirth in *Reynolds's Newspaper*: 'The idea of Victoria riding along on review day, the upper half of her dressed in a sort of military uniform and the

53 Queen Victoria giving meagre help to the Australian poor during preparation for the jubilee year of 1887. Beneath her throne are money bags; behind her Liberty draws the sword of vengeance.

lower half in the customary skirts, is so very absurd that no one but a member of the royal family would have thought of it.'[53] Other criticisms concentrated on the inappropriate nature of uniforms for men who were never likely to see a shot fired in anger. This point was often made with reference to the Prince of Wales.[54] Nevertheless, there was also a serious intent behind radical criticisms of military royals. The Saxe-Coburg heirs, princes and junior branches of the royal family were at the heart of the military command structure; Victoria's cousin, the Duke of Cambridge, who came to Britain from Hanover in the 1830s, remained Chief of Staff of the army for most of the high-Victorian period, from 1856 until his resignation in 1895. Cartoons in the satirical press pictured him as a German 'Beggar on Horseback' precariously astride the British lion (illus. 54).[55]

The question of the armed forces was central to the Australian republican experience. There could be no talk of sovereignty or independence without military provision. The Australian armed forces were involved through integration with the British army and service abroad in the interests of the empire. The subordination to the queen was real and direct through the Oath of Loyalty, the adherence to the queen's regulations and service under the command of British officers. By the 1890s colonial forces utilized British officers employed by the colonial governments, but responsible to the War Office and hence the Duke of Cambridge directly.[56] Moreover, the project of further involving the colonies in the defence of the empire was widely discussed in the 1880s.

The 1887 Colonial Conference in London, the first in a series held until recent times, was called to coincide with the queen's jubilee. Even before the conference it was known that the preferred British vision of imperial defence was for a system of payments by the colonies towards the strengthening of the Royal Navy. Nevertheless, it was difficult for the Australian colonies to evade sending delegates. In the eyes of its critics, the resulting Australian Naval Defence Agreement was taxation without representation, and it took four years of conflict to implement it in its entirety. For some Australians it was defence under the aegis of the queen, and for her empire, rather than for Australia. Domestically, radicals like George Black protested against the use of Australian troops in British imperial wars in the Sudan and South Africa.[57] The *Republican* in Sydney wrote: 'The Motherland has waged war with Egyptian patriots and our expressed wish for political emancipation will bring down upon us the iron-clads and warriors whose mission it is to preserve the old order of things [...] he would be little less than stupid who would believe that England would lightly yield to us our rights.'[58]

"A BEGGAR ON HORSEBACK !"
OR,
TRANSLATED FROM THE GERMAN.

54 The iconoclastic Matt Morgan depicted the British Lion as resentful of the command of a foolish Duke of Cambridge, wearing a paper soldier's hat and seeking to ride the armed services into the ground.

In 1889 the issue of military forces in the Australian colonies arose again in relation to the extension of responsible government to Western Australia. In a secret dispatch, the governor of New South Wales, Lord Carrington, questioned the wisdom of keeping British troops for an imperial arsenal in the event of colonial separation. The Colonial Office was less concerned with the idea itself, as with his having been so incautious as to commit it to paper. The 1897 Jubilee Colonial Conference, which was to a considerable extent concerned with the continuance and development of this colonial naval contribution, was again opposed by radicals. During the campaign in South Africa of 1899–1902 there were whispers amongst some socialists that there were marked similarities between the Boer Republics and Australia, and that Australia should seek its freedom in like manner. In the longer term Australian soldiers in the service of the Crown gained a reputation as the unwilling servants of empire in both the Boer War and the Great War.[59] During the Gallipoli campaign of 1915 British officers frequently commented on the insubordination, slovenliness and marked disrespect for king and country amongst Australian soldiers (illus. 55).

Another contrast between Australian and British anti-monarchism was the latter's failure to attract the support of the literary elite and key opinion formers. In Britain in the early part of the nineteenth century the flamboyant, anti-establishment element in literary culture was short-lived, whereas in Australia criticism of royalty in literary periodicals gradually gained acceptance. The 1890s witnessed a move away from a traditional colonial literature with an imperial sub-text that exalted the deeds of masculine frontier pioneers and miners, to a more explicitly Australian political and nativist agenda. Whereas poets like Henry Lawson and Victor Daley might once have been dismissed by London publishers as offering a debased version of Rudyard Kipling, by the end of the century they were beginning to be taken seriously as part of an authentic Australian tradition.[60]

During these years there was a proliferation of a new kind of literature increasingly free from the domination of a narrow colonial intelligentsia. Lawson, the key figure of the literary nationalism of the 1890s and the writer most often seen as Australia's first national bard, wrote his earliest published verse on republicanism and defended the cause in prose in the *Republican* newspaper. The plebeian character of much of this writing is very marked; Lawson was working as a carriage-painter when he wrote his republican poetry. Thereafter, he became a major figure in the mythology of the Australian Labour Party. His poems, which are still popular in Australian radical circles today, compare favourably with the outpourings of his near-contemporaries, the British Chartist poets. Lawson, like the British radical poet Ernest Jones, targeted the wealthy and over-privileged aristocratic elite, in his case, aristocratic society in Sydney, whose presence as

Young Officer: "Haw, haw, no shave?"
Australian: "He, he, no ——— razaw!"

55 The British officer's accent and bearing are derided in this cartoon from amongst the sketches and stories produced by Anzacs in World War I.

colonial administrators seemed irksome in the freer setting of the New World. For Lawson the corrupt and venal system they presided over was inextricably linked with the court patronage of the Old World. He discerned a web of corruption, with monarchy at its centre, stretching back to the British Isles. Australians, he believed, had to break this system for their own political health. The first step in that direction was to sever all existing links with the Crown. He wrote in his first published poem, 'A Song of the Republic':

Sons of the South, awake! arise!
Sons of the South, and do.
Banish from under your bonny skies
Those Old World errors and wrongs and lies
Making a hell in Paradise,
That belongs to your sons and you.

Women, too, were conspicuous in this literary explosion; in the words of John Docker the 1890s was 'a great age of feminist and pro-feminist literary production'.[61] Young male and female writers of the *fin de siècle* were 'offensively Australian' and, in their writing, hostile to the British connection, monarchism and to vestiges of imperial culture. Moreover, their work circulated throughout Australian society. The Lawsons, mother and son, respectively edited and wrote for the *Republican*. They were part of a group of urban bohemians writing about 'The Bush', who were prominent in defining a new kind of 'Australianness' at the end of the nineteenth century. George Black, one of their number, described them as 'a hard-reading crowd' who were held together by a mutual interest in a number of 'progressive' causes in the late 1880s. Some, like Tommy Walker, were freethinkers who drew their republicanism from the Paineite tradition via Bradlaugh and Annie Besant. In addition, they had strong links with urban crowd politics and were part of the mob that disrupted the jubilee meetings in 1887. The government's response to this episode was to close the theatres on Sunday evenings to impede the spread of their doctrines, thereby demonstrating the deep roots of republican-ism in Australian cultural and creative life. Republicanism, however, did not stand alone. It was strengthened throughout all classes of Australian society by its connection with a cluster of populist causes: anti-Chinese feeling, land nationalization, secularism, trade unionism and nationalism.[62]

Most debilitating of all for the anti-monarchist position in Britain, and offering a contrast to Australia, was the extent to which gender issues strengthened the position of the throne and deprived opponents of the monarchy of a lasting appeal to a purely female audience. Conventional representations of femininity stressed the depth of female attachment to the monarchical principle. These domestic and female aspects of royalty had better hopes of working for monarchism in Australia than some of the others. The role of women under the imperial contract was to produce children and to sustain their menfolk as servants of the empire.[63] Monarchy provided both example and inspiration for this. At the level of polite society, governors' wives such as Lady Carrington presided over the derided loyalist functions at

Government House. Nevertheless, the Australian colonial experience undermined bonds of loyalty to motherland and monarchy. Marilyn Lake has argued that the notion of the strong-minded, independent Australian woman, impatient with the constraints of empire, owed something to the frontier experience and contemporary depictions of female pioneers pushing civilization forwards into the interior.[64]

Women were conspicuous in republicanism from the late 1880s, and showed more sustained zeal on behalf of the cause than their British counterparts. The radical journalist Louisa Lawson continued her interest in republican issues after the riots of 1887, and in 1888 started *The Dawn: A Journal of Australian Women*, which had a continuous existence until 1905. During these years she was the leading light in the New South Wales women's suffrage movement. The Australian colonies were closer to giving the vote to women than was Britain or the rest of the empire, which led many political women to challenge both the imperial connection and the status quo.[65] In the 1890s, argues Helen Irving, the female suffrage campaign altered perceptions of Queen Victoria markedly; she was now respected by women, less for her position as monarch, than for her role as a powerful woman in politics. This is not to negate the role of women in republicanism. For women Australian federation held out the prospect of entirely new avenues for political activity. In 1897 the feminist Catherine Helen Spence stood as a candidate for election to the Convention drafting the Federal Constitution, and was subsequently responsible for designing a proportional representation system for the Australian voting system.[66] In 1888–9 she wrote *A Week in the Future*, forecasting a Commonwealth of Great Britain under an elected President, and she anticipated the same for Australia.[67] However, such women were often disappointed by the 'masculinist nature' of the new politics. The federal constitution did not prove to be republican, and the leaders of the organized women's movements were ambiguous about the federal proposal.[68]

A comparison between opposition to the throne in Britain and Australia is illuminating. In Britain anti-monarchism was always vulnerable to the charges of undermining the constitution, promoting disunity and importing alien systems into an otherwise stable political environment. Frequently republicanism was presented as an illegal and revolutionary threat to respectability. In a speech at Ashton in 1868 the apostate Chartist J. R. Stephens made this case strongly, commenting of 'republican institutions': 'Infidelity, communism, strife of classes, break-up of the holy ties of wedlock and of home: these, amongst many others, are some of the dangers that threaten us from the side of an openly avowed democracy.'[69] In Australia the opposite was the case.

Republicanism carried connotations of national unity in opposition to empire, home rule and civic renewal away from the corruptions of Europe. These elements were entirely absent from the British equation. A distrust of British rule and of the imperial framework often pervaded the relations between the two countries. In 1887 at the time of the Irish Coercion Bill, it led many Australians (particularly those of Irish descent) to question the whole notion of imperial federation (illus. 56). Opposition to the Crown thus touched a popular nerve and reflected aspirations to nationhood and legislative and legal autonomy from Britain. By the 1890s sufficient symbols of nationality were in place to construct a successful alternative patriotism. For Australians, especially those in New South Wales, the most significant celebration of the 1880s was the 1888 centenary of the British settlement of Australia, not Victoria's jubilee. Australian republicanism was, as Helen Irving remarks, 'based on an often intuitive assertion of egalitarianism, a labourist democratic ideal, opposition to absentee landlordism, aristocracy and monarchy, all associated with Britain'.[70] She perceives the federal movement leading to the formation of the Australian Commonwealth in 1901 as having many components in the utopian decade of the 1890s. Republicanism was, in her view, one of these, and it would be unduly narrow to exclude it from a reading of the federal debate simply because a self-governing Australia was fashioned as part of the British empire. There was, after all, an ambiguity in the term 'Commonwealth' and Joseph Chamberlain, the Colonial Secretary, had to meet Queen Victoria's concerns: 'I assured her that there was no anti-monarchical intention and that the most earnest desire of the Colonials was to have a member of the Royal Family as the first Governor-General – which unfortunately appears to be impossible [...]'[71] Many Australians did not share his dismay.

The varying history of anti-monarchism in different parts of the empire should not obscure both its periodic vitality and striking transfer of language and themes. In the age of empire, republicanism moved between Britain and its colonies. Robin Gollan has noted that: 'The English radical press, in particular *Reynolds's News* and Henry Labouchère's *Truth*, were the source of much of the Australian republicans' rhetoric.'[72] At the end of the nineteenth century the dream of an Australian republic was not realized. The federation of 1901 fell far short of a republic and co-joined the former colonies under the British monarch as head of state. Federation did, however, open up the issue of what constituted 'Australianness'. As part of that process the period up to the turn of the century was characterized by an Australian literary revival and a vigorous debate about the national soul. Despite a

"Graciously Pleased."—Again.

"Her Majesty has been pleased to give the Royal assent to the Irish Coercion Bill."—*Caldegram.*

56 A malevolent Victoria gives the royal assent to Lord Salisbury's 1887 Irish Coercion Bill. Whilst Salisbury celebrates, Gladstone turns his back in disgust and 'Australia' tears up a plan for Imperial Federation.

strong residual monarchism throughout the empire, that discussion continued after federation. Against the background of a continuing imperial framework and an alien head of state, republicanism was established as a subaltern doctrine co-existing with more loyalist tendencies within the Australian political system. These factors shaped a situation in which an English-inspired anti-monarchism made the imaginative leap from simple criticism of the expense of royalty, to a full-blown 'republican' form that made the attainment of nationhood possible.

6 'Lords of Misrule': Liberalism, the House of Lords and the Campaign Against Privilege 1870–1911

'We are all socialists now'.

(SIR WILLIAM HARCOURT on the death duties clause in the Liberal budget of 1894)

Private ownership in land rests ultimately on one of two claims, the claim of the spade or the claim of the sword. Right through the history of England these two claims have competed for recognition.

(*The Land: The Report of the Land Enquiry Committee, 1913*)

In late nineteenth-century Britain hostility to privilege, wealth, and the trappings of landed society transcended political opposition to monarchy. Anti-monarchism and anti-aristocracy were often conflated, using the same narratives of a traditional radical disdain for leisure, inherited wealth and the court. Opposition to the throne in the nineteenth century, however, never succeeded in making itself acceptable as a critique of the political system on its own terms. In part, this was a consequence of its own diffuse nature. Dislike of the hereditary principle among respectable politicians was more frequently expressed through attacks on the House of Lords. From 1832 onwards the House of Lords was seen by reformers of all hues as the unacceptable face of landed wealth and naked class interest. Whereas an attack on monarchy imperilled the foundations of the constitution, reform of the Lords could pass as a legitimate act of party politics used to curb the excesses of a retrograde and permanently Tory element within the legislature. In this way the Liberal 'Peers versus the People' rhetoric of the late-nineteenth and early-twentieth centuries was a substitute for an attack upon the monarchical state, and diverted attention away from the monarchy itself. At the same time it drew together existing radical criticisms of privilege to create a Liberal view of the constitution that, while loyalist in nature, sought acceptable alternatives to privilege deployed in support of party interest.

Political historians frequently portray the reform of the House of Lords as an unpopular issue that lacked real momentum and generated no lasting public debate. Lords reform is reduced to the level of a mere re-ordering of the legislature,[1] and the popular politics of the campaign against privilege is ignored. For historians of Liberalism, it is inextricably linked with the decline of the Liberal Party and the changes to the constitution resulting from the 1911 Parliament Act. On this reading, Liberal criticisms of the Lords after 1884 are seen as an ineffectual rhetoric that did little to arrest the steady decline of the party in the early part of the twentieth century. The 1909–11 campaign against the peers is sometimes represented as a backward-looking exercise that demonstrated Liberalism's failure to devise an agenda for the early-twentieth century, or to address the labour versus capital issues that were beginning to undermine the position of Liberalism and provide a platform for an emergent Labour Party. According to this analysis, the campaign against the Lords was a product of confusion, impelled simply by the weight of Liberalism's history and traditions (illus. 57). This view is compounded by the early socialist press's dismissive treatment of the Lords issue, and its occasional questioning of the Liberals' reasons for embracing it.[2]

For some radical newspapers the issue was simply a distraction. The *Christian Socialist* wrote: 'Royalty and the House of Lords both bear their character conspicuously on their foreheads, but the House of Commons is more likely of all to prove dangerous to the people's liberties, when it is essentially a class governing body.'[3] Many contemporary sources claim that the issue was greeted with apathy by the electorate in 1910.[4] In addition, the Lords issue is linked to the long-term structural weaknesses of the Liberal Party. With Henry Campbell-Bannerman's comment, 'when in doubt, slang the Lords', in mind, it is frequently represented as a blocking tactic that prevented the emergence of other more divisive policies that might upset the balance of interests within the Liberal coalition.

The Fabian Socialist Cecil Chesterton was in no doubt that the campaign against the Lords was another variant of Liberal 'faddism'. For him, House of Lords reform appeased 'faddist' groups within the party but failed to enthuse electorally. In 1905 he wrote: 'The objection to the House of Lords is not a reformer's objection, but a Liberal partisan's objection [...] With us to whom it is a matter of supreme indifference by which party reforms are carried, this consideration need not weigh.'[5] Paradoxically, the charge of 'opportunism' is sometimes levelled against Lloyd-George's radical Liberalism over this issue. Such a view acknowledges the popularity of the campaign but

NERVOUS WORK.

Peer (log.). "WELL, I SUPPOSE THEY'LL GO ON MISSING ME AS USUAL; BUT I MUST SAY IT'S GETTING RATHER WARM!"

57 The House of Lords as target and victim of Liberal Party history.

never satisfactorily explains the popular basis of its support. Only Eugenio Biagini has noted the strength of public hostility against the Lords as a significant component in a still vigorous popular Gladstonianism after 1884.[6]

Aristocracy was closely tied to monarchy through the royal bloodline and by traditions of service and the outward forms of court protocol. An aristocratic presence at court and in Parliament conferred a historic dignity and splendour on the offices of the Crown.

Aristocrats were present at all significant state occasions and during the public rituals of monarchy. Their centrality to the rites of passage that surrounded monarchs continued to unnerve reformers into the nineteenth century. In 1850 the *Freethinker's Magazine* condemned them as 'attendant flunkeys of the genus aristocratic' and wrote of their decorative function in parliament: 'The peers are like a volume bound in calf and splendidly "got-up" – the Commons like a people's edition of the self-same book.'[7]

Queen Victoria's funeral reiterated the importance of the British aristocracy at the beginning of the Edwardian period. Their assembled strength, alongside the 42 archdukes and two emperors of the royal houses of Europe, demonstrated the still very narrow concentration of wealth, power and land in the hands of a small number of titled families. At the turn of the century radicals remained conscious of this social aberration and frequently levelled charges of oligarchy against Parliament and the royal state. Moreover, radicalism realized that the survival of an unchanged and unchallenged aristocracy was conditional upon the persistence of an enduring royal power at the heart of government. The *Radical* commented in 1888:

On inquiry it will be found that in connection with our monarchical institutions there is an aristocracy, founded upon favouritism, and sustained by the royal will, an aristocracy of idlers, doing nothing to enrich the state, but absorbing much of its treasure – the result of the hard and patient toil of thousands of workers.[8]

Such criticisms were part of a long tradition. Greedy peers had figured prominently in radical rhetoric since the 1790s. Most reformers viewed them as part of a hierarchy of wealth and influence that conspired to deprive the people of their just rights. In the 1830s Richard Carlile christened this political edifice 'The Lump' and campaigned vigorously against aristocratic influence in politics and public life.[9] Viewed in these terms, the House of Lords acted as a bulwark against liberty that shielded the reactionary element within the constitution. The Chartists frequently held up the Lords as an object of ridicule. Ernest Jones criticized the entrenched aristocratic composition of the Upper House at the time of the 1858 debates surrounding the Jewish Disabilities Relief Bill, which was delayed several times in the Lords: 'The House of Lords as at present constituted is part of our glorious constitution. Touch it with an infant's hand and you sully its purity. Take the possibility of a Jew becoming a lord – it is horrible!'[10] The peers were an easier target than the monarchy. Throughout the nineteenth century the House of Lords was more overtly self-serving and nakedly opportunistic in its dealings with reformers than the Crown. As a result, it never inspired the same demonstrations of popular loyalty as monarchism. This gave radicals a pretext for attacks on aristocracy, and a firm basis of support for their actions that, unlike hostility to the throne, was not dependent upon the periodic unpopularity of individual monarchs. On occasion, a coded language operated that allowed covert criticism of hereditary privilege without explicit reference to the Crown. At the time of Dilke's visit to Birmingham at the end of 1871, this enabled him to project his message without fear of interruption by loyalists.[11]

Following the increased public visibility of Queen Victoria after the early 1870s and a subsequent revival in the monarchy's fortunes, much of the activity that had characterized the campaign against the throne was channelled into hostility to the Lords. In 1872 a conference of radicals in Birmingham declared for abolition of the second chamber in a measure that 'would equal a change greater than 1688'.[12] *Reynolds's Newspaper* and George Standring's *Republican* preserved this older political tradition intact into the 1890s. As in its descriptions of monarchy, *Reynolds's* rejoiced in the exposure of the disreputable hidden history of the peerage. Its *Reynolds's Peerage*, which directly lampooned *Debrett's Peerage*, the 'Bible of the Aristocracy', divulged the historical wrongdoings and misdeeds of eminent landed families. In 1897 it exposed the family link of the Earl of Bradford, Lord Chamberlain of the Queen's household, to the President of the Court of Regicides, responsible for the exhumation and violation of Oliver Cromwell's corpse.[13] In later editions there were similar revelations about the Marquis of Bute and other landed scions.[14] The centrality of this form of rhetoric has often been overlooked. Contemporary accounts of the formation of the Democratic Federation, the precursor to the SDF, demonstrate that it was originally established not for the purposes of disseminating socialism, but rather to campaign for the abolition of the House of Lords.[15] Here a recovered popular radicalism reminiscent of the 1830s lived on as an aspect of a vigorous plebeian democracy.

A crude rhetoric of popular egalitarianism also surfaced within Liberalism during the 1860s. By the beginning of his first ministry in 1868 Gladstone had become a shrewd operator in the political brinkmanship required to steer complicated measures through the House of Lords. As Chancellor of the Exchequer in 1860 he had already faced fierce opposition from the Lords for his budget abolishing the excise duty on paper, so making a cheap press possible. The Lords opposed this measure on the grounds that it would enable radicals to disseminate their ideas through the production of inexpensive printed literature. Subsequently Gladstone's first ministry presaged later Liberal attacks on landed and aristocratic privilege. Gladstone's reform programme struck directly at landed society with measures to prevent the purchase of army commissions in 1871, to extend rights of ownership to tenant farmers in Ireland, and to disestablish the Church of Ireland. These latter measures posed a threat to the landed Anglican establishment in Ireland but they also had a strong appeal for a radical audience. High Gladstonianism appeared to be implementing older reform agendas that had opposed the Church of England as the backbone of the establishment. It was also in touch with the shade of an existing radical style of agitation. Furthermore, such measures brought the Liberal Party into direct conflict with the House of Lords over issues that had strong popular support. Both the Church Disestablishment Bill of 1869 and the Irish Land Acts of 1870 were mutilated or delayed by the Lords, causing outcry in the popular press.

Gladstone's Irish policy has traditionally been dismissed as a mere distraction that simply obstructed the evolution of broader social welfare agendas within the Liberal Party. In reality, Ireland enabled Gladstone to portray the Liberal Party as radical in focus, and provided the opportunity for a change in direction that held out the prospect for similar land and church reforms on the English mainland. In fact there was sleight of hand here, and many radicals in the 1860s remained unconvinced by the vague promises made by the Liberals during and after Gladstone's first government.[16] Ireland remained Ireland, and the sphere of Irish politics, for most Liberals, an entirely separate arena of political debate. Gladstone was never radical enough to contemplate significant land reform in England or disestablishment of the Church of England on the Irish model. Rather he embraced a conservative agenda that trimmed off the worst excesses of privilege in church and state to make established institutions more easily defensible.

Before the 1880s there is no real evidence for any lasting accord between Liberalism and working-class radicalism on the basis of a shared and compatible reform agenda.[17] Indeed, such a policy appeared impossible while Gladstone continued in place as leader of the Liberal Party and remained true to his conservative inclinations. As to John Morley's argument that Gladstone became more radical as he grew older, this is now generally accepted as a product of Morley's wishful thinking.[18] After 1884, however, Gladstone's confrontation with the House of Lords created a continuing demand for significant constitutional reform measures that laid the groundwork for later Liberal successes against the Upper House. As Gladstone's hold on the party weakened, these came increasingly to dominate a shared discourse between radicals and Liberals that paved the way for the fused politics of Progressivism in the years before World War I. Gladstone himself featured as an icon of these Liberal/radical reforming impulses. Considering himself an outsider, he always resisted the notion of a peerage after his retirement. This delighted his working-class radical following. After his death the *Single Tax* wrote: '"The Great Commoner", to the joy of all democrats, has passed away without the tinsel ornaments of monarchy so dear to the hearts of men of feebler mind [... his title is] greater than that of a king.'[19] Disraeli acted as a contrast to Gladstone in this respect; his assumption of an earldom and his elevation to the House of Lords in 1876 reinforced the association of Gladstonian Liberalism with democratic virtues, and of Toryism with narrow privilege and a system of honours.[20] In Disraeli's case the peerage was seen as favouring the interests of a non-English outsider (illus. 58).

Gladstone's conservatism emerged most strongly over the issue of the constitution and the role of the House of Lords. Despite continuing obstruction of Liberal policies by the Lords into the 1880s, Gladstone was reluctant to open the doorway to reform of the Upper House or to seriously consider modification of their powers. For him, the basis of the House of Lords and the grounding of monarchy in the hereditary principle meant that these institutions were too inextricably

" Our language commands no expression of scorn which has not been exhausted in the celebration of your character : there is no conceivable idea of degradation which has not, at some period or other, been associated with your career."

Mr. Disraeli.

" Plain, and not honest."
Richard iii.

58 A hostile cartoon of Disraeli emphasizes his elevation to the peerage and his Jewishness. Such caricatures reaffirm his 'outsider' status and the worthlessness of titles.

59 Gladstone presenting prizes at a band competition on his estate at Hawarden in 1896. The castle and the crowd's acclamation indicate the fusion of popular politics and titled status that underpinned Gladstonian demagogy.

intertwined to make any such programme possible. In his view, Lords reform would imperil the very foundations of the monarchy itself. He wrote to Queen Victoria in 1884 that he would resist any attack on hereditary power 'for the avoidance of greater evils' and that 'organic change of this kind in the House of Lords may strip and lay bare, and in laying bare may weaken, the foundations even of the throne'.[21]

While countenancing a public reform campaign against the House of Lords following its rejection of the 1884 Reform Bill and condemning the institution as an 'irresponsible power' in his stump oratory, Gladstone was still not prepared to propose a blueprint for a reformed second chamber. His politics remained strongly coloured by his own aristocratic background (illus. 59). Throughout his career the substance of his oratory about the Upper House, though critical, never really progressed beyond the view he expressed strongly in 1869, that the real problem with the Lords was the chamber's remoteness from the legislative process. He commented then that 'from the great eminence on which they sit they can no more discuss the minute particulars of our transactions than could a man in a balloon'.[22] After 1893 when Gladstone encountered fresh obstruction from the Lords over his second Irish Home Rule Bill, he strenuously resisted pressure from radical Liberals to embrace a popular crusade against them. Gladstone's 1892–4 government reflected his aristocratic preferences in this regard. His second Home Rule Bill contained a provision for an unelected upper chamber in Ireland made up of Irish peers. In cabinet, he promoted peers to high office over the heads of long-standing reform Liberals. Moreover, in 1895 he sought to deter his successor, Lord Rosebery, from fighting a general election with Lords reform as its theme. Gladstone counselled John Morley that Liberals should learn to live with the Lords. Rather than seeking to abolish the Upper House altogether, Gladstone proposed keeping the Lords busy by wrong-footing them with a constant stream of small measures 'like pistols at the heads of the Lords [...] bills that the opposition in the Commons would find it embarrassing to obstruct or oppose'.[23] There could be no clearer symbol of the retreat from the notion of an election fought solely on the Lords issue[24] than Gladstone's last speech in the House of Commons in 1894, in which he spoke on the issue of the Lords's amendment of the Parish Councils Bill, praised their decisions and gracefully withdrew from the brink (illus. 60).

Toryism shared the concern of Gladstonian Liberalism that tampering with the Lords imperilled the fabric of the constitution.

60 Conservative cartoons often misleadingly showed Gladstone as a radical wrecker, keen to swamp the Lords with fellow radicals like the fraudulent 'Tichbourne Claimant', William Harcourt, Joseph Chamberlain and Charles Bradlaugh.

During the 1909–11 House of Lords crisis, Tories repeatedly claimed that the issue placed the throne under greater threat than at any time in recent British history. The death of Edward VII in May 1910 confirmed the mortal danger to the constitution posed by Liberal policies, prompting angry scenes in the Commons when Asquith spoke, and shouts of 'Who killed the king?' from the opposition benches.[25]

In the early 1880s radical and Liberal attitudes diverged significantly over issues of privilege and a hereditary second chamber. For working-class radicals, reform of the Lords held out the prospect of a more substantive renewal of government. Moreover, radicals were untroubled by the implied threat to monarchy that emerged from proposals to reform the hereditary element within the legislature. Many radicals believed that the reform of the monarchy might follow naturally from the dismantling of the aristocratic superstructure that cushioned the throne and court. For the reform community this was a development to be welcomed. At a lecture to the Paddington branch of the National Secular Society J. E. Woolacott asserted:

It is urged by some that the arguments used against the Lords apply equally to the Crown. If this is so, and these arguments are good arguments, all I have to say is 'so much the worse for the Crown'. I have but little sympathy with lords and kings. I believe in government for the people, and by the people.[26]

Challenging the notion that the House of Lords acted as a bulwark and first line of defence for the monarchy, the orator Mackenzie commented in similar vein at the time of the 1884 Reform Bill:

Unwise, I think, at least from a conservative point of view, are those who in these days, admit that the monarchy stands in need of any institution which is in itself prejudicial to the interests of the whole community. Our present sovereign may continue to reside quietly by the lovely shores of Osborne or her Highland house of Balmoral, but depend upon it, the days of monarchy are numbered, and as Shelley says: 'Kingly glare/will lose its power to dazzle, its authority/will silently pass by'.[27]

Implicit in these arguments was the notion, frequently reiterated elsewhere, that the monarchy and the House of Lords would sink or swim together. Some radicals argued during the Franchise Bill crisis of 1884 that once the initiative passed out of the hands of ministers and the matter was taken up by the populace then, 'however they may put a bold face on the matter, [it] must make the hereditary legislators look to themselves, and to the preservation of their privileges'.[28] Many ultra-radical pamphlets bore variations on the theme of 'What Shall We Do With It?' in their titles, in conscious emulation of the diatribes against monarchy in the 1870s.[29] For Liberals, in contrast, a wider reform of the royal state was only accidentally implied by the rhetorical assaults on the Upper Chamber that occurred with increasing frequency from 1884 onwards. Most Liberals exonerated the monarchy from complicity in Lords obstructionism altogether. A pamphlet produced by the Financial Reform Association in Liverpool during the Reform Bill crisis posited that the power formerly concentrated in royal hands was now the preserve of an unchecked aristocracy that ruled without restraint through its instrument of the Lords.[30]

Hostility to the throne was not unknown amongst Liberals. Queen Victoria's neglect of the more remote regions of Britain had led David Lloyd George to refer slightingly to 'royal vagabonds' in 1889 at the time of her visit to Wales,[31] but, in general, the Liberal Party remained strongly wedded to royal influences, despite Victoria's ostracism of the traditional Whig hierarchy and her personal dislike of Gladstone. In 1884 during the anti-Lords demonstration in Hyde Park, Lord Carrington urged reformers protesting against the Upper Chamber's opposition to the Franchise Bill to demonstrate their loyalism to spectators who included the Prince and Princess of Wales:

I had invited visitors to see the demonstration from my house [...] and I heard that the Prince and Princess of Wales would come to see the demonstration. I suggested to one of the organisers that it would serve to show the loyalty of the Liberal Party if, as the procession passed, it should take off its hats and cheer loudly. This happened and the procession took three and a half hours to pass the window.[32]

After 1894 Lord Rosebery was elevated to the leadership of the Liberal Party by the exercise of royal patronage, and despite his well known dislike of the Upper Chamber.[33] For the majority of mainstream Liberals, the House of Lords issue was simply about the partisan exercise of power by a branch of the legislature. They saw this as promoting the interests of the Tory Party, reducing the second chamber to an arm of political Conservatism, and impoverishing the constitution. In his premier's battle cry on the eve of the general election of November 1910, Asquith condemned the existing system as fostering the 'yoke of [a] Single Chamber-tyranny'.[34] Tory refusals to accept Lords reform accelerated the political confrontation emerging from the issues surrounding the entrenched power of the peerage in the Upper House. In 1884 at the time of the Third Reform Bill, the Lords re-emerged as the enemies of progress, reform and the rights of the people. Again in 1909 Lloyd George likened the Lords to a waiter who, 'if the cook is a Liberal one [...] insists upon showing the dish and ascertaining the views of the customer [...] until it gets quite cold. But if the cook happens to be a Tory one, [he] never ascertains the views of the customer. He has to take it.'[35] Many Liberals concluded that they 'found themselves in office only, but not in power'.[36]

A common opposition to privilege, however, helped overcome the deep cleavages between Liberalism and advanced radical culture. Radical images of the Lords as malign and interfering projected a different impression of the Upper Chamber from its sometimes benign and impotent depiction in popular culture.[37] Such narratives united the Liberal Nonconformist opposition to indolence and dislike of Church of England bishops resident in the Upper House with a broader radical hostility to unproductive wealth and inherited status. Nonconformists had long campaigned against the Lords Spiritual and their role as defenders of the interests of the Church of England within the executive. Even some Anglicans agreed, seeing the role of bishops within the House of Lords as inimical to civil and religious liberties.[38] The Lords's rejection of the 1908 Licensing Bill, which sought to increase licensing and spirit duties, confirmed the vision of the Peers and the Tory brewers working in tandem against the Nonconformist interest and the temperance crusade.[39]

Between 1909 and 1911 Liberals campaigned to undercut the moral authority of the Upper House. During this period hatred of a restrictive, idle, aristocratic presence retarding constitutional advance crystallized around hostility to the peers, with the Liberal Party acting as the vehicle for a marked levelling tendency. Fused Nonconformist and radical inspired notions of spirituality, temperance and self-improvement underpinned Lloyd George's remark in a speech at Newcastle that the House of Lords constituted 'five hundred men [...] chosen accidentally from among the unemployed'.[40] This image of the Lords, viewed from the perspective of a Welsh 'outsider' in politics, was one of moral laxity and malaise. The campaign against the Lords was suffused with a related sense of moral earnestness throughout. Condemning the 'Lords of Misrule', one Liberal pamphlet of 1884 drew attention to the image of the peerage that emerged from the aristocracy's own journals, advising that anyone who wished to know their true character 'will then learn what a compound of gossip, frivolity, conceit and superciliousness is the literature specially composed for them [...] If he wants to know anything of their moral influence let him turn to the turf, and to the divorce court.'[41] For Lloyd George such failings were hereditary, and he attacked members of the peerage as 'the ennobled indiscretions of kings'.[42] In a familiar image some Liberals employed the established rhetoric of opposition to hunting that featured strongly in anti-monarchism. Given that a Mountain Trap Pigeon Shooting Bill passed without amendment immediately prior to the rejection of the 1884 Reform Bill, such comparisons seemed appropriate. One pamphleteer wrote: 'Killing vermin and shooting birds is the work which they do perform; but what shall we say of the work they do not perform?'[43]

In 1894 opposition to a Liberal Death Duties Bill apparently confirmed the Lords's role as a selfish class bent only upon self-preservation. The old topsy-turvy images of carnival were again deployed here to illustrate this theme. Like the royals, peers were depicted as tramps with begging bowls, demanding handouts from the state and the public purse. In 1898 the *Single Tax* showed the Irish peerage taking money from the pockets of a blindfolded John Bull with the connivance of Lord Salisbury and the Tory party, under the caption 'Out-Door Relief for the Aristocracy' (illus. 61). After 1906 Progressivist Liberalism bridged the gap between radicalism and Liberalism still further, and accentuated the tendency towards distrust of aristocratic values. The New Liberalism celebrated the notion of a community of producers and encouraged an alliance of the middling sort and the respectable working-class against an idle rich and an

OUT-DOOR RELIEF TO THE ARISTOCRACY.

The sum of £400,000 will be taken by the Government out of the Imperial Exchequer—that is to say, out of the pockets of the people—every year to be given the Irish Landlords as the price of their support to the Irish Local Government Bill now before Parliament.

61 Irish landlords extracting money from the coffers of the Exchequer and a blindfolded John Bull with the encouragement of Lord Salisbury and the Conservative Party.

equally idle poor, who were incapable of responsibility and lacked any real stake in society. The political partnership of Asquith and Lloyd George was central to this message. Asquith provided a reassuring anchor for the voters of Middle England, while Lloyd George acted as the conduit for a more robust criticism of aristocracy rooted in the Welsh experience of high land rents, an alien Anglican Church and absentee landlordism.[44]

There were sufficient shared concerns and common reference points to make an alliance between radicalism and Liberalism desirable during the highpoints of anti-Lords hostility in 1884 and 1909–11. This co-operation drew its strength from a common vision of the constitution, an on-going narrative of national liberty, and a perception of Lords reform as a further stage in the battles for English rights and freedoms. The Lords reform campaigns were constructed around a memory of past achievements arising from the inherited highpoints of the national past. They were grounded particularly in memories of the victory over the Upper Chamber during the debates surrounding the 1832 Reform Bill. This measure, like the 1884 Reform Bill, was subject to delaying and blocking tactics in the Lords that were overcome by a popular campaign of political agitation throughout Britain's towns and cities. Memories of the 1832 Reform Bill riots were stirred by an outbreak of disorder at Aston Lower Ground in Birmingham during a Tory meeting in support of the Lords.[45] Even at the start of the campaign the radical *Newcastle Weekly Chronicle* discovered parallels between the 1832 riots and obstructionism in the Lords in 1884: 'The House of Lords in 1832 brought the country to the verge of revolution by their hostility to reform, and the motion which Earl Cairns is to introduce on Monday is simply a repetition of their tactics at that time.'[46] Between 1909 and 1911 contemporaries were also reminded of the three close-fought elections waged and won against vested interests in 1830–32 that presaged later Liberal electoral confrontation with the Lords during the constitutional crisis.[47] There was, however, more than just an appeal to constitutional precedent at work in the 1884 crusade against privilege.

According to a Whig reading of constitutional evolution the 1832 reform bill made progress as a consequence of a shared alliance between middle-class and working-class radical reformers working in tandem against an unrestrained and unjust power. Here it was the notion of the people locked in a struggle against a narrow caste interest that mattered most to a later generation of Liberal/radical reformers. The 1884 anti-Lords campaign was perceived as a renewal of past radical fervour against a common enemy and an attempt to regain

62 Demonstration against the Lords in London, July 1884, part of a sequence of images that are amongst the earliest photographic representations of a political march.

freedoms that seemed endangered by the peers. As part of this process of 'remembering', veterans of 1832 paraded at popular demonstrations, surviving banners were unfurled, and the theatre of popular street display made repeated reference to this earlier sequence of events. One old Warwickshire veteran of 1832 appeared on public platforms with the traditional *fasces*, or bundle of sticks, symbolic of the united will and determination of the people since the French Revolution of 1789.[48] The 1832 slogan 'the bill, the whole bill, and nothing but the bill' was revived and displayed on placards at the July 1884 demonstration against the Lords in Hyde Park (illus. 62). The same event featured coffins marked 'In Memory of the House of Lords AD 1884', but pride of place was given to 'a Brobdingnagian representation of Mr. Gladstone holding in his palm a peer wearing his coronet and with 50 dangling from his hand' (the majority in the Lords against the bill).[49]

Similar historical visions of the people versus privilege emerged from the attempt by the Lords to amend or restrict the Liberal budget in 1909. By convention money bills were in the control of the House of Commons alone. Moreover, the budget was a hallowed fiscal institution for Gladstonians, evoking the financial probity and restraint of the High-Victorian state.[50] As a consequence, Liberal budgets became the touchstone of the social contract between governors and the governed.

Budget day was, above all, a day of great national reckoning in which the compact between state and people was renewed annually before the public gaze. As part of this process, budgets and the theatricality that surrounded them served as reaffirmations of public and political accountability through a commonly recognized set of rituals and display. It was this compact that the Lords disrupted in 1909 with tactics that undermined the sanctity of mutual obligations between taxpayer and government.[51] Liberal election leaflets in the two general elections fought against the influence of the peers in 1910 underlined this point. In National Reform Union leaflets, Sir Wilfred Lawson was quoted as saying:

So long as the House of Commons has in its hands the power of the purse, it is strong enough to deal with the Lords whenever it is backed up by public opinion in doing so. Surely that is constitutional enough for anyone; for 'grievance before supply' is a kind of Commons Magna Charta, and there is, and can be, no greater grievance than the House of Lords.[52]

Significantly, banners from 1832 were again on display at anti-Lords demonstrations on Glasgow Green in 1909,[53] while the vision of the battles for English liberty and their role in overcoming the narrow second chamber animated Liberals into the middle years of the twentieth century and underpinned the party's declaration in 1927 that: 'Liberals stand for the supremacy of the House of Commons, on the fundamental ground that the people must govern themselves – whether for good or ill [...] nobody can tax the people except themselves.'[54]

Such joint memories knitted together the language of the Whiggery of the 1830s, Nonconformity, radical invective, and the vision of a pure and undiluted constitutionalism with its roots deep in the British past. The anti-Lords slogan, 'The Peerage and the Beerage', epitomizes the language and moral vision they shared. The Peers acknowledged the unanimity of sentiment around the anti-Lords platform and identified a composite 'Jacobinism' as the true threat to the history and traditions of the existing order.[55] In practice radicalism and Liberalism were indistinguishable over this issue. In the absence of any model for an alternative constitution within radicalism, there were no clear guidelines over the 'ending or mending it' debate. It is certainly difficult to chart lines of demarcation that separated one camp off from another. For Liberals, notions of 'divided powers' rooted in the discourse of the American and French Revolutions were not imperilled by proposals to reform the Upper House by merely ridding it of its hereditary dimension.[56] Those Liberals who suggested creating an elective Upper Chamber on the American model found many supporters within a broader radical culture that still sought inspiration in American democratic precedent. Above all, it was older notions of the 'Norman Yoke' that found their strongest expression in rhetoric of this kind. The most evocative appeals were to shared historical memories of 'William the Bastard' and an oppressive Normanism that featured strongly in both radicalism and the Whig history of the period. For radicals, the Norman invasion established a framework of injustice; for Liberals, it created a separate hereditary caste that, not for the first time, was engaged in upsetting the delicate balance between King, Lords and Commons. Restricting the power of the Lords offered the prospect of redressing this imbalance. In 1894 the Parish Councils Bill creating parish assemblies was represented by both radicals and Liberals as a reassertion of the Anglo–Saxon *folkmoot* against lordly Norman rule in the counties.[57] Study of the Norman origins of the Upper House also helped illuminate the second chamber's historical role in regard to the mixed constitution, and shattered its own myths about its legislative function. A 1910 Liberal election leaflet quoted the radical Goldwin Smith on this issue:

The House of Lords has been taken everywhere for a second chamber or senate. It is nothing of the kind. It is one of the estates of the feudal realm, reduced by the decay of feudalism to comparative impotence, such influence as it retains being that not of legislative authority, but of hereditary wealth. It has never acted as, what it is imagined by the political architects of Europe to be, an Upper Chamber revising with maturer wisdom, and in an impartial spirit, the hasty or ultra-democratic legislation of the more popular house. It has always acted as what it is, a privileged order in a state of decay and jeopardy, resisting as far as it dare each measure of change, not political only, but legal, social and of every kind.[58]

The career of Henry Labouchère, former editor of the Liberal *Daily News* and MP for Northampton, symbolizes this radical/Liberal fusion over constitutional ideas and demonstrates the ways in which Liberals and radicals united in defence of a legislative structure that was seen as 'historically' constructed. Labouchère became the most vocal Liberal opponent of the Lords, proposing private members bills to abolish the hereditary element in the Upper House on three separate occasions between 1884 and 1888. He stated in the Commons in 1884 that: 'Members of the House of Lords were neither elected nor selected for their merits. They sat by the merits of their ancestors, and, if we looked into the merits of some of those ancestors, we should agree that the less said about them the better.'[59] Such sentiments legitimized Labouchère's personal radical journey from Huguenot

Protestant stock, through exposure to English history and American democracy, to radical reformer intent on Lords reform.[60] In addition, it created the possibility for a working partnership with groups like the SDF who supported him over his stance on the Lords.[61]

The campaigns against the House of Lords came at a time when the steady leakage of landed and urban proprietors away from Liberalism into Toryism increased the influence of radical Liberals within the party. The Newcastle Programme of 1891, which also highlighted Lords reform, marked a high point of their significance.[62] During the 1892–5 Liberal government Rosebery's personal Whig legacy, as the son of a member of Lord Grey's reforming ministry of the 1830s, conferred a marked radical pedigree on this anti-Lords issue. Furthermore, the National Liberal Federation, which comprised the strong radical backbone of much Liberal organization in the regions, gave the campaign against the Lords their wholehearted backing in 1884 and during the 1895 election. During these years even irreconcilable radicals like Charles Bradlaugh, notorious for his atheism and hostility to the throne and the peers, were posthumously amalgamated into the pantheon of Liberal-radical heroes. Prominent local Liberals and the Whig hierarchy were conspicuous at the unveiling of a statue to his memory in Northampton in 1894, despite their many years of vocal opposition to him in Northamptonshire.[63]

The Liberal attacks on the House of Lords created a generalized narrative of liberty that knitted together the opposing expectations of Liberals and working-class radicals, and provided the framework for a fused vocabulary of co-operation culminating in Progressivism. The notion of wielding power on the basis of birth was challenged directly. Between 1910 and 1911 the role of the 'Ditchers' in resisting Lords reform to the bitter end confirmed the worst impression of the peers current among radicals. The image of 'the coronet' in satire, election material and the Labourite press became the lasting symbol of this 'nation within a nation' that defied the will of the people (illus. 63).[64] Liberal posters from the 1895 general election went further and used the image of St. George locked in mortal combat with the dragon, surmounted with the coronet of the peerage, to symbolize the eternal struggle between democratic imperatives and caste interests. This was a crusade.

The vocal Liberal hostility to the Lords, far from imperilling the throne, confounded Gladstone's prediction of the hereditary principle's vulnerability to scrutiny, and created an acceptable enemy that diverted attention away from the monarchy which rose above mere party conflict. Under the patronage of the Liberal government, royal

THE LAST WORD

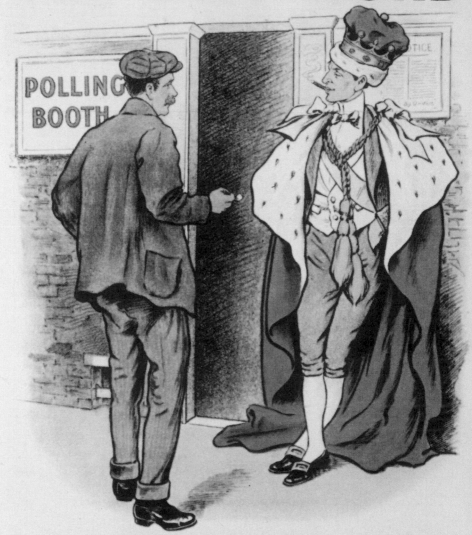

Tory Peer (to Voter): It's all right, my man, you may go and vote if you like, but however you vote, **I** always have the last word.
Why not have the last word yourself?

63 This 1910 Liberal election poster challenges traditional notions of deference to social superiors: a laconic aristocrat mocks a working-man on his way to the polls to unseat him.

events like the coronation of George V and the Investiture of the Prince of Wales in 1911 stabilized the Crown during a period in which the foundations of the dignified element within the constitution seemed open to question. In these ceremonies the Liberal vision of the United Kingdom was projected as decentralized, devolved and diverse, but nevertheless united, under the 'Liberal' monarch, George V.[65]

Far from promoting the cause of anti-monarchism, the creation of an acceptable Liberal opposition to privilege actually retarded the prospects of republicanism still further, making it seem irrelevant to the real struggle that arose from the peers versus the people campaigns. For Liberals, Lords reform was a safe project, displacing the necessity for a broader revision of the constitution. Moreover, it lifted the monarchy out of the mire of everyday politics and set up a false comparison in which the monarch remained resolutely aloof from politics, whereas the Lords retained an interest in deploying hereditary privilege in favour of the Tory interest. It was the Lords themselves who had committed a cardinal sin and hastened their own demise, while the fiction of royal impartiality was maintained.[66] In this way the Liberal Party managed to square the circle and laid the groundwork for a future Lib–Lab alliance rooted in a loyalist vision of the constitution in the years before 1914. Radicals like John Burns who favoured a republic realized Liberalism's limited potential as a vehicle for reform of the royal state, and were highly critical of Lloyd George's close relationship with George V during the planning of the Investiture at Caernarfon; 'he's had housemaid's knee ever since' was his cynical comment on Lloyd George's first meetings with royalty.[67]

Nevertheless, notions of democracy and democratic participation were central to the combined vision of Liberalism and Labourism. Recent research on the historical antecedence of turn–of–the–century Labourism has emphasized the strength of such democratic appeals.[68] The early Labour movement reclaimed conceptions of democracy, freedom and political accountability from Liberalism and Toryism. It is now acknowledged that the roots of Liberalism and Labourism are inextricably intertwined. This new scholarship revises existing analyses of the Labour Party as a trade-union-dominated crusade, intent upon the amelioration of economic and social grievances, and geared towards the redistribution of wealth.[69] The new reading of the Labour tradition emphasizes Labourism's debt to Liberalism and an inheritance that was inclusive of those strands of opinion that sought reform of the constitution, rather than simple modification of the economic superstructure. Labourism was never, however, simply a client in its early relationship with the Liberal Party. The Progressivist project of

1906–14, which was underpinned by the Lib–Lab alliance of 1903, is now accepted as a fundamental part of a joint culture. It provided a working partnership of ideas and a coherent strategy with consequences that continued to shape the direction of Labour policy after 1945.[70] No longer simply dismissed as a distraction from the forward march of Labour, this period of co-operation is now seen as a profitable interchange and evolution for both sides of the alliance. Without Labour's votes after 1910, when Asquith led a minority government, Progressivism would not have survived. The strength and mutual advantage gained from this partnership also explains Labour's failure to make progress in by-elections between 1906 and 1914.[71]

The Lords issue provides a further opportunity to reprise the politics of 1909–11 and to deepen our understanding of the importance of constitutional reform to the Labour pioneers. Asquith's 1910 declaration of war on the Lords in the second general election of that year signalled a convergence of intent on this subject between Labourism and Liberalism (illus. 64). Radical Liberals, radicals who owed a debt to the Chartist tradition, and Labourites were able to unite around a common strand of belief that saw the existence of the Lords as detrimental to the will of the people. For reformers whose views were moulded by an older radical milieu and who saw English and Irish democracy as co-joined, deliberate attempts by the Lords to overturn reform in Ireland perpetuated a vision of that country as difficult and unmanageable, while further accentuating its differences with the mainland. Many radicals and Irish Nationalists saw the presence of Irish peers in the Lords as constituting the major barrier to the resolution of the Irish Question.[72] George Standring noted even the 'blind, the lame and the halt' hurrying to Westminster 'in bath chairs and ambulances' to vote down the Compensation for Disturbances in Ireland Bill in 1880.[73] There was also a point of contact here for mainstream Liberals exclusively preoccupied with the Irish issue. W. T. Stead wrote:

It may be said that the House of Lords has been unable to persevere in its opposition to popular reforms excepting in the case of Ireland; and in the case of Ireland its success has been as signal as it has been pernicious. In England and Scotland it has delayed and marred measures of reform; in Ireland alone has it rejected them.[74]

For socialists within Labourism the abolition of the Lords was similarly an essential 'clearing away' of a body that thwarted the potential for eventual reform in England itself, and whose defeat made the realization of true socialism possible (illus. 65). Against this background, advanced radicals were willing to overcome their initial doubts about the Liberal

THE PREMIER'S BATTLE CRY

Mr. Asquith's Speech at the National Liberal Club, November 19th. 1910.

64 H. H. Asquith as leader of the anti-Lords crusade in 1910.

intent to transform the Lords into a Liberal 'House of Patronage', and embrace the reform crusade of 1909–11. In the eyes of Labour men like Ramsay MacDonald, steeped in a Chamberlainite radical tradition, it was the actions of the Lords, not the reformers, who upset the delicate balance of the constitution.[75] In part, such Labourite notions of a direct democracy were formulated in response to Conservative 'referendal' theories of the House of Lords as a supreme arbiter, expressive of the true will of the people, that occupied the constitutional high ground of

65 A 1910 election poster showing the House of Lords as a barrier to progress and reform.

politics in battles with the Commons. According to this argument, the Lords had a constitutional duty to refer measures directly to the electorate for its decision where the government of the day seemingly lacked a full electoral mandate. This reflected an instinctive distrust of the caucus politics of the Commons and, in effect, openly invited the Lords to rebuff legislation of which they disapproved.[76]

Labourite notions of a direct democracy forcefully contested this retrograde vision of the constitution. Devolved democratic participation was central to Labourite concerns. In the 1890s many Labour papers campaigned vigorously for referenda on all council and borough matters as a defence of local autonomy in the face of parliamentary intervention in local affairs. As Ian Bullock and Siân Reynolds have pointed out, the years after 1894 saw something of a vogue for referenda in Labourite circles.[77] For some Labourites referenda provided an opportunity to circumvent the power of the Lords in 'The Mangling House'; J. Morrison Davidson advocated a referendum based on the Australian model, in which two consecutive referrals of legislation by the upper chamber automatically triggered a ballot of the electorate.[78] Asquith sought to appease this tradition within Labourism in 1910 at the height of the House of Lords crisis when he suggested an immediate referendum on the position of the Lords.

Joint declarations and activity between Labourism and Liberalism against the Lords were strongest at the grassroots level. Officially, the

196

embryonic Labour Party remained aloof from attempts to reform the Lords. In 1910 Keir Hardie denounced the Liberals for seeking to enhance and consolidate the power of a Liberal-dominated Commons at the expense of the second tier of the executive, '[...] thus taking away the odium which inevitably attaches to obstructive powers and tactics when continuously exercised by a body of irresponsible legislators'.[79] For many working men, however, the Lords was as much a symbol of the ability of local employers to augment their wealth with estates and stately homes, as of landed privilege *per se*. From the turn of the century onwards this social transformation in the Lords, from a house of ancient pedigree to a bastion of former businessmen, had become a common theme amongst radicals.[80] Here issues of employment rights and constitutional reform became inextricably intertwined. Responding to the Liberal notion of flooding the Lords with new peers sympathetic to the government, the Fabian *New Age* demonstrated an abhorrence of new money and a strong tinge of anti-Semitism in its attacks on 'the prospect of a second chamber crowded with Jew stock-brokers, wealthy soap-boilers, men who have made their pile in the South African "swindle" and who (have) set up as "gentlemen of England"'.[81] At the local level, Labour periodicals in the West Riding fulminated against 'the [existing] assembly of successful lawyers, slum owners and varnished soap-boilers styled, surely in joke, the "Upper House"'.[82] The Lords' amendment and delay of the 1894 Employers' Liabilities Bill did much to mobilize a constituency of trade unionists and the disaffected within Liberalism who sought a final reckoning with the Upper House.

During the election of 1895, when Keir Hardie (1856–1915) cautioned in a speech at Sowerby Bridge against an excessive enthusiasm for Lords reform that might detract from the 'social question', West Riding radicals warmly embraced Lord Rosebery's crusade against the Upper House at an ecstatic meeting in Bradford.[83] In a strong appeal to the West Riding radical tradition, the Liberal *Bradford Observer* spoke of enthusiastic demonstrations from the crowd that 'expressed the long-smouldering fires of Old Liberal as well as New Liberal discontent [and] the long restrained revolt forced upon it by decades of arbitrary and despotic treatment'.[84] Post-Gladstone many Liberal and Labour activists felt liberated by the end of Liberal policies of tentative and uneasy co-existence with the Lords. Subsequently much pent-up anger and frustration was released by the radical activity surrounding Rosebery's campaign. Even Keir Hardie praised Gladstone at the time of his death in 1898 for his role in initiating these later attempts to curb the Lords; in an obituary in the *Labour Leader*, he gave the campaign his retrospective blessing and condemned the last Gladstone Cabinet for a lack of nerve in standing up to the peers:

The old warrior was thirsting for a fray with the Lords [...] The proud commoner would not brook that the haughty lordlings, themselves bankrupt of prestige and with no power behind them, mere shadows of things which had been, should thwart his will. But the little-souled crew who surrounded him, shrank in dismay from the contest and the consequences.[85]

In the general elections of 1910 fought on the Lords issue, the anti-peers campaign, while denting the Liberal majority of 1906, allowed the Liberals to consolidate their strength in working-class districts in Lancashire, Yorkshire, South Wales, Scotland and London on a high turnout of electors.[86]

The 1911 Parliament Act, which limited the ability of the Lords to retard Commons legislation, stopped short of a full root-and-branch reform of the Upper House. Liberal intentions of making the second chamber an elective body were never fulfilled. Progressivism was not a levelling creed, either in Britain or the US. Instead, it advocated a notion of social justice that sought to inform the propertied of their true responsibilities and obligations to the poor.[87] In Britain it never contemplated a full assault on the existing order, rather it hoped simply to humanize the establishment's role as guardian of a Liberal-led status quo.

After 1909 Liberals attempted to unblock the constitution by embracing a strategy of land reform that increased taxation of land values for the very rich. It was intended that this project would cause the wealthy landowners who monopolized the Lords to simply fade away and so resolve the problems posed by a predominantly landed Second Chamber. L. T. Hobhouse argued in 1907 that the land 'is the true battleground for a struggle with the Lords'.[88] Liberal land reform projects, however, moved away from the many expedients for the break-up of the landed estates proposed by extreme radicals from the mid-nineteenth century onwards. Land valuation, the necessary prerequisite to taxation based on the unearned increment of land, posed no threat to the principle of land ownership as such and was far removed from the notion of land nationalization advocated by Chartists like Bronterre O'Brien in the 1840s. The Liberal land reform programme was shaped instead by the transatlantic ideology of the American land reformer Henry George, which presented the case against a landowners' monopoly but avoided direct state confiscation of property. This represented the expansion of an established Liberal tradition with antecedence in Chamberlain's Unauthorized Programme of 1885 and the concerns raised by the Disraeli government's 1876 land register, *Return on Owners of Land*, which showed very high concentrations of land in a small number of hands.[89]

Chartists like Ernest Jones, who campaigned against the excessive waste of fertile land involved in conventional farming methods, became part of an acceptable radical pedigree on this issue. In 1910 his speech on 'The Hereditary Landed Aristocracy' from 1856 featured prominently in Liberal election leaflets.[90] Such precedents and the moral fervour of Georgeite belief appealed strongly to both Liberals and Labourites. Moreover Labour policy did not differ significantly from the Liberals over issues posed by the land. The Liberal-led Land Values Group included both Liberal and Labour MPs.[91] The 1909 budget thus awakened the long-held ancestral belief that the land was the rightful inheritance of the English people. The song 'The Land! The Land! God Gave the Land to the People' (set to the tune of 'Marching Through Georgia') was used by Lloyd George as the rallying cry of the Liberal Party in the two general elections of 1910, and featured prominently in radical pamphlets on the land issue.[92]

As with reform of the House of Lords, however, the implicit republicanism that was very conspicuous in Henry George's ideas was masked by the diminished radicalism of the land debate. George himself addressed his audience on a visit to London as 'members of the republic of man destined to federate the world'.[93] Liberal obfuscation thereafter diluted the important constitutional issues present in land reform proposals and conveniently ignored the role of the royal family as the country's largest landowners. *Reynolds's Newspaper* recognized this omission and implicated both the monarchy and the aristocracy in the traditional abuses of land holding:

The far larger portion of the rents derived from the enormous properties possessed by the Duke of Bedford in London was bequeathed [...] to the succour of the poor. Henry the Eighth reversed all this and bestowed it upon one of his favourite courtiers [...] What Mr. George contends is that this was robbery; that the king had no right to rob the poor of what lawfully was theirs; and that as no transfer of stolen property can be valid in law, and that the Bedford estates came within that category, their present owner is not entitled to their possession.[94]

Land nationalizers continued to view monarchy and aristocracy as linked through the Norman Conquest, with land nationalization leading inevitably to modification of royal power.[95] In Scotland in particular, where the vast royal estates stood at the apex of an apparently still feudal situation in the Highlands and the Borders, land reform was intimately connected to reform of the monarchy.[96] On the issue of the land therefore, as with its constitutional policy on the Lords, the Liberal Party's reform pledges united reformers in the Progressive camp, but failed to fulfil the radical potentialities present in the reformist discourses of Liberalism.

Other factors contributed to a weakening of the potential and actual vocabulary of an anti-monarchist stance, and of opposition to existing privilege outside Liberalism. Most potent here was the decline of the Cromwellian myth of republicanism within radicalism. In the past Cromwellianism had always sustained an oppositional stance critical of the throne, courtiers and the royal state. Such memories still featured strongly in the anti-Lords demonstration of 1884. Reformers pointed out that the constitutional precedents for the abolition of the second chamber were Cromwellian ones.[97] In 1649 the Commonwealth Parliament had taken the unprecedented step of dismissing the Lords, an action that demonstrated to radicals the effectiveness of resolute action on the constitution. To those who hoped for a broader assault on privilege, the anti-Lords campaign raised the possibility of modification or abolition of royal power in a similar style. *Reynolds's Newspaper* noted the memories stirred on the day of the radical demonstration in Hyde Park in July 1884, when the procession passed the site of Charles I's execution at the Banqueting House in Whitehall:

No man with the feelings of an Englishman seeing the procession traversing the historic roads of Whitehall, Charing-Cross and Piccadilly could not but be impressed with the recollection of another crowd that stood there in 1648 (*sic*) to witness the last act in a contest with the people. Except that Englishmen are now much more inclined to employ scorn and contempt rather than the scaffold and the headsman, they are very much what their forefathers were when privilege chose to attack the sacred rights of the people.[98]

By the end of the century, however, the image of 'The Man from Huntingdon' as a figure of unsullied radical zeal and integrity became harder to sustain. During these years historical scholarship rediscovered the role of groups like the Levellers, who, after the Putney Debates in 1647, suffered the consequences of Cromwell's wrath in much the same way as royalists and the Irish. The Levellers became immensely sympathetic figures for a new generation of Labourites and socialist pioneers at the turn of the twentieth century. Their advocacy of franchise extension, land reform and communal living mirrored the Georgeite concerns of millenarian socialism. These recovered memories of radical Cromwellian martyrs forced a reappraisal of Cromwell's influence that was debated and mapped out on the pages of the radical newspapers of the period. Cromwell now appeared less a benign figure than a despot, and for the first time radicals found themselves in agreement with previous Tory condemnations of his career. The *Single Tax* wrote of the Levellers in 1897:

They formed, indeed, the extreme left, the irreconcilables of the Puritan or Independent Party, in whose glorious struggles and victories many of them assisted. But, being opposed to all compromise, they stood in the way of that 'settlement of the nation' which was, at all events in the practical mind of Cromwell and his supporters, the most pressing necessity of the hour. Hence the iron hand of Cromwell fell upon them, and in the sacred name of 'law and order' they as a body, as a living factor of the politics of the time, were swept out of existence.[99]

The new vision of a strong, dictatorial Cromwell harmonized best with notions of vigorous leadership and decisive action in defence of state and nation. Such opinions were to be found increasingly on the extremist conservative fringe of politics, rather than on the left. By the end of the century Cromwellianism had moved into the mainstream. The erection of the statue of Cromwell outside the Houses of Parliament at the tercentenary of his birth in 1899 symbolized this progress. He was not respectable enough to warrant a place inside the Commons itself, but he was central enough to British historical memory to be acknowledged on its forecourt as a major architect of the constitution.[100] The new statue captured the imagination of those political figures who looked for national renewal in strong dictatorial control from the centre and a rejection of the existing party system. In a period of potential coalition politics, amid rumours of a national government, images of a saviour for the nation came increasingly to the fore. The Cromwellian legacy was now about naked power and its exercise (illus. 66). Lord Rosebery, who spoke at the unveiling and was the chief inspiration behind its erection, hoped to be the main benefi-ciary of such sentiments.[101] He unashamedly identified himself with Cromwell as a strong man who could win back British prestige abroad following international humiliation in the Boer War. His championing of the Cromwellian ethic did much to rehabilitate the 'Great Commoner' as a stern and fair dispenser of justice.[102]

Despite the failure of Rosebery's ambitions, Cromwell subse-quently became closely identified with national greatness, an assertive Britishness and the preservation of the empire that he in part had created. In 1911 Winston Churchill, then Navy Secretary, thought these fitting grounds for the construction of a dreadnought called *Cromwell* – a project that floundered under the weight of royal disap-proval.[103] Nevertheless these patriotic associations remained an entrenched part of the Cromwell myth into the middle years of the

66 'He who was then *protected* has become the *Protector*': Cromwell as a beneficent despot shows mercy to a former royalist who saved his life during the Civil War after intercession by his mother.

twentieth century. In 1914 the *Observer* newspaper described General Kitchener as 'Cromwellian', and in 1940 the code name selected to signal a German invasion was 'Cromwell'.[104]

The implications of anti-monarchism for national resources and the constitution were potentially significant. With an ascendant Liberalism dominating the high ground of politics and a Labourism in thrall to Liberal management strategies, it was, however, unlikely that these would ever be realized. Anti-monarchism was essentially oppositional rather than governmental in nature. Moreover, the throne cemented a strong state structure. In an age of constitutional reform, state welfare provision and total war, there was little place for a rhetoric that seemed incapable of practical implementation and resolution.

Some socialists sought to extend the rhetoric of hostility to the Crown into the field of social welfare provision and even pacifism during the re-armament phase before the Great War. The West Riding socialist Charles Glyde linked spending on the monarchy with a broader debate about old-age pensions and naval defence estimates. In 1903 he argued for the redeployment of state handouts to royal dependants into pensions and state provision for the elderly poor. He wrote:

While the aged poor have been starving, while they have been despised and neglected, while they have gone down to their grave with the hateful brand of pauperism upon them [...] after they have given their health and strength to build up the wealth of the country for someone else to enjoy, the relatives of the royal family have been reared in luxury, pampered and kept without doing a single day's honest or useful work during the whole course of their wasted, useless, aimless existences. They have had paradise, and the aged poor have had hell.[105]

In similar vein, Glyde extended the debate about monarchy into the arena of imperialism, drawing on traditional criticism of royalty's links with the armed forces:

We use the revenue from the business to keep the descendants of the prostitutes of Charles II, to keep in luxurious idleness a horde of royal drones, and to make the army and navy bigger, so that the classes can use the children of the poor to exploit, plunder and murder the natives of so-called heathen countries.[106]

By the turn of the century, however, such assessments appeared dated. Divorced from a genuine programme of action, it was difficult to see where they could lead. George Sims noted in his autobiography the outlandish and outmoded language of elderly reformers attacking monarchy in the London clubland of the 1900s. He recalled in particular:

An aged and eccentric anarchist who used to wear a red tie and a slouch hat and sell regicidal pamphlets on Sunday afternoons in Trafalgar Square and shout 'Death to Kings!' at Sunday evening democratic debates [and the occasion when] he leapt on the platform at the close of a lecture and proceeded to demand the blood, not only of the entire royal family, but of all the members of the British aristocracy.[107]

At the dawn of a new century this appeared as little more than 'sound and fury, signifying nothing'. Gradually such rhetoric faded into simple acknowledgement of the broader inequalities of wealth and power that characterized British society. Cecil Chesterton wrote of the 'hopelessly obsolete' nature of republicanism in 1905, adding: 'People have begun to realize that it is a little ridiculous to get violently excited because the king is given a few thousand in return for certain services [...] while we allow landlords, capitalists and financiers to pocket many hundred times as much in return for no services at all.'[108]

In addition, under the tutelage of the Liberals, the Labour Party once in office or sharing power adopted the same strategies of fixing, manipulating, and working with the Lords and the monarchy that had characterized Liberal governments of the 1880s and 1890s. During the First World War the House of Lords was praised by Labour politicians as a bastion of the people's liberties for their actions in defence of the right of trial by jury under the 1914 Defence of the Realm Act. Sidney and Beatrice Webb conceded that the Upper Chamber had legitimated its role on these grounds.[109] In many ways this vision of a working partnership between Lords and Commons was Liberalism's strongest direct legacy for Labour in government.

By 1914 the oppositional nature of anti-monarchism had driven it outside a Labourism now poised to reap the benefits of power. Instead it migrated to groups like the Irish Nationalists and the suffragettes, who were locked out of the formal avenues of protest and sustained a fierce dislike of royal power and authority. In Ireland the framework of separatist politics galvanized the rhetoric of anti-monarchism that had characterized the period of Victoria's jubilees into a potent language of opposition to British rule. Traditionally, the tone of hostility to the throne was much the same in Ireland as in England. In James Joyce's *Ulysses*, the character of Leopold Bloom fulminates against the 'Prooshians and Hanoverians' and asserts that Ireland has had enough of 'those sausageeating bastards on the throne'.[110] Nevertheless, republicanism in Ireland was grounded in the blood sacrifice of Irish martyrdom in 1798, 1848 and 1916. These experiences provided a foundation myth and a history for the new Irish state after 1922.

In the years of turmoil before the outbreak of the Great War songs and ballads continued to articulate a fierce, visceral dislike of royalty rooted in these experiences of British rule. In 1911 this sentiment surfaced strongly during King George V and Queen Mary's coronation tour, prompting hostile demonstrations in some areas and mass abstentions from the festivities in others. The compendium of Irish Nationalist verse, *The Voice of Banba*, records the following ironic song sung during the coronation tour:

> Put on the glorious English crown!
>   It bears no smirch or stain,
> 'Twas never cursed by fevered lips,
>   'Mid gory heaps of slain;

> 'Twas never cursed where roofless homes
>   Stand bare beneath the sky,
> 'Twas never cursed in dungeons dark
>   Where strong men starve and die!
>
> Put on the precious English crown!
>   No stolen gem it holds.
> Put on the priceless royal robe!
>   No blood is in its folds.
> Though voices cry from Irish graves,
>   From India's plundered plains,
> The Empire's crown and robe are clean,
>   They bear no murder stains![111]

In the poems of the collection, Ireland emerges as a colony with grievances like any other. The front cover shows the contrasting image of a supplicant, subject Ireland, tied by bonds of commerce to the mainland and fulfilling the role of a subservient West Britain. As a free, erect nation in control of her own trade, however, she emerges as an independent country in her own right. Whereas seated, the folds of the Irish beggar's dress assume the form of the union flag, once erect, her clothes become those of a Celtic warrior goddess (the 'Banba' of the title). This transformation also expresses the transition from kneeling subject status to one of full citizenship (illus. 67).

The dominant preoccupation of the incoming regime was self-definition against Britain. Discarding the oath to the Crown and removing the symbols of royal authority from public buildings, post boxes and law courts gave the reality to Irish republican sentiment in the Free State between 1922 and 1936. Moreover, in such actions Ireland occupied a continuing role as an 'anti-Britain' and 'other', expressive of the notion that hostility to the throne came only from across the Irish Sea.

On the British mainland the suffragettes were isolated in the consistent hostility they displayed towards the throne in the years before World War One. Suffragette organizations frequently targeted royal ceremonial. During George V's tour of Lancashire in 1913 special security arrangements were made to prevent disruption of events by suffragette action groups. Even so, local suffragettes secured a number of publicity coups, including hurling a bundle of pamphlets advocating women's suffrage into the royal car at Southport.[112] The only other protests on the tour came from charities and clergymen who regretted the king's inability to appreciate the scale of poverty and deprivation in the Liverpool slums. At St George's Church in Liverpool the Rev. Henry Dunnico preached against the king's visit, asserting that 'spectacular

67 The spirit of Ireland as the warrior goddess Banba.

visits [...] could not possibly enable a king to appreciate and understand the sufferings of the poor'.[113]

Apart from the suffragettes, the only real fervent anti-monarchist hostility in Britain at the turn of the century came from the ranks of the small English Anarchist movement. Anti-monarchism's connection with marginal Anarchism confirmed the beginning of the movement of this body of ideas outside the mainstream of politics altogether. In 1893 a series of 'indignation meetings' orchestrated by Anarchists to express outrage at 'the waste of wealth on these thieving royal vermin' during preparations for the marriage of the Prince of Wales's youngest daughter, Princess Maud, to Prince Charles of Denmark provided the pretext for the arrest of the most outspoken amongst the Anarchist community in London.[114] Subsequently, the *Commonweal* attacked the 'servile conduct' of 'Social Democratic and trade union flunkeys' who refused to condemn royalty, and inveighed against the leaders of organized labour in London, 'whose pet aim seems to have been to get the patronage of all the royalty, bishops, sky-pilots and snobocracy they can possibly obtain'.[115]

The vision of a compliant and passive Labourism on royal issues was similarly evoked during King George V's visit to Rochdale in 1913. At the end of the royal tour John Bright's former residence at One Ash was marked with a conspicuous red flag to attract the king's attention as the royal motorcade passed.[116] This image promoted the notion of an acceptable Lib–Labbery fused around notions of consensus, the status quo and the national interest. This was a John Bright idealized both by Liberals and Labourites. Here was the acceptable face of a radical tradition characterized by the virtues of restraint, dedication to the cause of the people and opposition to Irish Home Rule and the peerage, but remaining, above all, fundamentally loyalist in nature

In 1911 Lords reform was long overdue. However, at the beginning of the twentieth century the House of Lords issue provided a more significant and contentious political moment than hitherto realized by historians. In simple constitutional terms, the 1911 Parliament Act merely turned the convention of Lords non-interference in money bills into enforceable statute. Much conventional historiography has therefore concentrated on the long-term constitutional implications of the 1911 Act for the balance of power between the Lords and the Commons. This is to miss the point. Above all Lords reform provided the opportunity for unity between the contending factions of radicalism, Labourism and the New Liberalism behind a common purpose. The project of modernizing the state was as much a concern of early Labourism and later radicalism as it was of Liberalism. Re-visiting their common Enlightenment legacy and drawing together themes of public service, civic reform and popular accountability, Lords reform propelled the divided forces of radicalism, Labourism and Liberalism into a communality of ideas. In so doing, it drew the sting of popular anti-monarchism from radicalism, and provided the framework for future Labourite co-operation with the establishment. Moreover, rather than weakening or challenging the throne, the Liberal House of Lords crisis confounded Gladstone's predictions of the 1880s, with the result that the monarchy emerged from the dispute with the Commons revived, and with its prestige enhanced in the years before the outbreak of the Great War.

7 The Labour Party and the Failure of English Republicanism 1919–99

'My objection to the royal symbol is that it is dead; it is a gold tooth in a mouth filled with decay.'

(JOHN OSBORNE, 1957)

Walking through the East End of London during the 1935 jubilee celebrations, George V's private secretary, Sir Clive Wigram, noted the words 'Lousy but Loyal' on a banner slung between two poor back-to-backs.[1] He recorded this message as a manifestation of the patriotism that infused even the disadvantaged and dispossessed in Britain. Twentieth-century British governments have come to accept without question that an unostentatious popular loyalism provides additional support for the political consensus. According to this reading, the British are, their current circumstances notwithstanding, a nation of enthusiastic monarchists. This view has been particularly prevalent on the Left. In marked contrast, those conservatives who see loyalty to throne and altar as brittle and easily undermined fear the potential for unrest amongst the mass of the population resulting from such examples as the Russian Revolution and the 'Hunger Marches' of the 1930s.

Labour in government, however, was keen to bind itself closely to the rituals, pageantry and display of the throne and the national memory of monarchy. During the first two Labour administrations of 1924 and 1929–31, the party adopted an obsequious attitude to the throne that made it risible both to its opponents and to many among its own supporters. For Labour politicians like Ramsay MacDonald or Philip Snowden, this attitude demonstrated the party's maturity and fitness for office under existing constitutional arrangements. In a climate of continuing electoral hostility to Labourism, its ability to project a loyalist image became a cherished ambition in a political environment in which the Tories effortlessly occupied the patriotic highground.

The early years of the twentieth century seemed propitious for radicals who hoped to see Britain shed her monarchy. The Great War heralded a purge of Europe's ruling houses, who were seen as embodying national failure, defeat and economic collapse. The Russian Revolution of 1917 showed the fragility of the foundations of monarchical autocracy once popular approval had been eroded and the support of the army, police and judiciary shattered. Woodrow Wilson injected a robust note of New World republicanism into this process by his insistence upon the removal of many of the minor German royal dynasties, complicit in Germany's pre-war rearmament, as a condition for peace. In 1918 Kaiser Wilhelm II led Emperor Charles of Austria, King Ludwig of Bavaria, King Ferdinand of Bulgaria and a host of minor royalty into exile (illus. 68). This effectively removed the names of Guelph, Wittelsbach and Coburg from the political map of Europe for the first time in many centuries. There were implications for the German aristocracy and the courtiers of the small German states in this process. British newspapers revelled in the creation of a new 'titleless' Germany, overcoming their fear of a Bolshevik revolution in Central Europe to express approval of the abolition of titles in the Socialist Republic of Bavaria in 1919. The *New Illustrated* magazine commented:

It will be a new Germany indeed where titles have been obliterated. Bavaria, the cradle of the Hun revolution, has taken the lead in a movement to abolish titles by passing a law which wipes out the Bavarian nobility at one fell swoop.

68 'Rulers of Kingdoms, Principalities and Powers: Driven into Exile by War of Their Own Making', including Emperor Charles of Austria, the Kaiser, King Ferdinand of Bulgaria and King William of Württemberg.

69 Labour crowd at the Woolwich by-election of 1903.

Democratic newspapers in other parts of Germany are advocating that Bavaria's example be generally followed [...] Germans dearly love titles. Everyone, high or low, has one and the result is often, unintentionally, a little comic.[2]

In the inter-war period thrones continued to fall. In Italy Umberto, the 'May King', was tarnished by his association with Fascism; King Constantine I of Greece was finally deposed and a Greek Republic declared in 1924. Commenting on this pan-European movement against monarchy, Alfonso XIII of Spain observed after his abdication in 1931: 'It seems we have gone out of fashion.' The abiding popular image of the early twentieth century was of thrones tumbling before the unstoppable 'forward march' of the masses (illus. 69).

Events on the Continent revived arguments about English 'exceptionalism'. At a time when the spectre of republicanism haunted Europe, the preservation of monarchy in Britain seemed the exception rather than the rule. Only the British royal family appeared impervious to the erosion of traditionalism and to the attacks on established political institutions now characteristic of a European political scene in a state of flux. Building upon its Victorian strengths, the royal house renewed its attempts to win the affections of its subjects. In some ways the throne benefited from a nostalgic sentimental pastoralism in poetry and literature, and the conscious rejection of modernism in all its forms that coloured popular responses to World War One.[3] A monarchy of carriages in the age of the automobile and of ceremonial dress in the age of the lounge suit appealed to a sense of stasis and continuity that bound the post-war world closer to the Edwardian era.

As Gerald J. DeGroot has pointed out, following victory in 1918 a profound cultural conservatism re-established itself in British society, fanned by a belligerent attitude to Germany, anti-Bolshevism and the continuation of war-time political leadership. The cult of royalty provided an important aspect of this cultural shift.[4] In the inter-war years the British monarchy set about reasserting its Britishness and consciously redesigning itself as a focus for national sentiment and patriotism. The royal revival after the Great War in Britain was built around a series of festivals and displays that brought the monarchy into close contact with the people. This was a monarchy that was, above all, highly visible.

After World War One George V came to symbolize all that was best about a 'people's monarchy', rooted in national tradition, charitable works and dedication and self-sacrifice on behalf of the nation (this despite the king's covert negotiations for the lifting of royal tax burdens in 1910 and 1913). In the United Kingdom, in contrast to Europe, monarchy came to symbolize unity and coherence, rather than divisiveness and disarray. As part of this process, George V's adviser, Lord Stamfordham, the real architect of the modern monarchy, attempted to distance the British royal family from their unpopular continental cousins, and urged the jettisoning of surviving German titles and honours. At his prompting, the House of Saxe-Coburg-Gotha became transformed into the House of Windsor. The name was chosen for its historic English undertones and connections with a noted national landmark, Windsor Castle, whose origins lay deep in the Anglo-Saxon past. As part of this process the royal house abjured its Prussian roots altogether and re-packaged its history in a conscious denial of much of the Hanoverian past. On Empire Day 1919, the centenary of Queen Victoria's birth, and at a highpoint of the negotiations surrounding a European peace settlement involving Germany, an editorial in the *New Illustrated* magazine highlighted the monarchy's imperial functions and commented of Victoria's notorious pro-Prussian sympathies:

Without reference to, and often without knowledge of the events which occasioned them, they have been used, with not very scrupulous honesty, to disseminate and foster an idea that the queen was more German than British at heart, and that her idolization of her husband betrayed her into becoming the tool of people whose ultimate objective was the annihilation of her own country as a great power [...] Justice requires the flat contradiction of the suggestion. Queen Victoria was fiercely jealous of Britain's prestige and where she perceived that to be involved was as fiercely uncompromising as that other great queen, Elizabeth.[5]

The monarchy of the post-1919 period was a sanitized institution. Now distanced from its continental cousins, transformed into a symbol of national unity in the glow of victory and incorporated into the diplomatic service as a representative embodiment of the nation state, it was commonly seen as being above politics. Following the expansion of democracy in the 1919 Representation of the People Act, power apparently bypassed the throne altogether, migrating into the hands of governments. As Frank Prochaska has pointed out, the main concern of radicals was no longer the mere existence of the royal prerogative as in the past, but how governments used it.[6] Much of the disdain and dislike of ruling institutions that had once adhered to monarchy could now safely be transferred to politicians.

Although no direct challenge to the monarchy emerged from the strains imposed by the Great War in Britain, some republican enthusiasms were rekindled by events in Russia. The downfall of Tsarism was widely celebrated by radicals. Sympathy for the Bolsheviks was occasionally translated into hostility to the existing order and opposition to pro-White Russian politicians and British government machinations for intervention in the Russian Civil War. In 1919 the socialist councils of action seemed to presage a general slide into revolt and disorder.[7] The English move against monarchy came, however, not through popular revolution, but rather in the columns of the *Times* newspaper. In 1917 in an open letter the author and Fabian socialist H. G. Wells revisited many of the traditional themes of the anti-monarchist rhetoric of the nineteenth century. The royal court, he commented, was 'alien and uninspiring'; monarchy lacked democratic sanction and failed to enthuse the population with the necessary patriotic zeal needed to defend the mother country in time of war. Wells concluded his letter by calling for an 'end to the ancient trappings of throne and sceptre' and proposing a republican alternative to the royal state.[8]

The only vehicle capable of articulating and channelling such republican sentiments remained the Labour Party. The roots of the political wing of the party were intertwined with the anti-monarchist impulses of the nineteenth century. Keir Hardie was a strong republican throughout his life, occasionally embarrassing the party by the vehemence of his outbursts against the throne. In 1908 he was temporarily barred from the Commons for his role in orchestrating Labour attacks against Edward VII's state visit to Russia to consolidate friendly relations with the Tsar. As a result, Hardie's name was struck off the guest list for Windsor Castle garden parties open to all MPs, an action he challenged with the backing of the Parliamentary Labour Party in order to ostentatiously snub future invitations to palace functions.[9]

A. J. P. Taylor sees the eager support Hardie secured in later years from Labour front-benchers for a place at the royal table over the garden party issue as indicative of the party's early absorption into the establishment.[10] Nevertheless, an irreverent dislike of monarchy was instinctive among many Labour supporters. In 1910 there was opposition from trade unionists to mourning rituals for the deceased Edward VII. The *Labour Leader* contrasted the extravagant public homilies to the king with the lack of press interest in the 136 victims of the Whitehaven Colliery disaster that overshadowed the king's death in the north of England.[11] In 1917 several Labour orators were moved to hope for a red flag flying over Buckingham Palace during the political euphoria greeting the outbreak of the Russian Revolution. In an inflammatory outburst, the trade unionist Robert Williams revived memories of the 1870s, declaring: 'Praise God when there will be a notice "To Let" outside Buckingham Palace.'[12] Hostility to the throne, however, was strongest at the peripheries, rather than at the core of the party. As K. O. Morgan has pointed out, the experience of the First World War polarized, rather than integrated, attitudes and identities in the United Kingdom.[13]

In Scotland the same seventeenth-century Covenanting tradition that inspired Keir Hardie and Ramsay MacDonald preserved an essence of nationalist and anti-royal feeling that surfaced amongst the Red Clydesiders during the rent-strikes and campaign for shorter working hours of 1919–20. After the formation of the Scottish National Party in 1934 the traditions of a non-monarchical, even republican, Scotland were open to re-examination by both the Labourite and Nationalist alliances in Scottish politics. During these years some Nationalists sought to reclaim Keir Hardie for the Home Rule cause.[14] In a similar fusion of historical and nationalist enmity, unemployed miners in the South Wales valleys in the 1930s chanted, 'We'll make Queen Mary do the washing for the boys/ When the red revolution comes/ We'll put the King on the means test.'

By the 1920s, however, opposition to the throne, if it featured at all in Labourism, occurred as a partisan sentiment rather than doctrine. Most often it emerged during periods in which the throne was in a position to adjudicate between the parties in close-fought general elections. This frequently led to accusations of partiality by the reigning monarch towards Conservatism or some other anti-Labour alliance of

Toryism and Liberalism. Herbert Morrison was quite categorical that George V's outlook 'could best be summed up as that of a Tory of the *Daily Mail* school during the Northcliffe regime'.[15]

The elections that first brought Labour to power were close-fought affairs that resulted in acrimonious horse-trading, in the face of fierce opposition, before the party could take up the reins of government. The formation of the 1924 government generated particular antagonism amid accusations of media and establishment hostility to an incoming Labour administration.[16] During this election Cromwell made his last public appearance in his traditional incarnation as an anti-royalist radical. In the interim period between the collapse of the preceding coalition government and the formation of the 1924 Labour administration, Britain was briefly without a government at all. The press speculated about a constitutional crisis, and George Lansbury invoked the execution of Charles I to force the king's hand on a choice of party leader. At a meeting in Shoreditch Town Hall, which coincided with the huge popular success of John Drinkwater's play about Cromwell's life in the West End, he commented:

A king of England had once stood out against the will of the common people and he had lost his head. A discordant king [James II] had acted in a similar manner and he had been turned out. King George V would be well advised not to interfere [...] Such 'jiggery pokery' was to be resisted.[17]

These outbursts were counter-productive, giving ready ammunition to the Tories. Following the formation of the first Labour Government several local Conservative associations suggested that Lansbury had opened the door to a new civil war between royalists and anti-royalists.[18] At one meeting threats were made to shoot him. Such responses led the Labour Party to reconsider the advisability of anti-monarchist outbursts at election time. In the late 1920s the party leadership also speculated about partisan royal attitudes towards the Labour Party, but refrained from criticizing the throne openly.[19] In 1934 Stafford Cripps was the last Labour figure of note to wonder aloud if the monarchy had had its day in a speech highlighting potential barriers to Labour in office.[20]

As the Labour Party circled the centres of power from the 1920s onwards, it steadily shed its hostility to the throne. In both 1924 and 1929–31 the realities of Labour victory, and the necessity to form viable governments that fulfilled its pledges to supporters and voters, forced the party into closer proximity with the sources of stability within the executive. Labour leaders, who had previously attacked the royal state when outsiders in a rhetoric that sought primarily to mobilize the dispossessed, were now forced into uneasy co-operation with elements essential to the smooth running of government, notably the civil service, the court and the monarchy. Under these circumstances the myth of an impartial and non-political royal family vital to the political health of the country gained ground within Labour's governing circles.

Herbert Morrison's comment at the time of Elizabeth II's coronation that 'when the people cheer the Queen and sing her praises, they are also cheering our free democracy' was far more typical of the Labour outlook than Sir Stafford Cripps's outburst of 1934.[21] For socialists within the party this posed clear problems of conscience and direction.[22] Labour in power sought to moderate utterances against the throne that would previously have formed a major ingredient in its platform rhetoric. Moreover, the 'Moscow Gold' scare stories and the Zinoviev Letter of the 1920s forced Labour into ever more extravagant and excessive declarations of loyalty. The flamboyant Conservative MP Chips Channon detected not just docility among Labour MPs during debates on the Civil List, but sometimes a positive enthusiasm for all things royal. Noting Labour's 'extreme royalism' in 1936 during debates on the Civil List, he wrote in his diary: 'The Civil List was really passed with amazing smoothness, the majority of socialists tumbling over themselves in order to laud the royal family: one might think that they had invented them themselves.'[23]

Several Labour leaders attempted to push this process still further. Ramsay MacDonald's later career as leader of the National Government between 1931 and 1935 is perhaps best understood as a centrist strategy designed, in co-operation with other political parties, to moderate Labourism in office and to reject political polarities and extremes.[24] As a reflection of this project, the National Government adopted patriotic symbols like the Union Jack and was always closely associated with George V, who was instrumental in bringing the coalition into being. The position of five leading aristocratic politicians in the National Government's cabinet ensured a link through into the certainties and protocol of pre-war governments. New codes of conduct were required of those unused to wielding power. This tension within Labourism was a long-established feature of the Lib-Lab experience. Overwhelmed by his rapid elevation to the position of MP, the trade unionist John Hodge called his autobiography *Workman's Cottage to Windsor Castle*. The moral he drew from his own experience was that 'like every French *poilu* carrying a French Marshal's baton in his knapsack, the ordinary British boy can, by his own native gifts, be assured of rising to positions of eminence, birth being no barrier'.[25]

In both 1924 and 1929 Labour leaders were forced to temper former anti-monarchist sentiments and to reconcile themselves to court protocol. Some achieved this transformation to better effect and with a greater degree of success than others. Beatrice Webb recalled in her diaries the comic effect of the first Labour prime minister, Ramsay MacDonald, appearing in a frock coat to greet the king, and of the erstwhile Scottish revolutionary James Wheatley 'going down on both knees and actually kissing the king's hand'.[26] With the correct social codes and forms of address largely unknown to former miners and cotton spinners, Webb found herself running impromptu classes in etiquette for the wives of Labour MPs.[27] The pretensions of new Labour ministers and their unease in court dress were widely ridiculed. When Sidney Webb was nominated Rector of Glasgow University 'the Conservative students gleefully reproduced his photo in tall hat and knee breeches as one of their trump cards'.[28] *Punch* played with these topsy-turvy images of working-men in ermine, representing the former Liberal Party switcher Sir Stafford Cripps as a peer above and working-man below (illus. 70). This picture represented many of the confusions the rank and file felt about a party simultaneously outside and inside established structures of power.

Such embarrassments diminished the stature of the first Labour governments in the eyes of both supporters and opponents of the Labour Party. In the 1930s there was a widely held impression that Ramsay MacDonald and Philip Snowden, far from embracing the course of collaboration with the establishment as a necessary evil, actually relished their connections with the rich and powerful.[29] After 1931 there seemed more than a mere flirtation with celebrity culture at work here; MacDonald had apparently succumbed to the lure of London society. Well-connected aristocratic hostesses were his constant companions on the social circuit, and he was to be seen at all the best society functions.[30] Chips Channon wrote of MacDonald at the time of his death: 'I saw him sometimes in those early months of the first Labour Government when London society very wisely decided to take him up rather than to ignore him. Defiant at first he soon took to grandeur and high life and wallowed in it like a man who had been starving all his life.'[31]

The theme of 'betrayal' by working-class leaders became part of the mythology surrounding this period of 'fusion' with sympathetic figures from other political parties.[32] MacDonald's poor public reputation set the tone for later obsequious Labour leaders such as Clement Attlee or Harold Wilson. Some Labour ministers, such as the leader of the railway unions, J. H. Thomas, bragged of their intimacy with members of the court and ready access to George V. On one occasion

70 'Comrade Cripps ... "Nobody guessed when I began / That I should end as a Labour man"': the aristocratic former Tory Sir Stafford Cripps seen as a hybrid of working-man and aristocrat.

Thomas made him laugh so heartily after an operation that he burst his stitches.[33] Labour's intellectuals, such as Richard Crossman, despaired at what they saw as a fatal working-class susceptibility to the lure of royalty among those working-men who had progressed through the party hierarchy. He wrote in his diaries that too many Labour Privy Councillors enjoyed their meetings with the Queen and sought to extend them: 'It is the working-class socialists who are by and large staunchly monarchist. The nearer the Queen they get, the more working-class members of the cabinet love her, and she loves them.' Ultimately he was inclined to ascribe such remaining republican sentiment as existed within the party to the professional classes, who he believed were less deferential to the 'aristocratic embrace'.

A by-product of the Labour leadership's close bonds with monarchy was the increasing tendency to radicalize the heir to the throne. During periods in which Labourism was weak or excluded from power Labour leaders looked instead to a sympathetic Prince of Wales to redress imbalances within society or to fulfil notions of social justice. Medieval conceptions of an alternative court seemed to linger in such actions. In the middle 1930s a fragmented Labour Party exiled from power by the formation of the National Government put its faith in Edward, Prince of Wales, as a far-seeing monarch who would refuse to countenance the sufferings inflicted on his subjects by the depression. For the Labour Party his comment 'something must be done' on a tour of Dowlais, South Wales, in 1936 marked a sharp break with the culture of inaction that had characterized governmental responses to the slump.[34] In the 1980s and early 1990s Prince Charles seemed to occupy a similar position for a Labour Party marginalized by Thatcherite Conservatism.

Labour Party conferences sometimes reflected grassroots disaffection with an excessively royalist party hierarchy. It seemed to some party activists that former critics of royal grants and dowries now sought special dispensation for Civil List payments for members of the royal family. In 1936 the Labour Parliamentary Party fully supported the move of formalizing state support for royalty by bringing the revenues of the Duchy of Lancaster under the control of the Treasury, so making the heir to the throne directly payable by the state. Clement Attlee took this opportunity to reiterate Labour support for the monarchy and to distance the party from previous republican agitation, which he dismissed as the work of 'bourgeois radicals'.[35] Such measures were sometimes challenged at the party conference. In 1923 local branches of the party forced a debate on the issue of republicanism at the national conference in which criticism of the leadership's monarchist tendencies was articulated by Ernest Thurtle of Shoreditch:

The leaders of the party appeared to have what might be called 'a fear complex'. They feared that the great bulk of the people would not support them if they came out as true democrats and stood up for government of the people, by the people. He invited them to shake off their fear and could tell them that if they faced up to the question boldly and stated that in the twentieth century the monarchy was an anachronism and should be swept away, they would get the support of the people.[36]

In support of Thurtle, a motion to abolish the royal family was proposed by the Stockton and Thornaby MP, Mr J. Vipond (indicating the survival of Cowenite-style republicanism in the North-East into the 1920s). With insufficient support from delegates, the motion was subsequently dropped after a personal intervention by George Lansbury. Elsewhere anti-monarchism lingered inside the party as a politics that dare not speak its name. It sometimes surfaced in internal policy minutes and discussion documents which were still peppered with references to 'lickspittles' and the 'emptiness' of continual royal adulation.[37] Many ordinary members agreed with Frances Brooke, Countess of Warwick, that royal influence had led MacDonald and other senior members of the party to abandon their commitment to the rank and file Labour tradition in 1931. She wrote: 'Not unnaturally royalty brings one very close to forms and ceremonies which are a bulwark against democratic encroachment.'[38] Letters in Labour Party newspapers frequently expressed the disgruntlement of activists on royal issues. Recalling the fiery socialist demagogue J. Bruce Glasier, one correspondent to the Scottish Labour paper *Forward* wrote during Elizabeth's coronation in 1953 'I have always believed that the monarchy was one of the main pillars of the capitalist system. If so, why is the Labour Party prostrating itself before the royal family?'[39]

The absence of any real impetus to reform of the monarchy within the Labour Party is made apparent by the lack of inclination within Labour ranks to exploit the fracture in the royal superstructure resulting from the Abdication Crisis of 1936. Genuine criticism of monarchy was conspicuous by its absence from discussions about this issue, and there were no sustained attempts to precipitate a debate on the future of the royal house. While several Labour newspapers declared that they would like to see a commoner like Mrs Simpson as queen, there was never any suggestion that the institution of monarchy itself might be abolished.[40] The 'Red Clydesider' Jimmy Maxton, who did try to provoke a debate on royal reform, remained isolated in his calls for a republic. At the height of the crisis Conservative newspapers like the *Times* praised the Labour Party for its responsible attitude.[41] Generally, Labourites showed a tendency to support Edward VIII.

When political divisions for and against the king crystallized at the end of 1936, most Labour leaders of note took the king's side. They criticized as excessively backward-looking and traditionalist the church's view that Edward's marriage to a divorcée would entail the breaking of his coronation oath to defend the faith. Anti-clericalism thus drew the likes of Sir Stafford Cripps and Harry Pollitt, leader of the Communist Party, into the ranks of the 'king's party', as supporters of a 'freedom versus puritanism' agenda. During the crisis a primitive monarchism re-established itself among the most left-wing groups.

The populist Social Credit Unions, which argued for the global curtailment of international finance, urged the king to take up his traditional monarchical role to rebuff Europe's financial institutions and Britain's foreign creditors.[42] Far from being impaired, royal fortunes actually improved over the issue of the abdication, and after his accession the chronically shy and unprepared George VI benefited greatly from public sympathy.

Having accepted the myth of an impartial and disinterested monarch, the House of Lords and the royal household remained the sole bastions of unchallenged hereditary privilege for Labour politicians. The anomaly represented by this system was freely acknowledged by the Labour Party. Despite the elevation of some Labour politicians to high office within the royal household, their presence scarcely affected the balance of forces inside the centres of royal power. Edward Short, Chief Whip in Harold Wilson's governments of the 1960s, wrote of the appointment of Charles Gray, a former Durham coal miner, to the position of Comptroller of the Royal Household in 1964:

His presence in all this was a tiny sign that we now had a Labour government committed to radical change – but in all the glorious flummery it was scarcely discernible. We had won the election; we were now 'in power', as we put it. But here, in the vast British establishment, was another centre of power which rolled on inexorably like [a] procession. What happened in elections did not affect it. It was self-perpetuating and supremely self-assured.[43]

In line with their Liberal predecessors, Labour adopted the reflexes towards the Lords that had characterized them in office. A traditional rhetoric of hostility to landed wealth, titles and privilege continued to be very marked within Labourism. Jack Jones told the Labour Party conference in the 1970s that: 'Three quarters of the members of the House of Lords inherited their position by birth; their ancestors were, by and large, cattle robbers, land thieves, and a few were court prostitutes.'[44] In 1988 Labour calls for outright abolition of the Lords were renewed when the Conservative government packed the Upper House with non-active 'backwoodsmen', to ensure an unamended passage of the Poll Tax Bill.[45]

Aside from such periodic criticism, in the case of Labourism even more so than Liberalism, there was ambivalence about the way in which the hereditary centre of gravity within the establishment was to be treated. Peerages and honours were in the party's gift as they had been of previous Liberal and Conservative administrations. Like their Tory counterparts, many Labour politicians came to see a seat in the Lords as a deserved recompense for many years' service to the party.

Moreover, during the Labour governments of 1945–51 the House of Lords modified its traditional obstructionism, functioning as a complementary, rather than as a rival, body to the elected chamber.

The first Labour group was formed in the Lords in the 1930s, and during the Labour governments of the 1960s and 1970s friends and allies were rewarded with titles and influence. Harold Wilson's infamous 'Lavender List', following his retirement in 1976, became a benchmark of impropriety in such matters of honours manipulation. The episode considerably tarnished Labour's reputation for impartial administration of the honours system and devalued the political currency of honours themselves.[46]

As with earlier Liberal governments, the Lords issue provided a mask and an obstruction that gave the party the perfect target in its war against privilege, while ignoring the realities of the new accord between the two houses, and leaving the incumbent of the throne untouched. From 1964 onwards Labour routinely spoke out against the second chamber, despite the fact that Harold Macmillan's creation of Life Peerages in 1958 had diluted the hereditary dimension to the Lords and provided further avenues of patronage for non-Tory governments. At the same time the Labour Party in the 1960s only ever tinkered with the outward details of royal power and authority. Despite a manifesto pledge to nationalize the Palace of Westminster in 1964 and to remove it from royal control altogether, Labour in fact agreed to a joint parliamentary committee that administered the Houses of Parliament in conjunction with representatives of the royal household.[47]

With the Labour Party now installed as an integral element of the two-party system, the rhetoric of hostility to the throne disappeared from the lexicon of Labourism. For a Labour Party intent upon building up a state welfare system in the post-war period, a cohesive executive structure built around a head of state with an acknowledged historical pedigree in the British past provided a strong foundation. Moreover, some socialists could reconcile their support for the Crown by promoting the notion of a 'socialist monarchy', in which the royal family were prepared to share the privations of the people, both in wartime and during the period of shortages after the war. Anthony Barnett writes of the Left's acceptance of this myth: 'A centrally-organized, conscript-based victory, in which every family knew the feel of His Majesty's uniform meant that loyalty to the Crown was a logical extension of the war against Fascism.'[48] For men such as James Callaghan who served in the navy, and Denis Healey, who was a beachmaster at the Anzio landings, the Crown had an overwhelming moral legitimacy.[49] This made reform or abolition of the monarchy, in Paul

Richards's words, 'Labour's last taboo'.[50] Even suspicions that the royal family evaded rationing during and after the war, and public disquiet at the expense of Princess Elizabeth's marriage to Prince Philip in 1947 at the highpoint of post-war food shortages, failed to shake Labour's confidence in the institution.[51] Only marginal figures on the left of the party, notably Willie Hamilton and Tony Benn, have continued to extemporize about the inequities of monarchy and the role of the inner circle of the court. Under these circumstances opposition to the throne survived largely among fringe groups who regarded themselves as entirely outside the political system or who were dedicated to a complete transformation of society.

From the 1930s the majority of anti-monarchist utterances came from the British Communist Party. At the time of royal births, deaths and marriages the Communist Party issued swingeing denunciations of the monarchy, portraying it as an extravagant distraction from a collapsing social structure. In a 1935 attack on George V's royal jubilee, 'The Jubilee – and How', the royal family was portrayed as a malign Punch and Judy manipulated by the forces of monopoly capitalism, whose image was constantly massaged and reinvented by the media for public consumption (illus. 71). In their pamphlets Communists castigated the expense of public ceremony and reworked the traditional vocabulary of anti-monarchism. During the coronation of 1953, in a reference back to the 'What Does She Do With It?' campaign of the 1870s, the pamphlet 'One Happy Family' proposed other uses for the £20 million spent on the coronation under the title 'What We Could Do With It'. They included investment in new homes, nursery provision, hospital beds and increased unemployment benefits. However, the most vocal criticism of the throne in the years after 1945 came not from the Left, but from the Liberal aristocrat, John Grigg (Lord Altrincham). His 1957 article in the *English and National Review*, while stopping short of open republicanism, nevertheless criticized the 'grotesque' presentation parties at which debutantes were introduced into aristocratic society, the Queen's 'priggish schoolgirl' accent, and the 'social lopsidedness' of the court and the royal household. He proposed a complete royal overhaul and predicted:

The coronation induced a mood compounded of religiosity, vaingloriousness, and bobby-soxing, which of its very nature was vainglorious and impermanent. Those who care for the monarchy as an institution should look beyond the hideous coloured photographs of a glamorous young woman in sparkling attire to the more testing realities of twenty years hence. The monarchy will not survive, let alone thrive, unless its leading figures exert themselves to the full and with all the imagination they and their advisers can command.[52]

71 Communist Party propaganda of 1935 shows the royal family as the puppets of international capitalism.

In post-war Britain everything changed except the monarchy. In the 1960s an accelerated process of social transformation erased many of the class divisions that had allowed monarchy to flourish at the apex of an aristocratic and plutocratic pyramid. Aristocrats such as Lord

Snowden abandoned traditional values and embraced the *déclassé* lifestyle of 'Swinging London', alongside a new aristocracy of rock stars, fashion designers and cultural commentators. In the absence of any real current of criticism, only the monarchy remained immune from these profound changes in the social landscape of Britain. John Grigg was criticized and physically attacked in public by a member of the League of Empire Loyalists for his calls for reform. Indeed the monarchy became ossified, resisting the seismic changes taking place within British society.

After 1945 the monarchy reverted almost exclusively to its ceremonial and mystical functions. In a period of stable majority governments, and with the Crown's imperial and military aspects in abeyance, monarchy returned to the role of figurehead and constitutional totem.

A family-oriented royal household was central to the appeal of post-war royalty. During these years the Crown's ceremonial function was consolidated by a new familial outlook and feel in a regal household whose future hopes resided in the youthful Princess Elizabeth. The emphasis on family-values in turn grew out of the apparent disregard for the succession that had characterized the actions of Edward VIII and Wallace Simpson during the Abdication Crisis of 1936. There was a marked anachronism in the way in which previous royal history was reinvented to promote the notion of a seamless continuity in Windsor marital stability. Steadfastness, loyal family relations and a loving and self-contained family unit were projected as the keys to the success of the British monarchy. This process began in the 1930s after Edward VIII's abdication. It was considerably aided by the British film industry, which loyally sought to heal the wounds caused by the rift in the royal family by revisiting the apparently more balanced and stable period of the Victorian monarchy. In two successful British films, *Victoria the Great*, released in 1937 the year after the Abdication Crisis, and *Sixty Glorious Years*, Dame Anna Neagle, the foremost character actress of the day, portrayed a stoical 'Widow of Windsor' devoted to the memory of Prince Albert. This depiction, familiar from accounts of the Victorian era in the 1940s, scrupulously avoided any hint of impropriety in her relationship with John Brown.[53] The correct standards of morality were revived, and the monarchy distanced from morally suspect relatives. This re-writing of royal history coincided with a marked restoration of traditional values in the post-war years in all areas of public life.

Tom Paine's criticism of monarchy as a 'peepshow' seemed even more relevant in the post-war years. As he correctly pointed out, this element of royal show was at the core of the British monarchy's appeal. Increasingly, such royal ceremonial was conducted under an intensified public gaze. After 1953, when the coronation ceremony reached into people's homes as the first televised national event, the new technological medium of television became an important pillar of the monarchy, with the BBC acting as custodian and deferential commentator on royal affairs. Under Lord Reith BBC radio and television sought to create a national constituency of listeners and viewers who used the new medium of the electronic age to experience public rejoicing at second hand.[54] Through its involvement in state occasions, the institutional history of the BBC became intertwined with that of other national institutions like the monarchy.[55] From the war years onwards media coverage of royal attendance at public functions remained central to definitions of whether or not the royal family was perceived to be doing its job and fulfilling its contract with its subjects. Nevertheless, the balance of public duty and secluded private life was a difficult one to maintain. On occasion the enhanced media interest and coverage of monarchy helped undermine the dignity of the royal office. The coronation of Queen Elizabeth II teetered perilously on the borders of kitsch and mistakes in the crowning ceremony were exposed by the camera. Where the media intruded, tensions were also sometimes set up with the 'sacred' function of monarchy and its role as the remote and dignified part of the constitution. Royalty was compromised, rather than aided, by public scrutiny and popular interest in royal private lives.

This new monarchical consensus was typified by the coronation ritual of 1953, which enlivened the grey post-war world. It was portrayed by the national press as a royal fable inclusive of all sections of the population. While contemporary photographs captured expressions of loyalism from all sections of society, they concentrated especially on slum dwellers and residents of post-war prefabricated housing (illus. 72). In editorials and letters the poor were congratulated for their patriotism and thrift in saving up money for bunting and Union Jacks.[56] Contemporary coronation images reinforced this message of the universality of national rejoicing, showing pictures of Elizabeth in schoolrooms and department stores and numerous representations of her on civic monuments. In most descriptions the coronation procession was viewed as a culmination of centuries of royal history. Despite its apparently inappropriate positioning, the image of Queen Elizabeth's picture in a butcher's shop window from Izis Bidermanas's coronation photographs reiterated in updated form the traditional connotations of the roast beef of 'Old England', the roasted ox of the coronation festival, and the crowning of a new ruler (illus. 73). Central to such display was a celebration of decades of British national greatness that sought to restore something of Britain's

72 Even the poor, in this case living in a post-war prefabricated home, were included in popular representations of the coronation.

importance in world affairs and the broader links with the former empire and Commonwealth. Sir Edmund Hillary's successful ascent of Mount Everest made the event a moment of international achievement and strongly associated Coronation Day in the popular mind with a reassertion of the country's status as a great power.[57]

Subsequently, the coronation had strong ramifications for sociological and ethnographic views of kingship. It promoted an official

73 Poster of Princess Elizabeth on display in a butcher's shop during the coronation.

discourse of Britain as a unified nation of patriotic citizens, whose success as exporter or world policeman was bound up with continuing royal rule. In an influential article written during the coronation year by the sociologists Edward Shils and Michael Young, the Crown was described as integral to a distinctive British 'moral unity' that set the country apart from the continent.[58] Queen Elizabeth was seen as the embodiment of a British civic religion cemented by a 'democratic coronation' that united a diverse but patriotic populace.[59]

Nevertheless, the rhetoric of the 'New Elizabethan' age that surrounded Princess Elizabeth's coronation masked continuing discontent with the role and position of the British monarchy. On occasion, the 'other Britain' that remained excluded from the script of ceremonial occasions came to the fore. The Shils and Young vision of the function of the British monarchy was contested in a less well publicized article by N. Birnbaum in 1955. This highlighted the reluctance of some sections of the population to celebrate the coronation, and questioned the motives of those who did turn out to view the Queen.[60] In the text to Izis Bidermanas's coronation photographs, John Pudney emphasized the mixed feelings towards royalty traditionally expressed by London crowds, and their volatility during royal ceremonial:

Do not suppose, however, that the Cockney is a fulsome devotee of royalty or of those who move in high places. Some of the ancestors of those whose portraits you see in these pages no doubt lined the route when Charles I marched to his execution [...] These are people who expressed pity rather than reverence for the young Queen Victoria at her crowning. There were sly jokes about the worldly life of her son King Edward VII. These are people who listened with mixed feelings to the radio farewell of an abdicating king only a decade and a half ago. These are citizens, in fact, who like to judge on results, whose urban sophistication is so little swayed by glamour that they can ever so politely roar with laughter – as I remember – at the spectacle of the late King Carol of Rumania driving in state to be honoured by their own City Fathers.[61]

Traditional anti-monarchist criticism of the expense of the coronation ceremony and of the loss of productivity to manufacturing industry it entailed also featured in the mainstream press. David Low's cartoon 'The Morning After' in the *Manchester Guardian* (illus. 74) was condemned by some readers for its sceptical and sardonic tone on Coronation Day, but as Birbaum pointed out, it is impossible to estimate how typical such attacks were of public opinion more generally.[62] The Mass Observation archive at Sussex University contains letters from those who reiterated their belief that the coronation frenzy was designed to help the fortunes of the Conservative Party,

74 Low's 'Morning After' cartoon caused a storm of controversy for its criticism of the expense surrounding Elizabeth's accession to the throne.

but were sucked in despite themselves. Other comments reflected the stay-at-home mentality of those who opposed Queen Victoria's jubilees. More specifically animal welfare groups like the Kinship Humanitarian Circle were critical of the inept slaughtering and public consumption of oxen by coronation revellers.[63] For Birnbaum, the holiday atmosphere of the coronation pointed up the 'very absence of shared values' and provided 'some measure of surcease from that condition of conflict which is more or less permanent for complex societies'.[64]

The impact of the coronation and the vision of monarchy it portrayed have been felt throughout the subsequent history of the House of Windsor. In the official version, the 'coronation spirit' was evidence of a nation united behind throne and altar. Attempts were made to rekindle this spirit of national celebration on several occasions: in 1969 with the Investiture of the Prince of Wales at Caernarfon, in 1977 with the Queen's Silver Jubilee, and with two royal weddings during the 1980s.

Nevertheless, the coronation can be said to mark the post-war meridian of monarchy. Contrary to received wisdom on the recent royal crises, criticism of monarchy has seldom been a taboo subject. Discussing opinion poll evidence from the 1960s onwards, Edgar Wilson has discerned a small, but steady, slide in the royal family's popularity. Gradually the numbers who would like to see the royal family reformed or abolished outright have crept upwards, with a slight bias towards anti-royal feeling in areas of social deprivation.[65] This has had profound cultural resonances in areas of British civic life. The practice of standing during the national anthem in cinemas at the end of the feature, for example, was abandoned in the early 1960s; cinema managers were embarrassed by audiences making their way to the exits as the anthem played.[66]

The emergence of a new culture of indifference or downright disrespect for monarchy has proved most marked among the young. The contrasts with 1953 are very apparent. In the coronation year a uniform attitude of abasement to the throne was adopted in children's literature and comics. The *Eagle* comic founded in 1950 typified this response. Established by the evangelical Christian the Rev. Marcus Morris, it combined a proselytizing message with nostalgia for an imagined imperial past. Dan Dare, its most famous character, was an English Protestant crusader, whose exploits against a cold alien rationalism were steeped in memories of the British resistance to Hitler.[67] Moreover, the *Eagle* provided a total 'lived' experience for its readers in which imperial and monarchical messages were tied to merchandising opportunities and strategies. Boys fired by coronation frenzy could watch the coronation procession in a Dan Dare 'Coronation jacket' or follow the coach on a 'Coronation cycle' (illus. 75).[68]

By the 1970s this compliant attitude towards the Queen had collapsed amongst teenagers. During the 1977 silver jubilee the young no longer observed the traditional respect for the royal house that had characterized the 1950s generation. Such sentiments were most strongly expressed by the punk rock band the Sex Pistols in their 'Anarchy in the UK' single, which shot to number two in the charts and included the lyrics 'God save the Queen/A fascist regime/Made you a moron/A potential H bomb'. Derek Jarman's film *Jubilee*, released at the beginning of the festivities, envisaged an anarchic punk future, including the shocking image of Queen Elizabeth's corpse robbed of its crown by a marauding punkette. Punk culture revelled in its disdain for conventional patriotism and deference. Jarman's bleak vision was steeped in images of decay and national collapse. Two days before the Queen's crypto-Elizabethan royal progress by barge down the Thames on Jubilee Day, the Sex Pistols played 'Anarchy in the UK' on their own sardonic boat trip past the Houses of Parliament.[69] The 1977 jubilee itself is best remembered for punk designer Jamie Reid's enduring image of Queen Elizabeth with a safety pin through her nose.[70] Such 'subvertisements' undermined the gravitas of the occasion and provided the inspiration for anti-monarchist badges, which

75 Advertisements and features in children's comics from the coronation year reflect the 'empire and monarchy' theme that characterized the celebrations.

were much in evidence amongst the student population in colleges and universities (illus. 76).

Like many youth movements, punk exuded negativity. It was, above all, an anti-system rooted in fear of unemployment and a rejection of consumerism. Nevertheless, the 1970s showed that the monarchy was no longer above criticism, especially by the young. A trickle of royal stories, initially including less popular members of the royal family like the Duke of Edinburgh, reflected an increasing attitude of disdain by the public at large.

From the late 1980s the media has gradually broken down the taboo on reporting royal misdeeds. In part, the monarchy has been damaged by the very medium that it hoped would cement the Crown's position. Indeed, the press has become the main critic of monarchy at the end of the twentieth century. Whereas in 1953 Princess Margaret could be a revered 'TV Princess', now the royal family is fair game for lurid tabloid sensationalism, much of it centred around the unsuccessful marriages of Charles and Diana and of Andrew and Sarah Ferguson. Kitty Kelley's recent biography, *The Royals*, has, among other unsubstantiated claims, alleged adultery, illegitimacy and drug dependency amongst senior members of the royal family.[71]

In recent years the opinion-poll ratings of the royals have oscillated wildly. Yet the polling organization MORI claims to detect no more than a consistent 20 per cent who favour a republic; of these, it suggests that barely eight per cent could be described as committed republicans.[72] Most often, public discussion of royalty centres around the modernization, rather than the complete abolition, of the monarchy, with royal figures like Princess Anne frequently appearing as favoured candidates for the presidency of the first British republic.

Cultural commentators have seen the debates surrounding the royal family as profoundly symbolic. For Stephen Haseler or Tom Nairn,

76 An underground culture of hostility to the throne with a strong punk flavour flourished even during the height of royal ceremonial at the time of the queen's silver jubilee in 1977.

233

they are symptomatic of a wider malaise in British society, connected to loss of empire, insecurity about a future British role in Europe and the break-up of the United Kingdom. Here the main issue is one of British identity at the end of the twentieth century. Haseler quotes the famous maxim of Dean Acheson, President Truman's Secretary of State, 'Britain has lost an empire, but hasn't found a role.' Tom Nairn has christened the same phenomenon the 'glamour of backwardness' and suggests that monarchy stifles the spiritual and cultural progress of nations.[73] Such constructions enable the issue of monarchy to be linked to broader agendas of national decline, faltering competitiveness and diplomatic and military subordination to the United States – discussions that are hardly new or specific to the 1990s. Nor is there any real assessment of why the debate should take exactly this form, at precisely this point in time. Stephen Haseler has suggested that European integration has made the throne increasingly redundant and irrelevant. In reality, rather than weakening the throne, European issues, such as omitting the Queen's head from the British version of the Euro, show a tendency to rebound and restore the position of royalty as a symbol of embattled sovereignty.[74]

A long-term historical view suggests a familiarity about the issues that preoccupy the public when the monarchy is debated in the 1990s. They constitute a revival of the traditional anti-monarchist rhetoric of the nineteenth century, and perhaps have rather less to do with contemporary debates about identity. Three main areas of anxiety recur: morality, the expense of the throne and concern about whether or not the royals are fulfilling their public duties. These themes constitute the classic anti-monarchist critique of the Crown as articulated at the height of British power in the 1870s. In the 1990s such ideas have found a new resonance, emerging from the criticism of established British institutions that characterized Thatcherism in the 1980s.

Much of this can be laid at the door of the obsessive costing of British institutions that characterized the Thatcherite approach to big government. Thatcherism was essentially an anti-traditionalist movement. E. J. Hobsbawm has remarked:

Thatcherite Conservatism is anti-traditionalist, not only because its crazy economic neo-liberalism is the exact opposite of the old Toryism, but because it has junked the Disraelian sales-patter of queen, empire, church and the rest.[75]

During the years of Thatcherite Conservative rule there were strong suspicions of mutual hostility between the Queen and the prime minister.[76] In the absence of effective Labour or Liberal opposition to the Conservatives, established institutions that challenged New Right thinking, like the church and even the House of Lords, became an alternative opposition and fair game for the Tory press. The first anti-royal stories emerged against this background. In the early 1990s popular disaffection with the Crown was fanned by a section of the media that endorsed the Thatcherite experiment and the Conservatives' marginalization of the monarchy, the church and other openly critical institutions. Rupert Murdoch typifies this strand of thinking and has reputedly sworn vengeance against the establishment that rejected him. Popular disaffection fed by intrusive reporting of royal scandals has thus become the hallmark of the royal crises of the late 1990s. In the years 1992–7 the press was obsessed by the carnality of the heir to the throne and his relationship with his mistress, Camilla Parker-Bowles.

Excessive media interest in the subsequent royal divorce created the image of Charles's former wife, Diana, Princess of Wales, as an outcast from the royal household. In the tabloid press she was a Cinderella figure who could still command enormous respect and drew upon reserves of loyalty and devotion denied to the House of Windsor. She is perhaps best understood as a female 'pretender' to the throne, noble even without her title, whose actions provided the metre and register of opposition to the monarchy. Indeed, in his speech at Westminster Abbey during her funeral Earl Spencer made this role explicit, referring to her 'blood family' as the true guardians of the princes and of Diana's legacy. Above all Diana represented the monarch Britain hoped for, but could never secure under the strict laws of inheritance that governed the royal succession.

Rather than unifying public support behind existing notions of monarchy, Diana's function was to create a segmented and conditional loyalism that thrived on criticism of the older and staider members of the royal household. Echoes of Queen Caroline were apparent in this appeal and much discussed in the quality press. Diana's death in a car crash in September 1997 generated a cult of Diana as a flawed celebrity, victimized woman and secular saint, at a time when conventional religious attachments are collapsing. Commentators saw this as a renunciation of the Thatcherite project among the dispossessed, who suffered the most at Mrs Thatcher's hands, and as providing the bedrock for a national myth of Diana, who posthumously represented charitable enterprises, caring and vanished community values. Certain writers have gone further, detecting in the extravagant mourning surrounding Diana's funeral expressions of a latent republican sentiment and a belated 'floral' revolution against the monarchy, similar to the peaceful protests that brought down the Eastern European Communist states in 1989.

The British anti-monarchist constituency of the late twentieth century deserves re-examination. On closer inspection, it stands in fundamental opposition to the movements and agitations that adopted a similar rhetoric in the 1870s. For the first time in many decades opposition to monarchy is more than just a private ritual of dissent. Whereas failing to stand for the national anthem once signalled a stubborn refusal to conform, hostility to the Crown is now an acceptable sentiment, frequently articulated in public. Outspoken hostility to the royal family has, however, become hostage to a profound cultural conservatism. It comprises almost exclusively a constituency of disgruntled royalists who look to the restoration of fundamental monarchist virtues. In some cases, they are prepared to tolerate a slimming down of royal power and ceremonial. Nevertheless, their attitude is a reactionary one, and they wish to revive the traditional moral attributes of a reinvented (but less ostentatious) 1950s-style monarch.

In contrast, the forces that might logically have been expected to undermine the throne have become its staunchest defenders. Professed republicans are almost non-existent in progressive parties like the Labour Party and the Liberal Democrats. Under Tony Blair, the Labour Party has cosseted and defended the monarchy as part of a broader project to stake out a constituency on the centre and move into former Conservative territory. Some on the progressive Left have actively encouraged the notion of a monarchy beholden to the presentational skills of New Labour and revived by Blair's populist touch.[77] Even the Scottish and Welsh nationalist parties, where treasonable sentiments might reasonably be expected to persist, exude a residual loyalism. The Scottish National Party wishes to revisit the monarchy's Scottish roots and hopes to retain the Queen in a ceremonial function in an independent Scotland.[78] Senior SNP spokespersons have been disciplined for suggesting otherwise, and the subject of the monarchy is considered too problematic for open discussion at party conferences.[79]

The assumption of resurgent republicanism, while widespread, does not in fact accurately reflect the form taken by the current wave of discontent with the monarchy. True radical reformers exist, but outside or on the fringes of political parties. Some of their number even deserve the label of 'republicans', but their voices are seldom heard. Once again, anti-monarchism can take a form reminiscent of the extreme minority nineteenth-century criticisms of the throne, in which hostility to royal power was historically grounded in a recovered British past. However, the label anti-monarchist must be qualified. An

236

informed republican viewpoint is barely discernible in much of the coverage of recent royal scandals. Those who feel strongly about monarchy are currently unrepresented in the debate. They are often linked to campaigns against the hereditary principle, for freedom of information and for a written constitution.

Despite the recent travails of the royal family, popular disillusionment with monarchy and the continuing debate about the expense of the throne, a broader public interest in constitutional and institutional reform has conspicuously failed to ignite. Anthony Barnett in particular has commented on the way in which hostility to the monarchy is accompanied by a profound constitutional illiteracy that prevents any real analysis of power and sovereignty within the executive.[80] Consequently discussion of the archaic function of the Crown, or appeals for an elected upper house, a written constitution and a Bill of Rights find little public resonance. As in the nineteenth century the adjective 'cranky' is sometimes used to describe this blueprint for wider reform, and in a 1990s-spin has been linked to a dour 'political correctness' by the *Daily Telegraph*.[81]

In 1994 the *Guardian* ran a feature portraying the members of constitutional reform bodies like Charter 88 as earnest 'Puritans' in a new 'Civil War' against the throne. In the wider public arena, however, republicanism remains a creed incapable of expression. Groups like Charter 88 or the overtly Paineite fringe organization Republic are little more than talking shops. Their influence is confined to London, and their ambitions to recruit limited to the wooing of key opinion formers. Thus far, no organization has emerged that would seek, or could achieve, the role of the nineteenth-century political agitators who contested a broad popular monarchism on the open political platform and fused cerebral republicanism with the pot-house level dismay at royal misdemeanours. Far from promoting real and lasting change in the monarchy, criticism of the throne is unlikely to translate into a genuine reform programme. The direction of reform has been reversed towards the modification or shoring up of royal authority, rather than its removal. Significantly, the most recent proposal for reform of the royal state at the time of writing (from the Blairite think-tank Demos) seeks to square the circle of public disillusionment with particular royal figures and satisfy the demand for change by proposing an elective element before the accession of each royal heir. This misunderstands both the nature of a hereditary succession and the function of consultative democracy.[82]

In the 1990s there is no real opposition to the throne linked to political parties, practicable political agendas or significant pressure groups. The rationale for reform tends to be a modest financial one. Moreover, current disillusion is likely to be addressed by the increasing public visibility of Prince William, whose succession will eventually heal the divisions between supporters of Diana and those of the Prince of Wales. Against this background, debate about monarchy closes down, and the House of Windsor looks set to continue. Even recent speculation about the Queen's abdication in favour of Charles only reshuffles the cards in the pack, rather than fundamentally restructuring the royal state.[83] With a secure blood-line, and a genetic solution through the future role of the royal princes to the recent travails of the royal family now apparent, the monarchy seems set to fulfil its ambition, as A. J. P. Taylor once said of the Habsburgs, 'to survive in grandeur'.[84]

Conclusion: The Future of the Monarchy?

'Sell the lot – And that Yacht,
  Renew with the Republic!'
(Flyer for a demonstration in Kensington Gardens by the
Republican Party, February 1993)

Events of recent years have placed the issue of monarchy back on the political agenda for the first time since the Abdication Crisis of 1936. Republicanism is now fashionable. Today figures as diverse as Beatrix Campbell, Tony Benn and Rupert Murdoch describe themselves as 'republicans'. For defenders of the monarchy it is disturbing indeed to see satisfaction ratings with the royal family fall to levels unprecedented in the post-war period. In her book *The Queen and I* Sue Townsend has speculated about a republican future where the Queen and the royal family are brusquely abolished, stripped of their fortune, and forced to move to the notorious 'Hell Close' on a rundown council estate. At the end of the story the Queen awakes to find that this disturbing vision is only a nightmare.[1]

Yet do these musings truly amount to anything more than wishful thinking? It would be hard to discern the shape of the future British republic in recent complaints about the Civil List and the effect of royal infidelity on British family values. The fact remains that with the exception of Tom Paine the republican tradition in Britain has had no central texts since the 1790s. Moreover it remains the poor relation of its European counterparts, its periodic outbursts comparing unfavourably with the rights of citizenship and programme of land, church and legal reforms that have provided the essential tenets of French government for much of the nineteenth and twentieth centuries. Recent evocations of the 'Good Old Cause' are more sentimental than practical in nature. In January 1999 the 350th anniversary of the execution of Charles I passed almost unnoticed.[2] As Justin Champion has pointed out, the increasingly complex historiographical debates about the causes and consequences of the English Civil War compromise historians' 'ability to communicate with a wider non-scholarly audience' and have blurred the certainties of popular nineteenth-century readings of Oliver Cromwell's career.[3] In recent years through re-enactment groups like the Sealed Knot, the Civil War period has acted more as heritage culture than as a usable part of our national past.[4] With the traditional links with the radical culture of English liberties broken, the Labour Party has shown itself reluctant to grasp the nettle of royal reform. In the twentieth century some of its Prime Ministers, including Ramsay MacDonald and Harold Wilson, have been among the most unctuous of royal flatterers.

Current complaints about the monarchy have been heard before. This book has charted the course of the campaign against the throne of 1870–72 and finds in that episode many precursors of the current travails of the monarchy. It is almost as if the British monarchy has a life cycle, during the course of which criticism is incurred at regular intervals, addressed and rapidly defused. For constitutional experts the strength of the British monarchy resides in its ability to appear timeless and unchanging, and at the same time flexible and responsive in the face of criticism.[5] Despite high levels of public hostility, the Hanoverians survived the death of Princess Charlotte and the divorce scandal surrounding George IV and Queen Caroline. Equally, in the 1930s when society and politics were perhaps more polarized than at any other time in recent memory, the monarchy rode out the Abdication Crisis and overcame the presence of a king in all but name 'over the water'.[6] Even the most incorrigible of royals seem capable of rehabilitation. Once crowned king in 1902 Edward VII was transformed into the fun-loving 'dear old dad'; George VI, after initial disappointment with his ability to fulfil the role of head of state, became the rock of British survival in 1940. Public attitudes towards professed republicans are less forgiving; Sir Charles's Dilke's public reputation never recovered from his involvement in a sex scandal in 1885–6.

In practice criticisms of monarchy almost always assume the same form. Opposition to court and kingly corruption lies at the heart of their message. By demonstrating the fallibility of our 'betters' and directing attention towards their failings, they have an implicitly levelling effect that erodes the mystique of monarchy and makes us feel better about ourselves. This theme re-surfaced throughout the eighteenth and nineteenth centuries. George IV's clandestine marriage to Mrs Fitzherbert, a Catholic; his divorce from Queen Caroline; the murder of a footman by Queen Victoria's uncle, the Duke of Hanover, in 1811; and Edward, Prince of Wales's involvement in the Mordaunt divorce scandal find echoes in images of Prince Charles and Camilla Parker-Bowles, or of Fergie romping with her financial adviser. There is something almost traditional in the current wave of royal sex scandals. In this, as in so much else, royal history offers numerous precedents. The pedigree of Charles's mistress, Camilla Parker-Bowles, as the granddaughter of Alice Keppel, Edward VII's mistress, has revived memories of previous royal indiscretions and evokes the soiled and tarnished image of the Edwardian court. Andrew Morton's best-selling biography of Princess Diana and her own *Panorama* interview in 1995 re-awakened a popular consciousness of the remote and frozen emotional lives of the royals, and of the double standards of the aristocracy's code of conduct that tolerated sham marriages, adultery and the presence of royal mistresses. Morton's influential and subversive book brought this knowledge to the public, using the traditional form of the lavishly illustrated royal biography to project a subversive message about the survival of the monarchy itself.[7] As a new generation of satirists like Steve Bell have realized, there is great comic potential in the lurid details of royal sex in the public domain, and something irresistibly reminiscent of the engravings of Gillray and Rowlandson in the recent cartoon representations of regal couplings. Such images accrete. Then as now enemies of the throne used these incidents as ammunition against the Crown. They strengthened post-Napoleonic War radicalism, acted as a focus for the Chartist movement, and featured in the early Labour Party's attacks on royal privilege.

Nor is there anything new in criticism of the expense of royalty or in proposals to limit the Civil List. The revelation of the Queen Mother's million pound overdraft is only the latest in a long line of exposures of royal extravagance. Civil List provision in particular has traditionally prompted concern among reformers. In 1870–71 opposition to the state's expenditure on monarchy provided the basis for the most sustained challenge mounted to the current royal house since the 1790s. During these years Queen Victoria's withdrawal from public life and, in a marked break with parliamentary precedent, the government's application for donations from the Civil List to support the royal children and Princess Louise's new husband prompted a major debate about the expense involved in the upkeep of royalty. In its origins this was a debate purely about finance, but it rapidly assumed the proportions of a broader attack on the power, privilege and prerogative of the queen herself. Sir Charles Dilke was the mouthpiece of this British republican moment, and there is a curiously contemporary ring to his demands for a parliamentary inquiry into the expenses incurred by the royal household, and the provision, at a substantial cost to the taxpayer, of retainers to staff the royal yacht and train. Dilke's campaign generated such intense feelings, both for and against the throne, that some of the republican meetings of this period degenerated into pitched battles. At one of these in Bolton in November 1871 a republican, William Scofield, was killed by a stone-throwing pro-monarchist mob, thus becoming Britain's first republican martyr since the seventeenth century.

The strongest accusation levelled against the royal house prior to the twentieth century was, however, the assertion that the Hanoverians represented an alien German regime that had little real understanding of the British character and way of life. This charge was reinforced by Victoria's own preference for German courtiers and her marriage to a Saxe-Coburg prince. The royal family's service to the nation in two world wars has gone some way towards abating this slur, but the charges of 'alienness' have occasionally been revived since. In 1960 the monarchy's cosmopolitan ancestry came under intense scrutiny when an amateur genealogist pointed out that there was no clear family name to bequeath to Prince Andrew at his christening.[8] The view that the Hanoverians are simply usurpers remains prevalent in the Scottish context. There, despite the Queen Mother's Scottish ancestry, the House of Windsor has traditionally been seen by reformers as an illegitimate instrument of centralized control that reinforces the historical and ceremonial links between the two countries. The royal family's own historical opposition to Home Rule or devolved authorities that might compromise the unity of the kingdom merely accentuates this view of the royal figurehead as an outsider. These days, however, Tony Blair's constitutional reforms have incorporated, rather than excluded, the royal presence into his blueprint for a devolved United Kingdom. With the history of Britain as a unitary state ending, the royal family have been brought on board to ensure continuity, stability and timeless glamour for the new institutions of a Scottish Parliament. Rather than opposing the monarchy as an 'alien' and 'un-Scottish' power, as they did in 1953 when wanted notices 'dead or alive' for 'Elizabeth I of Scotland', as a royal impostor, were plastered over the walls of Edinburgh,[9] the Scottish Nationalists now embrace the monarchy as conferring stability, dignity and ultimately statehood on Scotland. Once in place, politicians in a Scottish Assembly will, like their British counterparts, manoeuvre to secure honours and preferment from the Crown.[10] Here again, therefore, the monarchy fulfils its traditional conservative function of ensuring the continuation of the Union.

The tendency of British reformers to draw on examples of European 'bicycling royalty' as a precedent for a slimmed-down House of Windsor further conflicts with an inherited version of the United Kingdom as a happy and untroubled monarchy envied by more turbulent and unstable societies across the Channel. Such notions were (and are) informed by a Burkean emphasis on an organic constitution promoting stability and harmony where steady growth is infinitely preferable to revolution (illus. 77). Today a pronounced Euro-scepticism still extends towards imported royal habits, retarding the possibility of reform of the monarchy still further.

Perhaps the effectiveness of attacks against the throne are less important than the fact that such disrespectful sentiments are uttered at all. Looking beyond the limitations of the reforms demanded, it becomes apparent that their chief significance lies in the important function they served within radicalism. In the nineteenth century popular political culture was rooted in a dialogue of disapproval that harnessed a robust criticism of the higher social orders alongside the disavowal of authority present in attacks on courtly and regal

77 Madame Republic, sliding towards chaos, tries vainly to restrain a turbulent Paris as Bismarck looks on avariciously.

A CONTRAST.
MADAME REPUBLIC ENVIES JOHN BULL AND HIS MONARCHY.

influences. Here a landscape was traversed that traded in non-royal historical constructions of the British past, dislike of royal indolence, and an innate feeling that governance was ill-served by the hereditary structures within the state. In the 1870s such notions, which were already embedded in the traditions of British radicalism, held the reform community together outside Liberalism during a period in which issues arising from the reform of Parliament were assuaged. Subsequently they passed through into the ambit of the early Labour Party and surfaced strongly in the years of Progressivist co-operation between Labourism and Liberalism. Here they laid the parameters for the debates about the House of Lords and the attacks on privilege that characterized the Liberal reforming government of 1906–14. In time Labour itself became compromised on this issue by the need to work with, rather than against, the structures of stability within the state. In short the platform and commemorative uses of anti-royal rhetoric were too fragile to translate effectively into a programme of government. Significantly Tony Blair's predecessor as leader of the Labour Party, John Smith, refused to countenance even the most modest reform of the Civil List, and Blair projects himself as a staunch royalist.

Within recent years the strongest currents of opposition to the British monarchy have come from Australia. In 1993 Labour Premier Paul Keating spoke of 'affectionately and gracefully retiring' the royals; a referendum on whether or not to become a republic is now scheduled for the year 2000. It is tacitly acknowledged, even by Prince Charles, that Australia will in all probability be a republic early in the twenty-first century (illus. 78). The Australian move against the royal connection signals a rejection of traditional notions of Australian identity as a subordinate aspect of Britishness in the Southern Hemisphere, where political and economic realities now point in the direction of Asia.[11] Recent polling evidence suggests that republican sentiments are also beginning to emerge in Canada, where the Canadian political parties are watching the Australian example closely.[12] This has profound implications for the dominions, but rather less importance for the monarchy domestically. These days the Commonwealth generates little real affection at home, and the Queen's fervour for the institution is viewed by the British public as merely an eccentricity. For most British citizens the Commonwealth is an empty symbol, whose break-up would serve as an acknowledgement of Britain's diminished role and of the realities of the post-colonial world order.

In the 1990s, as in the nineteenth century, criticism of the throne in Britain never transcends muted calls for curbing the outward excesses of royalty and has no broader proposals for reform of the hereditary

SYDNEY 2000

78 Premier Keating applying the pressure necessary to remove Elizabeth from her role as head of state before the 2000 Sydney Olympics. The staircase is an Aboriginal snake symbol used to market the games.

system (frontispiece, illus. 79). The success of the Queen's balcony appearance on the fiftieth anniversary of VE Day in 1995, the death of Princess Diana and the lack of popular interest in constitutional reform suggests that the recent crisis in the royal family's fortunes has passed. Indeed in recent months, now that the public has moved on from the frenzy of mourning that surrounded Princess Diana's death, there has been a modest revival in royal prestige. Opinion polls consistently show a strong residual monarchism even amongst critics of the throne, reflected in suggestions that Princess Anne, the most popular of the royals, might be a suitable candidate for a president, or even a regent. In Australia, on the other hand, appeals to republicanism have evoked a lively response rooted in recent experience of Governor General John Kerr's use of royal reserve powers within the constitution to dismiss Gough Whitlam's Labour government without public consultation in 1975; so successful has this appeal been that proposals by reformers for a non-monarchical head of state are now perceived as not far-reaching enough, and the majority of Australians wish to vote for a president themselves, rather than submit to one imposed by Canberra.[13] Moreover, in Australia republican sentiment has many cultural resonances, expressing itself in the media, literature and the poetry of Australia's uncrowned Poet Laureate, Les Murray.[14] In Britain constitutional reformers now look to the Australian example.

79 Sean Read, *Happy and Glorious*, 1997, life-size assemblage. Glasgow Gallery of Modern Art. An iconoclastic work somewhat in the manner of the *Spitting Image* puppets shows Elizabeth as literally 'divested' of her royal grandeur.

Given the incoherence of the equivalent British tradition of opposition to the throne they are likely to be disappointed.

At the end of the twentieth century the House of Windsor remains as splendid, as remote and as central to our governing institutions as it did at the end of the nineteenth century. None of the fiercely articulated criticisms of royalty have amounted to a sustained agenda for reform of royalty itself, then or now. In most instances the Windsors have managed to avoid searching and protracted examination of their finances, their role within the constitution and their very fitness to rule. Most reformers have been content with the merest cosmetic tinkering with the worst of their excesses: discarding the royal yacht *Britannia*, or whittling down the number of minor royals receiving Civil List pensions. On occasion the House of Lords has diverted attention away from the central core of inherited privilege within the executive. In many ways this is in keeping with the pragmatic and indeed conservative nature of British radicalism itself. Where governments have been prepared to act to modify the Civil List, the Windsors use concessions to wriggle off the political hook and to appease public unease about their role. If the Labour Party does not take up these issues, who else will? Perhaps a searching reappraisal of the monarchy might be linked to a Bill of Rights, a system of proportional representation in the voting system and legislation to protect freedom of information. This could provide a *true republican* alternative and even potentially open the way to cross-bench co-operation between Labour and such Liberal Democrats as Simon Hughes who are known to feel strongly about monarchy. Conventional political wisdom has always suggested that to embrace a republican platform in Britain is to commit political suicide. This assumption remains untested. Recent public disquiet about the monarchy could be channelled and directed towards positive ends; at the very least it provides a breath of fresh air in a political system that is perhaps the most atrophied in Europe. If allowed to fade, only the Windsors will be the real beneficiaries.

References

Introduction

1　The deficiencies of traditional scholarship towards royalty are discussed in Anthony Arblaster, 'The Fall of the House of Windsor', *New Left Review*, no. 208 (1994), pp. 127–32.

2　The fullest introduction to the history of British constitutional developments is Stuart Weir and David Beetham, *Political Power and Democratic Control in Britain* (London, 1999), chaps 1–2.

3　See Ian Buruma, *Voltaire's Coconuts or Anglomania in Europe* (London, 1999), pp. 36–7.

4　See Marilyn Morris, *The British Monarchy and the French Revolution* (New Haven and London, 1998), introduction and chaps 1–2.

5　David Cannadine, *History in Our Time* (New Haven and London, 1998); *idem*, 'Queen Croesus', *London Review of Books*, 13 February 1992, pp. 3–6 and *idem*, 'After the *Annus Horribilis*', *Times Literary Supplement*, 3 November 1995, pp. 3–4.

6　Norman St. John-Stevas, 'The Monarchy and the Present' in *The Monarchy and its Future*, ed. Jeremy Murray-Brown (London, 1969), pp. 211–27.

7　This has frequently troubled non-traditional educationalists. See Terry Hadyn, '"Nationalism Begins at Home": The Influence of National Curriculum History on Perceptions of National Identity in Britain 1987–1995', *History of Education Society Bulletin*, LVII (1996), pp. 51–61.

8　David Norbrook, *Writing the English Republic: Poetry, Rhetoric and Politics 1627–1666* (Cambridge, 1999).

9　Christopher Hitchens in *Power and the Throne: The Monarchy Debate*, ed. Anthony Barnett (London, 1994).

10　Ben Pimlott, *The Queen: A Biography of Elizabeth II* (London, 1997).

11　This point is made strongly in the standard account: Margot Finn, *After Chartism: Class and Nation in English Radical Politics 1848–1874* (Cambridge, 1993), pp. 13–59.

12　*Red Republican*, 1 December 1850, p. 214.

13　Jane Connors, 'The 1954 Royal Tour of Australia', *Historical Studies (Australia)*, XXV (1993), pp. 371–82 and reprinted in *Memories and Dreams: Reflections on Twentieth Century Australia*, eds Richard White and Penny Russell (Sydney, 1997), pp. 171–85.

14　For example, Brian Harrison, *The Transformation of British Society and Politics 1860–1995* (London, 1996), chap. 12.

15　For an introduction to this subject, see Rohan McWilliam, *Popular Politics in Nineteenth Century England* (London, 1998), chaps 1–3.

16　Joss Marsh, *Word Crimes: Blasphemy, Culture and Literature in Nineteenth Century England* (Chicago, 1998).

17 The field of mid-nineteenth-century popular politics has expanded rapidly in recent years. On the above themes see: James Vernon, *Politics and the People: A Study in English Political Culture c.1815–1867* (Cambridge, 1993), chap. 8; Miles Taylor, *The Decline of British Radicalism 1847–1860* (Oxford, 1995), chaps 1–4; Patrick Joyce, *Visions of the People: Industrial England and the Question of Class 1848–1914* (Cambridge, 1991), chaps 2–3; *idem, Democratic Subjects: The Self and the Social in Nineteenth-Century England* (Cambridge, 1994), pp. 153–213; Eugenio Biagini, *Liberals, Retrenchment and Reform: Popular Liberalism in the Age of Gladstone* (Cambridge, 1992), chap. 5 and *idem*, 'Introduction: Citizenship, Liberty and Community' in Biagini, ed., *Citizenship and Community: Liberals, Radicals and Collective Identities in the British Isles 1865–1931* (Cambridge, 1997), pp. 1–17.

18 Thomas Tiffany, *The Popular Temperance Reciter* (London, 1887), pp. 194–5.

19 Many of the standard studies of the temperance movement stress the anti-aristocratic and anti-feudal elements that featured in the movement's platform rhetoric; see Brian Harrison, *Drink and the Victorians: The Temperance Question in England 1815–1872* (London, 1971; new edition, 1994), p. 141.

20 Alex Hall, *Scandal, Sensation and Social Democracy: The SPD Press and Wilhelmine Germany 1890–1914* (Cambridge, 1977), pp. 130–96.

21 Quoted in Gareth Stedman Jones, *Languages of Class: Studies in English Working Class History 1832–1982* (Cambridge, 1983), p. 211.

1 Equivocations of Liberty 1800–1837

1 Adrienne Munich, *Queen Victoria's Secrets* (New York, 1996), pp. 144–7.

2 For example, the painting features on the front cover of Marc Ferro, *Colonization: A Global History* (London, 1997).

3 Clare Midgly, ed., *Gender and Imperialism* (Manchester, 1998).

4 Munich, *Queen Victoria's Secrets*, p. 96.

5 *Manchester Courier*, 3 April 1872, p. 8. Images of Bibles, altars and the Queen were also prominent on Tory banners during the Jingo agitation of 1877–8 in Manchester; see the *Manchester Examiner and Times*, 4 February 1878, p. 3.

6 *Ibid.*, 4 April 1872, pp. 4–5. The Earl of Derby, who was present at the meeting, noted that two hours out of the three hour, twenty minute speech were a 'somewhat unreal' meditation on the British constitution. He also suggested that: 'Most of his argument would not have been difficult to answer had anyone cared to take the republican side.' See John Vincent, ed., *A Selection from the Diaries of Edward Henry Stanley, 15th Earl of Derby, 1869–78* (Royal Historical Society, 1994), vol. IV, p. 103. The radical Charles Watts took issue with the Disraelian vision of the constitution outlined at Manchester in the *National Reformer*, 26 May 1872, pp. 326–7 and 2 June 1872, p. 347–8. Disraeli's plea for health and social reform – 'sanitas sanitatum, omnia sanitas' – is downplayed in the account of his speech in Robert Blake, *Disraeli* (London, 1966; re-printed 1978), pp. 522–4.

7 This point is made strongly in Linda Colley, 'We Love Your Country. When Can We Move In?', *The Observer Review*, 16 February 1997, p. 17.

8 For Stead's career, see A. J. P. Taylor, *The Trouble Makers: Dissent Over Foreign Policy 1792–1939* (London, 1957; re-printed, 1985), pp. 79–81 and 90–91.

9 William T. Stead, *Studies of the Sovereign and the Reign* (London, 1897; re-printed 1901), p. 18.

10 William Hone, *The Right Divine of Kings to Govern Wrong* (London, 1821), pp. 24–5. On the language and writings of Hone, see O. Smith, *The Politics of Language 1791–1819* (Oxford, 1984), p. 189.

11 R. Hole, *Pulpits, Politics and Public Order in England 1760–1832* (Cambridge, 1989), p. 106, and James E. Bradley, *Religion, Revolution and English Radicalism: Nonconformity in Eighteenth Century Politics and Society* (Cambridge, 1990), chap. 4.

12 For the comments of the radical and Nonconformist J. Morrison Davidson, see *Lives of Eminent Radicals In and Out of Parliament* (London, 1880), pp. 210–15.

13 William Hone, ed., *The Early Life and Conversion of William Hone [Senior]* (London, 1841); F. W. Hackwood, *William Hone: His Life and Times* (London, 1912), chap. 2, and Edgell Rickword, ed., *Radical Squibs and Loyal Ripostes: Satirical Pamphlets of the Regency Period 1819–21* (London, 1971), pp. 1–32. Ebenezer Elliott, 'The Corn-Law Rhymer', recalled a similar ultra-Protestant upbringing to Hone's that also inculcated radical versions of Old Testament history; see John Watkins, *Life, Poetry and Letters of Ebenezer Elliott* (London, 1850), p. 7.

14 Hypatia Bradlaugh-Bonner, *Penalties Upon Opinion: Or Some Record of the Laws of Heresy and Blasphemy* (London, 1934), and D. Lawton, *Blasphemy* (Brighton, 1993).

15 *Northern Star*, 4 March 1848, p. 1.

16 J. Morrison Davidson, 'The New Book of Kings' (Pamphlet, London, 1884), pp. 3–4. Morrison Davidson's pamphlet ran to ten editions; see Kingsley Martin, *Britain in the Sixties: The Crown and the Establishment* (London, 1962), p. 183. In similar vein, George Bernard Shaw recalled conversing with an old Chartist who described Shelley's classic republican and anti-religious poem 'Queen Mab' as 'The Chartists' Bible'; see George Bernard Shaw, *Pen Portraits and Reveries* (London, 1932), pp. 236–46.

17 Palmerston's role as protector of British interests abroad is outlined in E. D. Steele, *Palmerston and Liberalism 1855–1865* (Cambridge, 1991), especially pp. 215–41.

18 For Palmerston's sometimes amiable relationship with British radicalism, see Antony Taylor, 'Palmerston and Radicalism 1847–1865', *Journal of British Studies*, XXXIII (1994), pp. 157–79.

19 Kingsley Martin, *The Triumph of Lord Palmerston: A Study of Public Opinion in England before the Crimean War* (London, 1924; re-printed 1963), pp. 210–12.

20 'Lovely Albert'. Ballad (821 04 BA1) in the Pearson Collection, Manchester Central Reference Library.

21 Obituary of Thomas Jones Barker in the *Times*, 29 March 1882, p. 10.

22 J. G. A. Pocock, '"British History" and the Limits and Divisions of British History: In Search of the Unknown Subject', *Journal of Modern History*, XL (1975), pp. 601–8; Hugh Kearney, *The British Isles: A History of Four Nations* (Cambridge, 1989); B. Levack, *The Formation of the British State: England, Scotland and the Union 1603–1707* (Oxford, 1987), especially the introduction and chap. 6; Raphael Samuel, '"British Dimensions": Four Nations History', *History Workshop*, no. 40 (1995), pp. iii–xxii; *idem, Island Stories: Unravelling Britain* (London, 1998), parts I and II, and E. Evans, 'Englishness and Britishness c.1790–1870' in *Uniting the Kingdom: The Making of British History*, ed. A. Grant and K. J. Stringer (London, 1995), pp. 224–43. For a critical appraisal from an Irish point of view of approaches to the history of the British state and English identity see Steven G. Ellis, 'Writing Irish History: Revisionism, Colonialism and the British Isles', *Irish Review*, 19 (1996), pp. 1–21.

23 Gerald Newman, *The Rise of English Nationalism: A Cultural History 1740–1830* (London, 1987).

24 Lois G. Schwoerer, 'Celebrating the Glorious Revolution, 1689–1989', *Albion*, XXII (1990), pp. 1–20.

25 Linda Colley, *Britons: Forging the Nation 1707–1837* (London, 1992), chap. 5.

26 Linda Colley, 'The Apotheosis of George III: Loyalty, Royalty and the British Nation 1760–1820', *Past and Present*, no. 102 (1984) and *Britons*, p. 217.

27 Dorothy Thompson, *Queen Victoria: Gender and Power* (London, 1990), chaps 1 and 2.

28 Stephen C. Schrendt, *Royal Mourning and Regency Culture: Elegies and Memorials of Princess Charlotte* (London, 1997), chaps 4–5.

29 Ronald Hutton, *The Rise and Fall of Merry England: The Ritual Year 1400–1700* (Oxford, 1994), pp. 251–60. This point is also highlighted in David Cressy, *Bonfires and Bells: National Memory and the Protestant Calendar in Elizabethan and Stuart England* (London, 1989), and *idem*, 'The Fifth of November Remembered', in *Myths of the English*, ed. Roy Porter (Oxford, 1992), pp. 68–90.

30 Tim Harris, *London Crowds in the Reign of Charles II: Propaganda and Politics from the Restoration to the Exclusion Crisis* (Cambridge, 1994).

31 P. H. Gosse, 'Schooldays in Dorset 1818–1823', *Longmans' Magazine*, XVII (1889), p. 517.

32 These traditions crystallized in a number of nineteenth- and early twentieth-century treatments of the Monmouth Rising that condensed much of the surviving oral lore surrounding the revolt. Some Monmouth material was also re-published during the early 1820s during the period of maximum disillusionment with the Prince Regent. See Anon., *An Historical Account of the Heroick Life and Magnanimous Actions of the Most Illustrious Protestant Prince, James, Duke of Monmouth* (London, 1820), pp. 1–5, and for the West Country traditions surrounding his return, Allan Fea, *King Monmouth: A History of the Career of James Scott, 'The Protestant Duke' 1649–1685* (London, 1904), pp. 379–80.

33 The Calvinist tradition also shaped the Scottish republicanism of the period; see Liam McIlvanney, 'Robert Burns and the Calvinist Radical Tradition', *History Workshop*, no. 40 (1995), pp. 133–49.

34 B. H. Bronson, *Joseph Ritson: Scholar-at-Arms* (Berkeley, 1938), p. 112.

35 Nicola Richards, '"A Sense of Belonging": National Identity, Popular Culture and Literature in England and Scotland in the Late Eighteenth and Early Nineteenth Centuries' (Unpublished Ph.D. Thesis, University of Manchester, 1997).

36 Colley, *Britons*, pp. 195–228.

37 Marc Baer, *Theatre and Disorder in Late Georgian London* (Oxford, 1992), chaps 2 and 4.

38 'The Coronation Carnival! Or Novel Scenes at Newcastle'. British Museum Ballad Collection (BL.1474.d.14(5)). My thanks to Nicola Richards for this reference. For an examination of the festivities surrounding coronation rituals, see George Tressider, 'Coronation Day Celebrations in English Towns 1685–1821: Elite Hegemony and Local Relations on a Ceremonial Occasion', *British Journal for Eighteenth Century Studies*, XV (1992), pp. 1–16.

39 The association between monarchy and fairy tales is remarked on in Angela Carter, ed., *The Virago Book of Fairy Tales* (London, 1991), pp. xix–xx.

40 Diana Donald, 'The Power of Print: Graphic Images of Peterloo', *Manchester Region History Review*, III (1989), pp. 21–30 and *idem*, *The Age of Caricature: Satirical Prints in the Age of George III* (London, 1996), chaps 4, 5 and epilogue.

41 Charles Hindley, *The Life and Times of James Catnach* (London, 1878), pp. 52–75.

42 Cruikshank was best known to contemporaries for his illustrations in the first English edition of the Grimms' fairy-tales translated by Edgar Taylor, see *German Popular Stories* (London, 1823) and for an account of the place of Cruikshank in children's story book illustration Pamela Trimpe, 'Victorian Fairy Book Illustration' in *Victorian Fairy Painting*, ed. Jane Martineau (Royal Academy, 1997), pp. 17–55.

43 T. Dolby, 'Jack and the Queen Killers' (Pamphlet, London, 1820), pp. 5–30.

44 Unsurprisingly Queen Caroline has lived on in children's nonsense rhymes and doggerel like 'Queenie, Queenie Caroline/Dipped her hair in turpentine/ Turpentine to make it shine/Queenie, Queenie Caroline.' Iona and Peter Opie, *The Lore and Language of Schoolchildren* (Oxford, 1959; re-printed 1987), p. 20.

45 The best general account of Queen Caroline's life is Flora Fraser, *The Unruly Queen: The Life of Queen Caroline* (London, 1996). Also see for an introduction to the historiography surrounding the case McWilliam, *Popular Politics in Nineteenth-Century England*, chaps 1 and 5.

46 There is now a vast literature on the Queen Caroline divorce case, but see in particular Thomas W. Laqueur, 'The Queen Caroline Affair: Politics as Art in the Reign of George IV', *Journal of Modern History*, LIV (1982), pp. 417–66; Ian McCalman, *Radical Underworld; Prophets, Revolutionaries and Pornographers in London 1795–1840* (Cambridge, 1988), pp. 162–77; Anna Clark, 'Queen Caroline and the Sexual Politics of Popular Culture in London, 1820', *Representations*, no. 31 (1990), pp. 47–68; Tamara Hunt, 'Morality and Monarchy in the Queen Caroline Affair', *Albion*, XXIII (1991), pp. 697–722 and Dror Wahrman, *Imagining the Middle-Class: The Political Representation of Class in Britain c.1780–1840* (Cambridge, 1995), chap. 11.

47 The role of public opinion in the Queen Caroline case is examined in Dror Wahrman, 'Public Opinion, Violence and the Limits of Constitutional Politics' in *Re-Reading the Constitution: New Narratives in the Political History of England's Long Nineteenth Century*, ed. James Vernon (Cambridge, 1996), pp. 83–122.

48 Ballad 'The Rogue Who Insulted the Queen', Pearson Collection, MCRL.

49 John Watkins, *The Life and Times of William the Fourth: England's 'Patriot King'* (London, 1831), pp. 494–502.

50 William Hone, 'The Political "A, Apple-Pie"; or the Extraordinary Red Book Versified' (Pamphlet, London, 1820), p. 15.

51 *Figaro in London*, 21 September 1833, pp. 149–50.

52 Roger Fulford, *Royal Dukes* (London, 1933), p. 238.

53 Thompson, *Queen Victoria*, pp. 19–20 and McCalman, *Radical Underworld*, pp. 34–5 and 39–41.

54 Arthur Aspinall, ed., *The Correspondence of George, Prince of Wales 1770–1812* (London, 1970), vol. VII, appendix 1, pp. 373–8. The original manuscript version of Major Charles Jones's memoir is in the Royal Library at Windsor.

55 There is a report of the accident that led to Captain Jones's death in the *Times*, 17 February 1843.

56 *People's Paper*, 1 November 1856, p. 4. In addition, there is much opposition to royal figures in Ernest Jones's poetry; see his 'Labour's History' in Ernest Jones, 'Chartist Songs and Fugitive Pieces' (Pamphlet, London, 1848), pp. 9–10.

57 This ambivalence in Ernest Jones's outlook is highlighted in George Jacob Holyoake's review of his life at the secularist Cleveland Hall, London in 1869; see the *National Reformer*, 18 April 1869, p. 251. Also see on this theme Antony Taylor, '"The Best Way to Get What He Wanted": Ernest Jones and the Boundaries of Liberalism in the Manchester Election of 1868', *Parliamentary History*, XVI (1997), pp. 185–204.

58 The radical Cato Street Conspirators were publicly executed in 1820 under the
    treason laws. Their fate remained a salutary lesson for radicals into the 1830s.
    V. A. C. Gatrell, *The Hanging Tree: Execution and the English People 1770–1868*,
    (Oxford, 1994), chap. 11.

59 Hindley, *Life of James Catnach*, p. 327.

60 There is a retrospective on the case in the *Newcastle Weekly Chronicle*, 16 August
    1884, p. 7.

61 Hindley, *Life of James Catnach*, pp. 329–30.

62 The episode of 'The Boy Jones' was immortalized in Arthur John Arbuthnott
    Stringer's famous children's novel *The Mudlark* published in 1932. This was later
    produced as a film entitled *The Mudlark* (1950), starring Irene Dunn as Queen
    Victoria, Alec Guinness as Benjamin Disraeli and Andrew Ray as 'The Boy
    Jones'. In these later depictions of the episode the subversion of the ballads
    surrounding the boy's original entry into Buckingham Palace is lost and the
    action is transferred to the period of Victoria's seclusion in the 1870s. Against a
    background of impending world war in the 1930s and British post-imperial
    decline in the 1950s, 'The Boy Jones' was elevated into a patriotic icon, keen to see
    the queen now in seclusion, and instrumental in coaxing her back into public life.

63 *Newcastle Weekly Chronicle*, 16 August 1884, p. 7.

64 R. G. G. Price, *A History of Punch* (London, 1955), chap. 2, and Susan and Asa
    Briggs, eds, *Cap and Bell: Punch's Chronicle of English History in the Making
    1841–1861* (London, 1972), pp. xi–xxx.

65 McCalman, *Radical Underworld*, chaps 9 and 10.

66 This was often tinged with a marked pro-Irish sentiment. See Roy Foster, *Paddy
    and Mr. Punch: Connections in Irish and English History* (London, 1993), chap. 9.

67 Thompson, *Queen Victoria*, chaps 1–3.

68 Dorothy Thompson, *The Outsiders: Class, Gender and Nation* (London, 1993),
    pp. 164–86, and Nicola J. Watson, 'Gloriana Victoriana: Victoria and the
    Cultural Memory of Elizabeth I' in *Re-Making Queen Victoria*, eds Margaret
    Homans and Adrienne Munich (Cambridge, 1997), pp. 79–104.

69 Edward Parry, *Royal Visits and Progresses to Wales from the First Invasion of Julius
    Caesar to the Friendly Visits of Her Most Gracious Majesty, Queen Victoria* (Chester,
    1850), p. 21 and pp. 434–80, and Raphael Samuel, 'Grand Narratives: History, the
    Nation and the Schools', *History Workshop Journal*, no. 29 (1990), pp. 120–33.

70 Ballad 'Mr. Ferguson and Queen Victoria' in Charles Hindley, *Curiosities of
    Street Literature: Facsimiles of Nineteenth Century English Broadsides* (London,
    1871; re-printed 1966), p. 63.

71 For the role of philanthropy in the appeal of Victoria and Albert, see Frank
    Prochaska, *Royal Bounty: The Making of a Welfare Monarchy* (London, 1995),
    chaps 3–4.

72 *Punch* (1841), vol. I, p. 103.

73 There are echoes of these early notions of Victoria as a 'Just Monarch' in press
    treatments of the mourning following her death. A contemporary review of
    public affairs wrote: 'It is right to say that the feeling of forlornness which
    pervaded the country was alike, in its diffusion and in its depth, of a kind such as
    has not been known in Britain since the death of King Alfred a thousand years
    ago.' See the *Annual Register 1901* (London, 1902), p. 8. For a study of the cult of
    Alfred and his association with myths of lost pre-Norman liberties see Thomas
    Hughes, *Alfred the Great* (London, 1881) and Asa Briggs, *Saxons, Normans and
    Victorians* (Historical Association Pamphlet, Hastings and Bexhill, 1966), pp.
    3–9. This article is re-printed in Asa Briggs, *The Collected Essays of Asa Briggs*
    (London, 1985), vol. II, pp. 315–35.

74 'Mr. Vincent's Speech in Reply to Lord John Russell's Declaration that the Middle and Working-Class of the Country Want No Reform' (Pamphlet, Manchester, 1848), p. 11.

75 The phrase 'domestic exemplar' is used by Wiliam T. Stead; see Stead, *Studies of the Sovereign and the Reign*, p. 115.

76 The death of Princess Charlotte during childbirth was expressive of this feeling. Her death in 1817 established many of the precedents for popular mourning of royalty, including black-borders for the newspapers that announced her death and popular subscriptions for posthumous statues of her. See Colley, *Britons*, pp. 268–73.

77 'Another Present for Old John Bull: Birth of the Duke of York' (Ballad BR F821 04 BA1) vol. IV, in the Pearson Collection, MCRL.

78 George Potter, 'History of the Tory Party' (Pamphlet, London, 1877), p. 9.

79 Anon., *The Crowning of King George V in Westminster Abbey: Why and How it is Done* (London, 1911), p. 18.

80 Ralph Waldo Emerson, *Works* (London, 1882), vol. III, p. 50. Emerson toured Britain on a number of occasions and became an important influence on the self-improvement culture of Liberals and Progressives; see William J. Sowder, *Emerson's Impact on the British Isles and Canada* (Charlottesville, Va, 1966), chap. 1 and Joyce, *Democratic Subjects*, pp. 46–8.

81 Richard G. White, *England Without and Within* (London, 1881), pp. 373–4.

2 Republicanism Reappraised: Anti-monarchism and the English Radical Tradition 1830–75

1 Edward Thompson, 'The Peculiarities of the English' in his *The Poverty of Theory and Other Essays* (London, 1978), pp. 245–301.

2 The standard introduction to this subject is N. J. Gossman, 'Republicanism in Nineteenth Century England', *International Review of Social History*, VII (1962), pp. 553–74.

3 For example, John Belchem, 'Republicanism, Popular Constitutionalism and the Radical Platform in Early Nineteenth Century England', *Social History*, VI (1981), pp. 1–35.

4 This idea is first set out in detail in Edward Thompson, *The Making of the English Working Class* (London, 1968), p. 88, but for its implications for later interpretations of anti-monarchism, see Edward Royle, *Radicals, Secularists and Republicans: Popular Freethought in Britain 1866–1915* (Manchester, 1980), pp. 198–206, and Fergus D'Arcy, 'Charles Bradlaugh and the English Republican Movement', *Historical Journal*, XXV (1982), pp. 367–83.

5 Stephen Cottrell, 'The Devil on Two Sticks: Francophobia in 1803', in *Patriotism: The Making and Unmaking of British National Identity*, ed. Raphael Samuel (London, 1989), vol. 1, pp. 259–74.

6 A new appreciation of Paine's work that emphasizes the range and subtlety of his ideas as well as their inherent populism has emerged from two new biographical studies of his life; see Jack Fruchtman, *Thomas Paine: Apostle of Freedom* (London, 1994), and John Keane, *Tom Paine: A Political Life* (London, 1995), chaps 9–11.

7 Vernon, *Politics and the People*, chap. 8.

8 There is now a large literature on this subject, but see in particular: Jack Fruchtman, 'The Revolutionary Millenialism of Thomas Paine', *Studies in Eighteenth Century Culture*, XIII (1984), pp. 65–77; Ian McCalman, 'New Jerusalems: Prophecy, Judaism and Radical Restorationism in London

1786–1832' (Paper presented to the Manchester University Modern History Seminar, March, 1992), and Ian Dyck, 'Local Attachments, National Identities and World Citizenship in the Thought of Thomas Paine', *History Workshop Journal*, xxxv (1993), pp. 117–35.

9 Tom Paulin in Barnett, ed., *Power and the Throne*, pp. 178–81.

10 For a comparison of such images in a British, Australian and European context, see W. D. Rubinstein, 'British Radicalism and the Dark Side of Populism' in his *Elites and the Wealthy in Modern British Society* (Brighton, 1987), pp. 339–73, and Robert Darnton, 'The High Enlightenment and the Low Life of Literature in Pre-Revolutionary France', in *French Society and the Revolution*, ed. Douglas Johnson, (Cambridge, 1976), pp. 53–87.

11 I disagree with Rubinstein's assertion that the power and coherence of such images was beginning to fade by the 1860s. See W. D. Rubinstein, 'The End of Old Corruption in Britain, 1780–1860' in his *Elites and the Wealthy in Modern British Society*, pp. 265–303.

12 *Northern Star*, 1 July 1843, p. 5.

13 See McCalman, *Radical Underworld*, pp. 204–31.

14 In the ballad 'A New Song on the Mordaunt Divorce Case' (Q 821 04 B2) in the Manchester Central Reference Library, Broadside Collection. For images of cuckoldry and their place in the criticism of monarchy more generally see Hunt, 'Morality and Monarchy', pp. 697–722.

15 *Newcastle Weekly Chronicle*, 5 March 1870, p. 4. The Mordaunt divorce proceedings received considerable exposure in other surviving radical papers; see in particular *Reynolds's Newspaper*, 6 March 1870.

16 Thompson, *Queen Victoria*, p. 98.

17 Andrew Carnegie, *Autobiography* (London, 1920), pp. 9–12.

18 The central importance of memories of the English Revolution for a later generation of reformers is emphasized in Finn, *After Chartism*, pp. 13–59.

19 The Unitarian pastor and Chartist fellow traveller Adam Rushton regularly referred to Cromwell's legacy in his sermons; see Adam Rushton, *My Life as Farmer's Boy, Factory Lad, Teacher and Preacher* (Manchester, 1909), pp. 108-9, 170 and 239.

20 Stead, *Studies of the Sovereign and Her Reign*, p. 10.

21 *Liberator* (1908), vol. 104, p. 168.

22 For Joseph Arch's invocation of the legacy of the English Commonwealth, see his reminiscences, *From Ploughtail to Parliament: An Autobiography* (London, 1898, re-printed, 1986), pp. 3–4. John Bright also drew extensively upon memories of the Civil War period in his speeches, see William Robertson, *The Life and Times of John Bright* (London, 1877, re-printed, 1912), p. 228 and p. 279.

23 Edwin Paxton Hood, *Oliver Cromwell: His Life, Times, Battlefields and Contemporaries* (London, 1882; reprinted 1895), chaps 15–17, and *idem*, 'Instincts of Liberalism: A Lecture' (Pamphlet, Manchester, 1879), pp. 21–2. Also see on this theme Raphael Samuel, 'The Discovery of Puritanism 1820–1914: A Preliminary Sketch' in his *Island Stories*, pp. 276–322.

24 *Bristol Examiner*, 9 March 1850, pp. 1–2.

25 The Irish, of course, were very largely excluded from the cult of Cromwell-worship. For this reason English radicalism's emphasis on the Interregnum sometimes stretched the working relationship between English and Irish reformers. The Young Ireland rebel John Mitchell recalled befriending a Chartist prisoner of 1848 in prison whose pro-Irish sympathies were rapidly reversed when another Irish inmate spat in his face, leading him to invoke the

name of Cromwell and to suggest that he hadn't 'been stern enough' with the Irish in the 1640s; see *Justice*, 21 February 1885, p. 1. For Irish attitudes to Cromwell more generally see T. Barnyard, 'Irish Images of Cromwell', in *Images of Oliver Cromwell: Essays By and For Roger Howell jr*, ed. R. C. Richardson (Manchester, 1993), pp. 180–206 and John Mitchell, *Jail Journal: Prisoner in the Hands of the English* (Dublin, 1913; reprinted, 1983), p. xviii.

26   These conflicting images of Cromwell are examined in Alan Smith, 'The Image of Cromwell in Folklore and Tradition', *Folklore*, LXXIX (1968), pp. 17–39.

27   Hackwood, *William Hone*, pp. 42–3. Many traditional elements of English Protestant martyrdom also surrounded the execution of the Cromwellian radical Henry Vane; see the *Newcastle Weekly Chronicle*, 27 July 1878, p. 7.

28   Peter Karsten, *Patriot Heroes in England and America: Political Symbolism and Changing Values Over Three Centuries* (Wisconsin, 1978), pp. 139–55; I. Roots, 'Carlyle's Cromwell' in *Images of Oliver Cromwell*, ed. Richardson, pp. 74–95; Samuel, *Island Stories*, pp. 276–322, and Finn, *After Chartism*, pp. 42–3. There was a previous outbreak of Cromwell worship in the 1790s when many radicals referred to him in connection with events in France; see McCalman, 'New Jerusalems', *passim*.

29   Images of a Tory Cromwell are discussed in Samuel, *Island Stories*, pp. 287–8.

30   There is an account of Cromwell's career that makes these points in the *National Reformer*, 30 April 1876, p. 273.

31   John B. Leno, *The Aftermath* (London, 1892), p. 79.

32   William Dorling, *Henry Vincent: A Biographical Sketch* (London, 1879), p. 44.

33   The *Northern Tribune*, vol. 1 no. 5, 1854, p. 147, and the *People's Paper*, 20 September 1856, p. 1.

34   *McDouall's Chartist and Republican Journal*, 3 April 1841, pp. 6–7.

35   For a recent assessment of popular constitutionalism that seeks to define it almost entirely in loyalist terms, see Colley, *Britons*, pp. 283–308.

36   *People's Paper*, 22 May 1858, p. 1.

37   Gregory Claeys, 'Thomas Evans and the Development of Spenceanism 1815–1816: Some Neglected Correspondence', *Bulletin of the Society for the Study of Labour History*, XLVIII (1984), pp. 24–30.

38   *Poor Man's Guardian*, 30 June 1832, p. 445. King Alfred remained an important radical icon into the 1870s; see a sketch of his life in the *Newcastle Weekly Chronicle*, 21 July 1877, p. 4.

39   It is referred to by Sir Charles Dilke in his 'Cost of the Crown Speech' at Newcastle in 1871, see the *Newcastle Weekly Chronicle*, 11 November 1871, p. 5.

40   The opposition that emerged towards Victoria during the 1866–7 reform campaign is examined in Walter Arnstein, 'Queen Victoria Opens Parliament: The Disinvention of Tradition', *Historical Research*, LXIII (1990), pp. 178–94.

41   *Manchester Examiner and Times*, 20 August 1866, p. 3.

42   'A List of the Departments and Branches of the National Reform League 1867' in the Howell Collection, Bishopsgate Institute. For James Finlen's lecture on Cromwell to the Holborn branch of the Reform League see the *Commonwealth*, 29 September 1866, p. 8.

43   *Bee-Hive*, 3 October 1868, pp. 4–5.

44   For accounts of the controversy surrounding Queen Victoria's private income in the 1870s, see William M. Kuhn, 'Ceremony and Politics: The British Monarchy 1871–1872', *Journal of British Studies*, XXVI (1987), pp. 133–62; *idem*, 'Queen Victoria's Civil List: What Did She Do With It'? *Historical Journal*, XXXVI (1993), pp. 645–65 and *idem, Democratic Royalism: The Transformation of the British Monarchy 1861–1914* (London, 1996), chap. 2.

45 E. A. Smith, *The House of Lords in British Politics and Society 1815–1911* (London, 1992), pp. 22–4.

46 S. Gwynn and G. M. Tuckwell, *The Life of the Rt. Hon. Sir Charles W. Dilke* (London, 1918), vol. II, p. 140.

47 Regional variations in patterns of support for republicanism are examined in M. P. Smith, 'Republicanism in Victorian Britain' (Unpublished Ph.D. thesis, University of Toronto, 1979), chaps 10 and 11.

48 *National Reformer*, 26 February 1871, p. 139 and 12 March 1871, p. 171 for the opening of the Birmingham republican club, and *ibid.*, 2 April 1871, p. 220 for the activities of the Leicester republicans.

49 Howell – Goldwin Smith, 25 February 1871, HC, BI.

50 There are accounts of the formation of the Tyneside and Sunderland republican clubs in the *Newcastle Weekly Chronicle*, 4 March 1871, p. 3 and 5 August 1871, p. 3.

51 *Ibid.*, p. 4 and for details of a meeting in Hyde Park in opposition to the Prince of Wales's tour of India in 1875, the *National Reformer*, 25 July 1875, p. 50.

52 The disturbances at Dilke's constituency meeting are described in the *Times*, 29 November 1871, p. 10, but also see for the disorder at Derby the *Manchester Guardian*, 5 December 1871, p. 8, and for the riots at Reading and Bolton the *Newcastle Weekly Chronicle*, 16 December 1871, p. 4, and the *Bolton Evening News*, 1 December 1871, p. 4. There are Home Office files on these events in the Disturbance Books [H.O. 45/939/2/] at the Public Records Office.

53 *National Reformer*, 10 December 1871, p. 381.

54 Elizabeth Longford, ed., *The Oxford Book of Royal Anecdotes* (London, 1991), p. 415.

55 James Epstein, 'Radical Dining, Toasting and Symbolic Expression in Early Nineteenth Century Lancashire: Rituals of Solidarity', *Albion*, XX (1988), pp. 271–91. A controversy generated by the booing of the royal family and titled army officers at a dinner in honour of the compositors of Ernest Jones's *London News*, is reported in the *London News*, 16 October 1858, p. 8, and 30 October 1858, p. 3.

56 *Saturday Review*, 22 April 1871.

57 Finn, *After Chartism*, pp. 273–303. A more eclectic approach locating republicanism in the context of previous radical agitations is followed in a study of Tyneside radicalism by Nigel Todd, *The Militant Democracy: Joseph Cowen and Victorian Radicalism* (Tyne and Wear, 1991).

58 Kuhn, 'Ceremony and Politics: The British Monarchy 1871–1872', pp. 140–41. The full text of Dilke's speech at Newcastle and initial responses to it are in the *Newcastle Weekly Chronicle*, 11 November 1871, p. 4 and p. 5, and the *Times*, 9 November 1871, p. 6 and p. 9; Dilke's speech at Leeds is reported in the *Leeds Mercury*, 24 November 1871, pp. 2–3.

59 For radical opposition to the expense of William IV's coronation ceremony, see the *Poor Man's Guardian*, 18 July 1831, p. 1.

60 The radical trades unionist James Aytoun recalled the dislike of Queen Adelaide made apparent during the Reform Crisis of the 1830s in his article in the *Bee-Hive*, 11 November 1871, pp. 1–2. Edmund Baines's role in leading the booing of the queen at meetings in 1832 was also recalled by the press following his patriotic outbursts against Dilke in 1871, see the *Bolton Evening News*, 27 November 1871, p. 3.

61 *People's Paper*, 4 October 1856, p. 4. Popular ballads of the Crimean War period also sought to discredit Prince Albert's peace mission to the Russians by suggesting that there was a conspiracy between the Coburgs and the Tsar to dismember

Turkey and convert it into a Russian protectorate. See on this theme the ballad 'Lovely Albert' in the Manchester Central Reference Library, Broadside Collection, vol. 5 [BR F 821 04 BA1], p. 296.

62   *Commonwealth*, 30 June 1866.

63   Charles Bradlaugh, 'The Impeachment of the House of Brunswick' (Pamphlet, London, 1871), p. 129.

64   Anna Clark, 'The Rhetoric of Chartist Domesticity: Gender, Language and Class in the 1830s and 1840s', *Journal of British Studies*, XXXI (1992), pp. 62–88, and *idem, The Struggle for the Breeches: Gender and the Making of the British Working-Class* (Los Angeles, 1995), pp. 220–32 and 248–63.

65   Thomas Wright, *Our New Masters* (London, 1873; reprinted 1969), p. 171.

66   The right of men to marry a deceased wife's sister had been a controversial one since the Reformation. Lord Lyndhurst's Act of 1835 made such marriages illegal with the result that the issue became a long-running public campaign in the nineteenth century. From the 1860s Lyndhurst's Act was regularly debated in Parliament until such marriages were finally legalized in 1907. The contemporary ramifications of this issue are discussed in Matthew Arnold, *Culture and Anarchy* (London, 1869; new edition, 1932), pp. 180–84.

67   *Newcastle Weekly Chronicle*, 4 March 1871, p. 4.

68   The controversy surrounding the republican riots in Bolton meant that the activities of the republican club there were closely monitored by the local press, which noted these aspects of female involvement in the movement in its reports. See the *Bolton Evening News*, 1 December 1871, p. 4, and 2 December 1872, p. 4.

69   There is an account of the formation of the London republican club in the *National Reformer*, 23 April 1871, p. 271.

70   The Eleusis Club, Chelsea was the site of a conference of metropolitan republicans in April 1871 reported in *Reynolds's Newspaper*, 30 April 1871. See Andrew Rothstein, *A House on Clerkenwell Green* (Marx Memorial Library, 1976; new edition, 1983), pp. 44–8, for the conversion of the Patriotic Club into a republican branch.

71   For the incipient republicanism of the Mile End and Sir Robert Peel branches of the Land and Labour League, see the *National Reformer*, 13 November 1870, p. 318.

72   *Bolton Evening News*, 7 November 1872, p. 3.

73   For Welsh republicanism, see R. Wallace, *Organize! Organize! Organize!: A Study of Reform Agitation in Wales 1840–1886* (Cardiff, 1991), and for the Teeside Republican Club, Malcolm Chase, '"Dangerous People?" The Teeside Irish in the Nineteenth Century', *North-East Labour History Bulletin*, XXVIII (1994), pp. 27–41.

74   *Republican Chronicle*, 1 April 1875, pp. 1–2.

75   *Ibid.*, p. 8.

76   *International Herald*, 10 August 1872.

77   Description in the *Times* quoted in the *Bradford Times*, 25 November 1871, p. 3.

78   These features of republican meetings were reinforced by the constant police scrutiny and harassment to which republican branches were subject. For an example of a police presence at a meeting of the Republican League in the Wellington Tavern, Brook Street, London, see *Reynolds's Newspaper*, 9 April 1871.

79   The decorations at the inaugural meeting of the London republican club are described in the *National Reformer*, 23 April 1871, p. 271. The design for Linton's republican banner is described in F. B. Smith, *Radical Artisan: William James Linton 1812–1897* (Manchester, 1973), p. 108, and its presence at the Sheffield conference of 1872 is noted in the *International Herald*, 30 November

1872, p. 3. For an example of a republican meeting ending with the singing of the 'Marseillaise' see a report of the Mile End branch of the Land and Labour League in the *National Reformer*, 29 May 1870, p. 349.

80 Wright, *Our New Masters*, p. 178.

81 These aspects of the martyrdom of William Scofield are reported in the *Bolton Evening News*, 5 December 1871, p. 3; 14 December 1871, p. 3, and 2 December 1872, p. 4. His funeral is reported in the *Bolton Journal*, 16 December 1871, p. 3, and there is further radical comment on the affair in the *International Herald*, 30 March 1872, p. 4, and 17 August 1872, p. 3.

82 George Odger, 'Odger's Monthly Pamphlets On Current Events No 1: Republicanism Versus Monarchy' (Pamphlet, London, 1872), p. 3.

83 For these aspects of the case, see the *Bolton Evening News*, 9 December 1871, p. 3.

84 I am grateful to the National Museum of Labour History, Manchester for sight of an election photograph of George Odger's by-election committee at Bristol in 1870 which contains this information.

85 Davidson, *Eminent Radicals*, pp. 31–3.

86 *Ibid.*, p. 50. There is a similar contemporary assessment of Joseph Cowen Jr's radicalism in *Biography and Review*, vol. 1 (1879), pp. 381–6. The link between phrenology and popular radicalism is explored in Roger Cooter, *Cultural Meanings of Popular Science: Phrenology and the Organization of Consent in Nineteenth Century Britain* (Cambridge, 1984).

87 Davidson, *Eminent Radicals*, p. 39.

88 James Epstein, *The Lion of Freedom: Feargus O'Connor and the Chartist Movement 1832–1842* (London, 1982), pp. 90–93 and 216–20.

89 The current scholarship in this field is summarized in John Belchem and James Epstein, 'The Nineteenth-Century Gentleman Leader Revisited', *Social History*, XXII (1997), pp. 174–95. For my own work on this theme see Antony Taylor, 'Modes of Political Expression and Working-Class Radicalism 1848–1874: The London and Manchester Examples' (Unpublished Ph.D. Thesis, University of Manchester, 1992), chaps 1–4.

90 For details of John de Morgan's career, see St Clair, *Sketch of the Life and Labours of John de Morgan*, pp. 1–2.

91 For these aspects of Dilke's career, see Gwynn and Tuckwell, *The Rt. Hon. Sir Charles Dilke*, vol. 1, pp. 94–168.

92 *Bolton Evening News*, 1 December 1871, p. 4.

93 George Odger's remarks at Bolton in *ibid.*, 27 November 1871, p. 3.

94 For a sense of Liberalism's move away from Whiggery's past associations with republicanism, see J. G. A. Pocock, *The Ancient Constitution and the Feudal Law: A Study of English Historical Thought in the Seventeenth Century* (Cambridge, 1957, revised 1987), especially pp. 229–51. This theme is developed in Jonathan Parry, *The Rise and Fall of Liberal Government in Britain* (New Haven and London, 1994), chaps 2–4.

95 The best account of the difficulties Palmerston experienced in working with Victoria remains Lytton Strachey, *Queen Victoria* (London, 1921), pp. 130–61.

96 Freda Harcourt, 'Gladstone, Monarchism and the "New Imperialism" 1868–1874', *Journal of Commonwealth and Imperial History*, XIV (1985), pp. 20–51 and Kuhn, *Democratic Royalism*, chap. 2.

97 *International Herald*, 27 July 1872, p. 5.

98 Bright's strongly worded defence of Victoria at a meeting at St James's Hall is reported in the *Bee-Hive*, 8 December 1866. His letter in reply to invitations to assume the position of President of the British republic is recorded in Robertson, *The Life and Times of John Bright*, p. 299. A fanciful list of appointments to an

imaginary Republican Provisional Government in the Charles Bradlaugh papers omits Bright's name altogether and lists Sir Charles Dilke as President, with Bradlaugh as 'Lord Chancellor and Keeper of the Nation's Conscience' and Edward Miall, rather incongruously, as President of the Board of Trade. See the Bradlaugh Papers, envelope 223, National Secular Society Archives, BI.

99 *People's Advocate*, 18 September 1875, p. 6.

100 Donald Woodruff, *The Tichborne Claimant: A Victorian Mystery* (London, 1957), pp. 392–3.

101 For example, *Reynolds's Newspaper*, 27 March 1887, p. 1 and the *Clarion*, 19 March 1892, p. 1.

3 'What Does She Do With It?': Radicalism, Republicanism and the 'Unrespectable' 1870–80

1 Kuhn, 'Queen Victoria's Civil List', pp. 645–65.

2 Robert Hough, *Victoria and Albert* (London, 1995), pp. 211–12.

3 The best account of the significance of wall-chalkings and anonymous placards remains Edward Thompson, 'The Crime of Anonymity' in *Albion's Fatal Tree: Crime and Society in Eighteenth Century England* by Douglas Hay, Peter Linebaugh, John G. Rule, Edward Thompson and Cal Winslow (London, 1975), pp. 255–308.

4 Patrick Joyce, *Work, Society and Politics: The Culture of the Factory in Later Victorian England* (London, 1980), pp. 292–301; Neville Kirk, *The Growth of Working-Class Reformism in Mid-Victorian England* (Brighton, 1985), chap. 7, and C. O'Leary, *The Elimination of Corrupt Practices in Elections 1868–1910* (Oxford, 1962).

5 Thompson, *Queen Victoria*, chaps 6 and 7.

6 David Cannadine, 'The Context, Performance and Meaning of Ritual: The British Monarchy and the Invention of Tradition' in *The Invention of Tradition*, eds Eric Hobsbawm and Terence Ranger (Cambridge, 1983), pp. 101–64 and Colley, *Britons*, pp. 195–228.

7 Quoted in Robert Woodall, 'Republicanism in Victorian Britain', *Historian*, XIII (1986), pp. 6–8.

8 John W. Burrow, *A Liberal Descent: Victorian Historians and the English Past* (Cambridge, 1981), pp. 167–8.

9 Royden Harrison, *Before the Socialists: Studies in Labour and Politics 1861–1881* (London, 1965), chap. 5.

10 W. E. Adams, *Memoirs of a Social Atom* (London, 1903), vol. II, pp. 229–30.

11 P. R. Williams, *The Contentious Crown: Public Discussion of the British Monarchy in the Reign of Queen Victoria* (Aldershot, 1997), chaps 1 and 2.

12 On the changing perceptions of 'Old Corruption' at mid-century, see Philip Harling and Peter Mandler, 'From Fiscal-Military State to Laissez-Faire State 1760–1850', *Journal of British Studies*, XXXII (1993), pp. 44–70, and Philip Harling, 'Rethinking "Old Corruption"', *Past and Present*, no. 147 (1995), pp. 127–58.

13 Complaints about his evident boredom and decision to leave an exhibition at the Royal Academy early appear in the Tory *Manchester Courier*, 22 May 1866, p. 3.

14 For example, the Liberal *Coventry Herald*, 1 December 1871, p. 5.

15 *Bee-Hive*, 9 Jan. 1864, p. 1.

16 For Victoria and Albert's borrowings from an invented Medieval past, see Munich, *Queen Victoria's Secrets*, pp. 23–54.

17 *Ibid.*, 16 Jan. 1864, p. 1.

18 *Bury Times*, 30 June 1866, p. 4.

19 Ernest Kantorowicz, *The King's Two Bodies: A Study in Medieval Political Theology* (Princeton, 1957), chap. 4.

20 Thomas Milton Kemnitz, 'Matt Morgan of "Tomahawk" and English Cartooning 1867–70', *Victorian Studies*, XIX (1975), pp. 17–22.

21 *People's Paper*, 8 November 1856, p. 1.

22 *Ibid.*, 29 November 1856, p. 1.

23 For the Conservative roots of Gladstone's thinking on the constitution, see Peter Clarke, *A Question of Leadership: Gladstone to Thatcher* (London, 1991), pp. 11–41.

24 This episode generated numerous radical pamphlets and squibs critical of monarchy and royal princes. See P. A. Taylor, 'The Dowry for the Princess Louise: Speech of Mr. P. A. Taylor MP in the House of Commons' (Pamphlet, London, 1871), especially pp. 2–10; Anon., 'A Parallel Case by a Penitent Whig' (Pamphlet, London, 1871), pp. 1–16 and W. L. Sargant, 'The Princess and Her Dowry' in *idem*, *Essays of a Birmingham Manufacturer* (London, 1871), vol. III, pp. 167–94. The Regency tradition of disrespectful alphabet books and children's rhymes was also revived. One example that coupled together Princess Louise and the hated anti-reformer Robert Lowe, who had publicly defended the union, read 'L for Louise and her money making beau, and for the matchless prince of matches, Old Bob Lowe'; see H. C. G. Matthew, ed., *The Gladstone Diaries* (Oxford, 1982), vol. VIII, p. 60.

25 Hall, *Scandal, Sensation and Social Democracy*, pp. 130–39.

26 In Britain Spanish republicanism was frequently referred to in both hostile and positive terms during the 1868 election which was fought on the merits of the expanded franchise arrangements of 1867; see, for example, the *Manchester Guardian*, 5 October 1868, p. 5.

27 David Tribe, *President Charles Bradlaugh MP* (London, 1971), pp. 146–8; Charles Bradlaugh, 'Through the Carlist Lines' in *Our Corner*, 1 June 1883, pp. 350–53, and H. S. Salt, *The Life of James Thomson* (London, 1889), pp. 98–103.

28 Charles Gavan Duffy, *My Life in Two Hemispheres* (London, 1897), vol. II, pp. 327–9. Also see Mark McKenna, *The Captive Republic: A History of Republicanism in Australia 1788–1996* (Melbourne, 1996), chap. 6.

29 For example, the *Bradford Observer*, 5 December 1871, p. 2.

30 For anti-German sentiment and opposition to royalty, see Antony Taylor, 'Republicanism Reappraised: Anti-Monarchism and the English Radical Tradition 1850–1872', in *Re-Reading the Constitution: New Narratives in the Political History of England's Long Nineteenth Century*, ed. James Vernon (Cambridge, 1996), pp. 154–78.

31 The popular view of 'republicanism' continued to be influenced by the poor public reputation of the Third Republic; see the defence of the Third Republic in P. Nord, *The Republican Moment: Struggles for Democracy in Nineteenth Century France* (Cambridge, Mass., 1995), pp. 245–54.

32 J. V., 'Is Monarchy an Anachronism?', *Fraser's Magazine*, XII (1875), pp. 411–36.

33 This tradition continued in the invasion-panic literature of the early 1880s inspired by plans to build a Channel Tunnel; this used lurid depictions of Communards and fantasized about a Commune-style event taking place in London; see J. Drew Gay, *How John Bull Lost London, or The Channel Tunnel* (London, 1882).

34 S. C. Hall, *The Trial of Sir Jasper: A Temperance Tale in Verse* (London, 1872), p. 7.

35 Finn, *After Chartism, passim.*

36 *Manchester Examiner and Times,* 10 April 1871, p. 4.

37 Kali Israel, 'French Vices and British Liberties: Gender, Class and Narrative Competition in a Late Victorian Sex Scandal', *Social History,* XXII (1997), pp. 1–26.

38 For example, Charles W. Dilke, *Problems of Greater Britain* (London, 1890), vol. I, p. 185.

39 Nord, *The Republican Moment,* chap. 8.

40 Charles Booth, *Life and Labour of the People in London: Poverty* (London, 1902), vol. I, p. 99.

41 The *Times* quoted in the *Bradford Observer,* 25 November 1871, p. 3.

42 Disillusioned in later life, Stead, who had seen the anti-monarchist rhetoric of the 1870s wither and die in the 1880s, became a staunch royalist. See Stead, *Studies of the Sovereign and the Reign,* p. 10 and p. 23.

43 David Nicholls, *The Lost Prime Minister: A Life of Sir Charles Dilke* (London, 1995), pp. 55–6.

44 *National Reformer,* 31 March 1872, p. 198. Radical sympathizers made verbal word-play of Fawcett's blindness in this debate. J. Morrison Davidson wrote: 'Who can ever forget the evening when the blind member was the only representative of the people who *saw* his way into the lobby where Sir Charles Dilke and P. A. Taylor were tellers against the dowry to the Princess Louise?'; see the sketch of Fawcett in Davidson, *Eminent Radicals,* p. 80. The acrimonious exchanges about the Civil List seriously undermined Fawcett's position as MP for Hackney; see Lawrence Goldman, ed., *The Blind Victorian: Henry Fawcett and Victorian Liberalism* (Cambridge, 1989), pp. 1–38.

45 *Birmingham Daily Post,* 7 December 1871, p. 5. The House of Lords and the aristocracy were also much debated at club level; see the deliberations of the Norwich and Birmingham Republican Clubs in the *National Reformer,* 10 December 1871, p. 375 and 378.

46 T. A. Jenkins, *Parliament, Party and Politics in Victorian England* (Manchester, 1997), p. 12.

47 Charles W. Dilke, 'The House of Lords' in *Speeches by Sir Charles Dilke, March 1871–March 1872* (London, 1872), pp. 70–78.

48 Angus Mclaren, *Birth Control in Nineteenth Century England* (London, 1978), pp. 174–6.

49 *Truth Seeker,* 1 April 1895, pp. 1–3.

50 Robert Allen, 'The Battle for the Common: Politics and Populism in Mid-Victorian Kentish London', *Social History,* XXII (1997), pp. 61–77.

51 Philip Guedalla, *The Queen and Mr Gladstone* (London, 1933), vol. II, p. 182.

52 *Newcastle Weekly Chronicle,* 29 July 1871, p. 4, and the *National Reformer,* 12 June 1887, pp. 379–80. Public access campaigners feared moves to develop the Crown Estates further and warned balefully of precedents on this issue under the Stuarts who had threatened to fence off Hyde Park for private use: 'There was once a Queen of England who asked her Lord Chamberlain what it would cost to enclose Hyde and St James's Parks, and preserve them for the private use of the royal family. The Lord Chamberlain is said to have replied that it would be rather expensive, for it would certainly cost two Crowns'; Taylor, *The Dowry of the Princess Louise,* p. 7. There is a version of the same story in *Reynolds's Newspaper,* 4 September 1881, p. 4. The monarch involved is usually identified as Charles I acting at the instigation of his wife, Henrietta Maria.

53 The Duke of Connaught, for example, was a ranger of Epping Forest; see the *Times,* 24 March 1882, p. 12.

54 Correspondence from a Cornish tin-miner, John Clapham, complaining about the Prince of Wales' dual income from both the Duchy of Cornwall and the Civil List in *Reynolds's Newspaper*, 20 March 1870, p. 1.

55 Antony Taylor, '"Commons-Eaters", "Land-Grabbers" and "Jerry-Builders": Space, Popular Radicalism and the Politics of Public Access in London 1848–1880', *International Review of Social History*, XL (1995), pp. 383–407, and Owen R. Ashton, *W. E. Adams: Chartist, Radical and Journalist 1832–1906* (Whitley Bay, 1990), chaps 4 and 5. For the Agricultural Labourers' Union campaign against enclosures by the Duchy of Cornwall in Somerset, see the *English Labourers' Chronicle*, 26 January 1878, p. 2.

56 R. Thorold Rogers, 'Report of a Public Meeting Held at the Exeter Hall, London, 18 March 1873' (Pamphlet, London, 1873), and Daniel Chatterton, 'Chatterton's Letter to the Prince of Wales and All Other Aristocratic and Royal Paupers' (Pamphlet, London, 1882), pp. 2–6.

57 Laurence M. Geary, 'O'Connorite Bedlam: Feargus and His Grand Nephew Arthur', *Medical History*, XXXIV (1990), pp. 125–43 and for contemporary accounts of the assassination attempt the *Manchester Examiner and Times*, 1 March 1872, p. 5, and 2 March 1872, p. 5. Further death threats were made against the queen by Edward Bryne Madden in December 1878. Most of Queen Victoria's eight potential assassins were in some way inspired by radical politics, or on occasion by erotic longings; see F. B. Smith, 'Lights and Shadows in the Life of John Freeman', *Victorian Studies*, XXX (1987), pp. 459–75, and Trevor Turner, 'Erotomania and Queen Victoria: Or Love Among the Assassins', *Psychiatric Bulletin*, XIV (1990), pp. 224–7. For examples of battles fought over the memories and corpse of the Chartist movement in the radical press of the 1870s, see the *Republican*, 1 June 1871, pp. 1–2, and 1 July 1871, p. 3.

58 There is an exploration of this theme with reference to the life of Joseph Rayner Stephens in Michael S. Edwards, *Purge This Realm: A Life of Joseph Rayner Stephens* (London, 1994), chaps 7 and 9.

59 This point is made strongly in David Nicholls, 'The New Liberalism – After Chartism?', *Social History*, XXI (1996), pp. 330–42. Significantly, the campaign against the Crown of 1870–71 is omitted altogether from the discussion of popular Liberalism as a broad church in Parry, *The Rise and Fall of Liberal Government*, chap. 10.

60 John Belchem, *Popular Radicalism in Nineteenth-Century Britain* (London, 1996), chap. 6.

61 *Manchester Courier*, 5 July 1872, p. 5 and p. 7.

62 The Liberal press in Birmingham used the opportunity afforded by the royal visit to correct prevailing impressions of the city as a 'republican town'; see the *Birmingham Daily Post*, 4 November 1874, pp. 4–5 and p. 8, and 6 November 1874, p. 4.

63 Chamberlain's 'republicanism' is explored in Peter Marsh, *Joseph Chamberlain: Entrepreneur in Politics* (Yale, 1994), pp. 60–61 and 87–8. For an exploration of his actions at the time of the visit of the Prince of Wales to Birmingham in November 1874, see Davidson, *Eminent Radicals*, pp. 88–9.

64 Richard Whiteing, *My Harvest* (London, 1915), p. 126.

65 For the controversy surrounding Victoria's refusal to open the Town Hall and the erection of the Cromwell statue in Manchester, see W. E. A. Axon, 'The Mayor of Manchester and His Slanderers' (Pamphlet, Manchester, 1877), pp. 3-12; 'The Life of Oliver Cromwell' (Pamphlet, Manchester, 1875), p. 14; the *Manchester Examiner and Times*, 2 December 1875, pp. 4-5, and the *Freelance*, 10 December 1875, pp. 393-4. Not until the visit of George V to

Manchester in July 1934 did any reigning monarch actually see the statue. Popular memory has it that it was always kept draped when a member of the royal family visited the city. In the 1940s it was exiled to Wythenshaw Park after allegedly becoming an impediment to traffic. Other variations on the story suggest that Victoria disliked Manchester Council's actions in making Garibaldi a freeman of the city in 1864.

66 Gary S. Messinger, *Manchester in the Victorian Age: The Half-Known City* (Manchester, 1985), pp. 154-5. Similar stories were current about Huntingdon, the birthplace of Oliver Cromwell, and Newcastle the site of Dilke's 'Cost of the Crown Speech' and the power-base for the noted republican Joseph Cowen Jr. It was commonly believed that Victoria would draw the blinds of her railway carriage when passing through Newcastle so as not to set eyes on the city. For republicans such snubs were badges of local pride; see Todd, *The Militant Democracy*, chap. 7.

67 Roy Jenkins, *Sir Charles Dilke* (London, 1958), pp. 83-4.

68 Chatterton, *Chatterton's Letter to the Prince of Wales*, p. 6.

69 This point has been reiterated in Nicholls, *The Lost Prime Minister*, chap. 4.

70 Joseph Cowen, 'Speeches on Public Questions and Political Policy Delivered by Joseph Cowen MP' (Pamphlet, Newcastle, 1874), pp. 77-8 and Anon., 'Mr. Cowen MP: Apostle or Apostate?' (Pamphlet, Newcastle, 1880), pp. 3-48.

71 Goldman, ed., *The Blind Victorian*, pp. 1-38.

72 Lawrence Goldman, *Dons and Workers: Oxford and Adult Education Since 1850* (Oxford, 1995), p. 109.

73 J. C. Cox, 'The Marriage of the Duke of Edinburgh: The Cost of the Royal Household, Royal Annuities and Crown Lands' (Pamphlet, London, 1873), p. 5.

74 Elizabeth Wallace, *Goldwin Smith, Victorian Liberal* (Toronto, 1957), pp. 150-55.

75 John Lawrence and Miles Taylor, eds, *Party, State and Society: Electoral Behaviour in Modern Britain* (Aldershot, 1996), introduction.

76 For the events at Derby, see Joseph Howe, *Twenty-Five Years' Fight with the Tories* (Leeds, 1907), pp. 3-7.

77 Silvester St Clair, 'Sketch of the Life and Labours of John de Morgan' (Pamphlet, Leeds, 1880), p. 6.

78 *Republican*, 1 February 1883, pp. 465-6.

79 *Newcastle Weekly Chronicle*, 9 November 1871, p. 4. Murphy's death and the campaign surrounding it is described in Donald MacRaild, 'William Murphy, the Orange Order and "Communal Violence": The Irish in West Cumberland 1871-1884' in *Racial Violence in Britain in the Nineteenth and Twentieth Centuries*, ed. Panikos Panayi (Leicester, 1993; reprinted 1996), pp. 44-64.

80 *Dart*, 25 October 1879, p. 7.

81 *Bolton Guardian*, 16 December 1871, p. 3 and p. 8, and 30 December 1871, p. 7. There is a file on the riot at Bolton in the Home Office Disturbance Books at the Public Record Office (HO 45/9296/9391).

82 *Bolton Guardian*, 23 December 1871, p. 8.

83 *Derby Mercury*, 6 December 1871, p. 8, and 15 January 1873, p. 2.

84 Henry Jephson, *The Platform: Its Rise and Progress* (London, 1892), vol. II, chaps 20 and 21.

85 *Reynolds's Newspaper*, 25 February 1900, p. 2 and p. 4.

86 McWilliam, *Popular Politics in Nineteenth-Century England*, pp. 69-70.

87 For example, the *Yorkshire Factory Times*, 15 January 1904, p. 4.

88 Andrew Carnegie, *Triumphant Democracy or Fifty Years' March of the Republic* (London, 1886), p. 240.

89   Kevin Gilmartin, *Print-Politics: The Press and Radical Opposition in Early Nineteenth Century England* (Cambridge, 1992), pp. 91–2.

90   Sir Charles Dilke's speech at Leeds in November 1871 in the *Newcastle Weekly Chronicle*, 2 December 1871, p. 4.

91   *Times*, 6 February 1872, p. 5. Again the comparison with France is an important one here. There the national treasures and paintings of France had passed into public hands after the revolution. Their public ownership by the state and its citizenry was reaffirmed in 1848.

92   Eric de Maré, *The London Doré Saw* (London, 1973), pp. 22–3.

93   Peter Mandler, *The Rise and Fall of the Stately Home* (London, 1997), pp. 101–3.

94   For the role of ruins and romantic castles in contemporary narratives of the national past, see Anne Janowitz, *England's Ruins: Poetic Purpose and the National Landscape* (Oxford, 1990), chaps 2 and 3. The implied link with contemporary republicanism is very strong in the report of the burning of Warwick Castle in the *Derby Mercury*, 6 December 1871, p. 3 and p. 6.

95   For example, the *Manchester Guardian*, 5 December 1871, p. 8.

96   *Coventry Herald*, 8 December 1871, p. 4.

97   *Derby Mercury*, 29 November 1871, p. 5. For the cult of Derby loyalism more generally, see J. Johnstone, *Memories of the Rebellion of 1745 and 1746* (Derby, 1820).

98   The republican debates at Preston are described in the *National Reformer*, 9 June 1872, p. 362. English radicalism had an ambivalent relationship with the 1745 Jacobite rising. In areas like Lancashire and Derbyshire, where there were vivid memories of the events of 1745–6, the progress of the Jacobite rebels through the north of England was recalled with fondness and was occasionally cited as a precedent for marches and demonstrations against the government of the day. In 1817 the Manchester 'Blanketeers' consciously followed the Jacobite line of march via Ashbourne and Derby; see Daniel Szechi, 'The Jacobite Theatre of Death' in *The Jacobite Challenge*, eds Eveline Cruikshanks and Jeremy Black (Edinburgh, 1988), pp. 66–70.

99   *Manchester Guardian*, 7 December 1871, p. 5.

100 *Bolton Guardian*, 16 December 1871, p. 8. Orangemen were also very visible in an attack on a Liberation Society meeting at Bacup in 1872; see the *Manchester Examiner and Times*, 11 March 1872, p. 7.

101 *Bolton Guardian*, 23 March 1872, p. 2.

102 Broadside F1868/6, MCRL, Local History Broadside Collection. For a display of traditional Protestant monarchism during a visit by Queen Victoria to Manchester, see the *Protestant Witness and Watchman*, 4 October 1851, pp. 638–9.

103 Kuhn, *Democratic Royalism*, chap. 3.

104 G. Howell – Goldwin Smith, 12 December 1873, HC, BI.

105 *Reynolds's Newspaper*, 21 July 1889, p. 3.

106 The interview was noticed and discussed by some of the regional newspapers; see the *Birmingham Daily Post*, 21 November 1871, p. 6. The trades unionist George Potter was also named as a 'republican' by Karl Marx.

107 Stead, *Studies of the Sovereign and the Reign*, pp. 19–20.

108 Anne Janowitz, 'William Morris and the Dialectic of Romanticism' in *Cultural Politics at the Fin de Siècle*, eds Sally Ledger and Scott McCracken (Cambridge, 1995), pp. 160–85.

109 On disillusionment with American republicanism, see Smith, *Radical Artisan: William James Linton 1812–1897*, chaps 7 and 8; Gregory Claeys, 'The Example of America a Warning to England? The Transformation of America in British Radicalism and Socialism 1790–1850' in *Living and Learning: Essays in Honour*

of *J. F. C. Harrison*, eds Malcolm Chase and Ian Dyck (Aldershot, 1996), chap. 6, and McKenna, *The Captive Republic*, pp. 203–4.

110 H. C. G. Matthew, *Gladstone 1809–1874* (Oxford, 1986), pp. 186–8; M. M. Robson, 'The "*Alabama* Claims" and Anglo-American Reconciliation', *Canadian Historical Review*, XLII (1961), especially pp. 8–9; A. Denholm, *Lord Ripon 1827–1909* (London, 1982), pp. 94–8, and the *National Reformer*, 2 June 1872, p. 343.

111 James Finlen, 'A Warning and an Example! Dedicated to the Dynasties of Christendom: Maximilian, His Life and Death' (Pamphlet, London, 1867), p. 15.

112 Adulation for Switzerland was in a long tradition. The romantic poets and the Chartists traditionally admired Switzerland as a classic example of a 'Paineite decentralized democracy'; see Iorwerth Prothero, *Radical Artisans in England and France 1830–1870* (Cambridge, 1997), p. 313.

4 The Crown, the Radical Press and the Popular Anti-jubilee 1876–98

1 Denis Judd, 'Diamonds Are Forever? Kipling's Imperialism', *History Today*, LXVII (1997), pp. 37–43, and C. Carrington, *Rudyard Kipling: His Life and Works* (London, 1986).

2 Denis Judd, *Empire: The British Imperial Experience from 1765 to the Present* (London, 1997), chap. 3, and Asa Briggs, ed., *Fins de Siècle: How Centuries End* (London, 1997), introduction and chap. 1.

3 *Halifax Guardian*, 26 June 1897, p. 3.

4 This point is made in Benjamin Wilson, *Struggles of an Old Chartist* (Halifax, 1887); re-printed in David Vincent, ed., *Testaments of Radicalism: Memoirs of Working-Class Politicians* (London, 1977), pp. 195–242.

5 For the life of John West and his later decline, see Rushton, *My Life as Farmer's Boy*, pp. 68–9, and his obituary in the *Times*, 24 January 1887, p. 10. There is an appreciation of West by former radical veterans in the *Macclesfield Courier and Herald*, 22 January 1887, p. 5. Also see John Earles, *Streets and Houses of Old Macclesfield* (Leeds, 1915), pp. 117–18.

6 For a commentary on the fringe nature of 'republican' thinking in the British radical tradition, see Belchem, 'Republicanism, Constitutionalism and the Radical Platform in Early Nineteenth Century England', pp. 1–32.

7 The classic statement of this view is Keith Laybourn and John Reynolds, *Liberalism and the Rise of Labour 1890–1918* (London, 1984), pp. 1–94.

8 David Howell, *British Workers and the Independent Labour Party 1888–1906* (Manchester, 1983), pp. 363–88.

9 This view has received consideration in Jon Lawrence, 'Popular Radicalism and the Socialist Revival in Britain', *Journal of British Studies*, XXXI (1992), pp. 163–86, and Mark Bevir, 'The British Social Democratic Federation 1880–1885: From O'Brienism to Marxism', *International Review of Social History*, XXXVII (1992), pp. 207–29.

10 Elaine Showalter, *Sexual Anarchy: Gender and Culture at the Fin de Siècle* (London, 1990), chap. 9, and Philip Hoare, *Wilde's Last Stand: Decadence, Conspiracy and the First World War* (London, 1997). The last true political expression of opposition to 'Old Corruption' may well have been the public revelations surrounding the Duke of Cambridge's mismanagement of the armed forces that was commonly seen as contributing to the poor performance of the British army in the Boer War; see G. R. Searle, *The Quest for National Efficiency: A Study in British Politics and Political Thought 1899–1914* (London, 1971; new edition, 1990), pp. 45–6.

11 The Scottish radical John McAdam wrote to Joseph Cowen in 1871 of 'the load which will be kicked off whenever the queen dies'. See Janet Fyfe, ed., *Autobiography of John McAdam 1806–1883* (Edinburgh, 1980), p. 179.

12 Max Nordau, *Conventional Lies of Our Civilization* (London, 1895), chap. 3.

13 They were very evident, for example, at the time of Edward's alleged involvement with Lady Mordaunt in 1869, which recalled the similar infidelities of the Prince Regent fifty years before, and generated a wave of popular semi-pornographic works that traded heavily in such comparisons. See S. D. Beeton, A. A. Dowty and S. R. Emerson, 'The Coming K... A Set of Idyll Lays', *Beeton's Christmas Annual* (London, 1872). This used heavy-handed sexual innuendo to satirize Tennyson's fawning 'Idylls of the King' that compared Edward's imminent accession to the throne to the return of King Arthur.

14 *Reynolds's Newspaper*, 7 June 1891, p. 1.

15 The most recent analysis of Edward's public role attempts to rehabilitate him on these issues and others; see Simon Heffer, *Power and Place: The Political Consequences of King Edward VII* (London, 1998).

16 On radical populism, see Baer, *Theatre and Disorder in Late Georgian London*, pp. 189–221, and McCalman, *Radical Underworld*, pp. 101–3 and 170–73.

17 *Gauntlet*, 13 October 1833, pp. 570–71. Also see for inverted images of royal poverty, *Punch* (1846), vol. X, p. 89.

18 The background to Victoria's assumption of the title of Empress of India is discussed in D. Washbrook, 'After the Mutiny: From Queen to Queen Empress', *History Today*, XVII (1997), pp. 10–15.

19 For example, Napoleon III is described as 'the personal friend of the Queen of England, the ally of the Crimean War, the free-trader, the special constable who beat the Chartists' in General Gustave-Paul Cluseret, 'My Connection with Fenianism', *Fraser's Magazine*, vol. VI (1872), pp. 31–46.

20 Joseph Cowen, *Speech on the Royal Titles Bill* (Pamphlet, Newcastle, 1876), pp. 3–10; the *Newcastle Weekly Chronicle*, 24 June and 5 August 1871, and Stead, *Studies of the Sovereign and the Reign*, pp. 10–11. The Palace responded to this criticism by dissuading the Prince of Wales from attending Napoleon III's funeral in January 1873.

21 *Newcastle Weekly Chronicle*, 1 April 1876, p. 5.

22 *Ibid.*, 8 April 1876, p. 4.

23 *Justice*, 14 June 1884, p. 4; there is a reference to Henry Vane as a model for nineteenth-century republicans in Morrison Davidson, *New Book of Kings*, pp. 3–4.

24 Cromwellianism still strongly defined G. M. W. Reynolds's political stance in the 1850s; see *Reynolds's Political Instructor*, 20 April 1850, p. 189. Also see on this subject Charles Bradlaugh, *Cromwell and Washington: A Contrast* (Pamphlet, London, 1883 edition), pp. 15, 16, and 19–20.

25 Correspondence signed 'Oliver Cromwell' in the *Radical*, 1 January 1881, p. 7; there are references to the Cromwell club at Plaistow in *Justice*, 21 June 1884, p. 7, and to a London-based Cromwell republican club in the *National Reformer*, 9 January 1881, p. 29. In 1881, *Reynolds's Newspaper* featured a sympathetic obituary of Dean Stanley of Westminster Abbey that praised his attempts to erect a monument in the abbey precincts to commemorate Cromwell's death; see *Reynolds's Newspaper*, 24 July 1881, p. 4. The continuing relevance of Cromwellianism for radicals in the 1880s is explored in Carolyn Steedman, *The Radical Soldier's Tale: John Pearman 1819–1908* (London, 1988), pp. 86–103.

26 *English Labourers' Chronicle*, 29 June 1878, p. 2.

27 *Radical*, 5 February 1881, p. 4.

28 For the continuing significance of *Reynolds's Newspaper* to a new generation of
    radicals at mid-century, see Virginia Berridge, 'Popular Sunday Papers and
    Mid-Victorian Society', in *Newspaper History from the Seventeenth Century to the
    Present Day*, ed. George Boyce, James Curran and Pauline Wingate (London,
    1978), pp. 252–64, and Louis James and John Saville, 'G. M. W. Reynolds', in
    Dictionary of Labour Biography, eds John Saville and Joyce Bellamy (London,
    1976), vol. III, pp. 146–51. The best recent study of G. M. W. Reynolds is Rohan
    McWilliam, 'The Mysteries of G. M. W. Reynolds: Radicalism and Melodrama
    in Victorian Britain', in *Living and Learning: Essays in Honour of J. F. C.
    Harrison*, eds Malcolm Chase and Ian Dyck (Aldershot, 1996), chap. 13.

29 This aspect of *Reynolds's* is overlooked in recent work that seeks to claim the
    paper for popular Liberalism; see Biagini, *Liberty, Retrenchment and Reform*,
    chaps 1–5.

30 This claim was made in *Reynolds's Newspaper*, 10 April 1864, p. 5.

31 *People's Advocate*, 17 July 1875, p. 6.

32 The 'republican' aspect of *Reynolds's Newspaper* is explored in Anne
    Humphreys, 'G. M. W. Reynolds, Popular Literature and Popular Politics',
    Victorian Periodicals Review, XVI (1983), pp. 78–89.

33 E. Reitan, 'The Civil List in Eighteenth Century British Politics', *Historical
    Journal*, IX (1966), pp. 318–37.

34 Kuhn, 'Queen Victoria's Civil List', pp. 645–65.

35 The standard radical compilation of Civil List recipients is John Wade, *The
    Black Book or Corruption Unmasked* (London, 1820), especially pp. 110–41, but
    also see Richard Carlile's *Gauntlet*, 29 December 1833, pp. 739–42.

36 *National Reformer*, 9 April 1876, p. 225. Sir Charles Dilke made the point at a
    meeting in Chelsea that his remarks were part of radical orthodoxy and 'he had
    said nothing stronger than was said by Lord Brougham in 1850'; see the
    Manchester Guardian, 24 November 1871, p. 3.

37 *English Labourers' Chronicle*, 17 August 1878, p. 7.

38 See his speech at Dundee in *Reynolds's Newspaper*, 14 September 1890, p. 1.

39 *Ibid.*, 30 April 1882, p. 1.

40 In the 1860s the entire length of the track outside Balmoral was patrolled by men
    on foot before the royal train was allowed to pass. See R. W. Clark, *Balmoral:
    Queen Victoria's Highland Home* (London, 1981), p. 83.

41 A vigorous campaign was waged against the royal yacht in the *Newcastle Weekly
    Chronicle*; see the *Newcastle Weekly Chronicle*, 21 August 1875, p. 8; 4 September
    1875, p. 4, and 15 April 1876, p. 4. There are also attacks on the royal yacht in
    Reynolds's Newspaper, 31 May 1882, p. 5.

42 *Newcastle Weekly Chronicle*, 15 April 1876, p. 4.

43 Joyce, *Visions of the People*, chaps 2 and 3.

44 For example, the *Northern Star*, 3 September 1842, p. 7, and 1 July 1843, p. 5.

45 For example, the *People's Advocate*, 19 June 1875, p. 1; *Reynolds's Newspaper*,
    11 March 1888, p. 2, and 28 September 1890, p. 3, and the *Radical Leader*, 1
    September 1888, p. 3.

46 *Reynolds's Newspaper*, 7 May 1882, p. 8.

47 *Ibid.*, 3 April 1881, p. 3.

48 *Radical*, 5 February 1881, p. 2. Similar attacks were made on the illegitimate
    parentage of the Duke of St Albans by Richard Carlile in the *Gauntlet*,
    13 October 1833, pp. 570–71.

49 Rohan McWilliam, 'The Tichborne Claimant and the People: Investigations
    into Popular Culture' (Unpublished D.Phil. thesis, University of Sussex, 1990),
    pp. 85–100.

50 *Reynolds's Newspaper*, 11 August 1881, p. 2. These charges are repeated in the *Radical*, 8 January 1881, p. 6.

51 *Newcastle Weekly Chronicle*, 1 April 1876, p. 1. Similar sentiments were expressed in *Reynolds's Newspaper*, 12 March 1876, pp. 4–5, and 7 May 1876, p. 1.

52 A. S. Wohl, '"Dizzy-Ben-Dizzy": Disraeli as Alien', *Journal of British Studies*, XXXIV (1995), pp. 375–95.

53 *Reynolds's Newspaper*, 6 June 1897, p. 1.

54 For example, the *Radical Leader*, 11 Aug. 1888, p. 7. The eighteenth-century origins of opposition to the Scottish element at court are discussed in Colley, *Britons*, pp. 195–228.

55 Quoted in *Reynolds's Newspaper*, 19 June 1887, p. 4.

56 *Ibid.*, 14 September 1890, p. 1.

57 *Ibid.*, 30 April 1882, p. 4.

58 *Ibid.*, 26 June 1887, p. 4.

59 *Ibid.*, 27 March 1881, p. 5.

60 Morrison Davidson, *The New Book of Kings*, p. 7.

61 *Liberty*, 28 April 1883, p. 6. Similar charges against Dilke were made in the *Radical*, 18 December 1880, p. 6.

62 *Reynolds's Newspaper*, 27 February 1887, p. 1, and 6 March 1881, p. 2, and 27 November 1887, p. 2.

63 George Lansbury, *My Life* (London, 1928), pp. 140–41.

64 Coral Lansbury, *The Old Brown Dog: Women Workers and Vivisection in Edwardian England* (New York, 1985), chaps 3 and 4.

65 This attack upon the royal passion for hunting coincided with increasing sympathy for the plight of animals prompted by the work of Thomas Martin, Richard Erskine, and the founders of the RSPCA. See on this point Brian Harrison, 'Animals and the State in Nineteenth Century England' in his *Peaceable Kingdom: Stability and Change in Modern Britain* (Oxford, 1982), pp. 82–122.

66 *Reynolds's Newspaper*, 5 March 1876, p. 5.

67 Quoted in the sketch of E. A. Freeman in Morrison Davidson, *Eminent Radicals*, p. 259.

68 *Liberty*, 5 May 1883, p. 5.

69 Hilda Kean, *Animal Rights: Political and Social Change in Britain since 1800* (London, 1998), pp. 156–7.

70 Attacks on 'Hunnish sports and fashions' at court in Henry Salt, *Seventy Years Among Savages* (London, 1921), pp. 152–3. There is also an attack on foreign monarchs who brought their hunting retinues with them on visits to Britain in *Reynolds's Newspaper*, 5 March 1882, p. 5.

71 *Clarion*, 26 December 1891, p. 1. Sir Charles Dilke also drew attention to the cruelty of the Hurlingham meets in the 1870s. See his 'Cost of the Crown' speech at Newcastle in the *Newcastle Weekly Chronicle*, 2 December 1871, p. 4.

72 For example, a column on shooting accidents in the *Clarion*, 2 January 1892, p. 1.

73 Williams, 'Public Discussion of the British Monarchy', chap. 1, and Thomas Richards, 'The Image of Victoria in the Year of Jubilee' in his *The Commodity Culture of Victorian England: Advertising and Spectacle 1851–1914* (London, 1991), pp. 73–118.

74 For example, Colley, 'The Apotheosis of George III', pp. 114–29.

75 R. B. Haldane, 'Is a National Party Possible?' *Fortnightly Review*, XLII (1887), pp. 317–28 and G. R. Searle, *Country Before Party: Coalition and the Idea of 'National Government' in Modern Britain 1885–1987* (London, 1995), chap. 3.

76   For derision of the Duke of Cambridge's visit to Stockton in 1842, see the *Northern Star*, 3 September 1842, p. 7, and for attacks on Victoria's visit to Glasgow in 1847 *ibid.*, 21 August 1847, p. 3.

77   *McDouall's Chartist and Republican Journal*, 3 April 1841, pp. 6–7.

78   *Northern Star*, 27 June 1840, p. 1.

79   *English Chartist Circular*, vol. II (1843), p. 371.

80   Freda Harcourt, 'The Queen, the Sultan and the Viceroy: A Victorian State Occasion', *London Journal*, V (1979), pp. 35–56.

81   Sarah A. Tooley, *The Personal Life of Queen Victoria* (London, 1897), pp. 244–5.

82   The origins of traditional Protestant ceremonial and their relationship to the public personage of the monarch are outlined in Cressy, *Bonfires and Bells*, *passim*.

83   For example, the imaginative recreation of Medieval Manchester described in Alfred Darbyshire and George Milner, *A Booke of Olde Manchester and Salford* (Manchester, 1887), pp. 13–17 and p. 133.

84   Alan Kidd, 'Between Antiquary and Academic: Local History in the Nineteenth Century', *Local Historian*, XXVI (1996), pp. 3–14.

85   Edwin Rainbow, ed., *City of Coventry: Official Account of the Celebration of the Queen's Diamond Jubilee* (City of Coventry, 1898), pp. 58–71.

86   Stanley Weintraub, *Victoria: Biography of a Queen* (London, 1987; re-printed 1997), pp. 22–3.

87   John Davis has disputed the radicalism of the Parliamentary Debating format in Working-Men's Clubs and Local Parliaments of the 1880s. Nevertheless, even those clubs that passed motions of support for the throne debated the case for a reduction in the expense of royalty; see John W. Davis, 'Working-Class Make-Believe: The South Lambeth Parliament 1887–1890', *Parliamentary History*, XII (1993), pp. 249–58.

88   For an explanation of the absence of widespread formal celebrations in 1888–9, see Schwoerer, 'Celebrating the Glorious Revolution', pp. 8–12.

89   *Reynolds's Newspaper*, 24 July 1898, p. 8. For the background to the event see *ibid.*, 17 July 1898, p. 2, and 31 July 1898, p. 4.

90   Sydney was a favourite hero of the Chartists; see Karsten, *Patriot-Heroes in England and America*, pp. 129–30.

91   *Reynolds's Newspaper*, 13 November 1887, p. 4.

92   *Ibid.*, 27 June 1897, p. 2.

93   *Ibid.*, 13 June 1897, p. 1.

94   *Ibid.*, 13 November 1887, p. 4.

95   Peter Mandler, *Aristocratic Government in the Age of Reform: Whigs and Liberals 1830–1852* (Oxford, 1990).

96   *Reynolds's Newspaper*, 7 August 1881, p. 2, and 28 September 1890, p. 3.

97   Wade, *The Black Book*, p. 110.

98   *Reynolds's Newspaper*, 27 June 1897, p. 1.

99   John Mackinnon Robertson, 'The Lesson of the Jubilee' in the *National Reformer*, 10 July 1887, pp. 21–2.

100 Edward Thompson, *William Morris: Romantic to Revolutionary* (London, 1955; reprinted 1976), pp. 479–82. James Thomson recalled spending Thanksgiving Day in 1872 at 'a concert far away' and immersed in 'a moral French novel'; see Salt, *The Life of James Thomson*, p. 68.

101 For the controversy around this issue in 1872, see the *National Reformer*, 24 March 1872, pp. 185–6, and 21 April 1872, p. 249.

102 *Reynolds's Newspaper*, 29 May 1887, p. 1.

103 There is a report of the working-men's festival at the Crystal Palace in the *Times*, 27 June 1887, p 7. See for Holyoake's response to critics of his role in this event, George Jacob Holyoake, *Sixty Years of an Agitator's Life* (London, 1906),vol. I, pp. 270–71.

104 *Reynolds's Newspaper*, 18 June 1897, p. 4.

105 The origins of radical jubileeism are discussed in Malcolm Chase, 'From Millennium to Anniversary: The Concept of Jubilee within British Radical Thought in Late Eighteenth and Nineteenth Century England', *Past and Present*, no. 107 (1990), pp. 132–47.

106 *Reynolds's Newspaper*, 16 January 1887, p. 4.

107 *Labour Leader*, 19 June 1897, p. 205.

108 *Newcastle Weekly Chronicle*, 18 June 1887, p. 3.

109 Support for this project was simply assumed rather than solicited; see William Golant, *Image of Empire: The Early History of the Imperial Institute 1887–1925* (Exeter, 1984), pp. 5–11.

110 *Reynolds's Newspaper*, 27 March 1887, p. 1.

111 *Ibid.*, 27 June 1897, p. 5.

112 *Radical*, 1 July 1887, p. 84.

113 *Bulletin*, 27 August 1887, p. 2. See for the aggressively hostile tone of the *Bulletin* to all things aristocratic, Alisa G. Zainu'ddin 'Early History of the Bulletin', in *Historical Studies, Australia and New Zealand: Selected Articles*, ed. M. Beever and F. B. Smith (Melbourne, 1967), pp. 199–216.

114 *Bulletin*, 9 July 1887, p. 6.

115 *National Reformer*, 12 June 1887, p. 379. There is an account of the political career of Joseph Symes by F. B. Smith in the *Australian Dictionary of National Biography 1851–1890*, ed. G. Serle and R. Ward (Melbourne, 1976), vol. IX, p. 237.

116 The Sydney riots are described in detail in C. M. H. Clark, *A History of Australia* (Melbourne, 1987), vol. IV, pp. 396–407. Also see for a contemporary Australian account of these events, the *Bulletin*, 18 June 1887, p. 6, and 25 June 1887, p. 4.

117 *Reynolds's Newspaper*, 14 August 1887, p. 2.

118 *Ibid.*, 16 January 1887, p. 4.

119 For example, *ibid.*, 20 February 1887, p. 1.

120 *Ibid.*, 9 January 1887, p. 3, and 16 January 1887, p. 11.

121 *Macclesfield Courier and Herald*, 5 March 1887, p. 3. The power exercised by rate-payers in the new industrial towns of the North-West is discussed in John Garrard, *Leadership and Power in Victorian Industrial Towns 1830–1880* (Manchester, 1983), chaps 6 and 7.

122 *Reynolds's Newspaper*, 6 February 1887, p. 7.

123 *Ibid.*, 13 June 1897, p. 3.

124 *Ibid.*, 16 January 1887, p. 8.

125 *Ibid.*, 20 June 1897, p. 5, and 27 June 1897, p. 5.

126 *Loc. cit.*

127 Vernon, *Politics and the People*, pp. 208–12, and Michael Winstanley, 'The Factory Workforce', in *The Lancashire Cotton Industry: A History since 1700*, ed. M. Rose (Preston, 1996), p. 121.

128 Longford, *Oxford Book of Royal Anecdotes*, pp. 397–8.

129 *Reynolds's Newspaper*, 27 June 1897, p. 5.

130 Ben Brierley, 'Walmsley Fowt Welcomes the Prince of Wales' in *'Ao-o'-th'-Yate Sketches* (Oldham, 1896), pp. 170–78.

131 The monarchy's problematic relationship with Scots Gaelic culture in the Highlands in the nineteenth century is explored in Grant Jarvie, *The Making of*

a *Myth: The Scots Highland Games* (Edinburgh, 1991). The fullest study of anti-royal sentiment in Wales is John Davies, 'Victoria and Victorian Wales' in *Politics and Society in Wales 1840–1922*, ed. Geraint H. Jenkins and J. Beverly Smith (Cardiff, 1988), pp. 7–28. Also see R. R. Davies, ed., *Welsh Society and Nationalism* (Cardiff, 1994).

132   *Radical Times*, 26 February 1887, p. 4.

133   *Ibid.*, 19 February 1887, p. 1.

134   Nonconformist opposition to Victoria's tour of Wales in 1889 was reported in the *Times*, 17 August 1889, p. 8, 23 August 1889, p. 7 and p. 10, and 24 August 1889, p. 10.

135   For other manifestations of Welsh republicanism, see Jan Morris, *The Matter of Wales: Epic Views of a Small Country* (London, 1984), pp. 393–5.

136   The ringleaders were tried in Chester; see the *Chester Chronicle*, 4 June 1887, p. 8, and 23 July 1887, p. 6.

137   *Reynolds's Newspaper*, 19 February 1887, p. 1.

138   *Commonweal*, 26 February 1887.

139   The role of monarchy in cementing the antagonisms between Ireland's religious communities is discussed in James Loughlin, *Ulster Unionism and British National Identity since 1885* (London, 1995), pp. 17–21 and 40–43.

140   *Justice*, 28 February 1885, p. 1.

141   *Weekly Freeman*, 26 June 1897, p. 6, and Desmond Greaves, *The Life and Times of James Connolly* (London, 1961), pp. 70–74.

142   Nuala C. Johnson, 'Sculpting Heroic Histories: Celebrating the Centenary of the 1798 Rebellion in Ireland', *Transactions of the Institute of British Geographers*, XIX (1994), pp. 78–93.

143   *Reynolds's Newspaper*, 16 Jan. 1887, p. 11; 6 Feb. 1887, p. 7; 27 June 1897, p. 5.

144   *Loc. cit.* and 13 June 1897, p. 3. Also see the *Weekly Freeman*, 12 June 1897, p. 8.

145   Irish Home Rule papers ran sardonic headlines on jubilee day in 1887 that emphasized the sufferings of the peasantry in the Land War; see a 'Jubilee Eviction Number' in *ibid.*, 18 June 1887, p. 1.

146   *United Irishman*, 24 March 1900, p. 5.

147   *Justice*, 19 January 1901, p. 5.

148   *Labour Leader*, 2 February 1901, p. 37, and 29 June 1901, p. 203.

149   The description of him as 'a born courtier with that deference which he has inherited from his Highland ancestry' is in L. McNeill Weir, *The Tragedy of Ramsay MacDonald* (London, 1938), p. 138.

5 Anti-monarchism in the Colonies: Anglo-Australian Dimensions 1870–1901

1   A recent example is Vernon Bogdanor, *The Monarchy and the Constitution* (Oxford, 1995).

2   Peter Spearritt, 'Royal Progress: The Queen and Her Australian Subjects', in *Australian Cultural History*, ed. S. L. Goldberg and F. B. Smith (Cambridge, 1988), pp. 138–57; Connors, 'The 1954 Royal Tour of Australia', pp. 371–82, and Luke Trainor, 'Republicanism: Models and Traditions', in *Republicanism in New Zealand*, ed. Trainor (Palmerston North, 1996), pp. 27–46.

3   David Cannadine and Simon Price, 'Introduction: Divine Right of Kings', in *Rituals of Royalty: Power and Ceremonial in Traditional Societies*, eds Cannadine and Price (Cambridge, 1987).

4   Bernard S. Cohen, 'Representing Authority in Victorian India', in *The Invention of Tradition*, ed. Hobsbawm and Ranger, pp. 165–209.

5 Sasthi Brata, 'The Jewel in the Crown' in *The Monarchy and Its Future*, ed. Murray-Brown, pp. 29–40.

6 *People's Advocate*, 15 April 1876, p. 5.

7 *Liberator*, 7 August 1897, p. 10449.

8 Searle, *The Quest for National Efficiency*, chaps 2–3, and for the background to the Boer War, Bernard Porter, *The Lion's Share: A Short History of British Imperialism 1850–1983* (London, 1975; new edition, 1984), chaps 3–4.

9 Richard Price, *An Imperial War and the British Working-Class: Working-Class Attitudes and Reaction to the Boer War 1899–1902* (London, 1972), chap. 10, and Arthur Davey, *The British Pro-Boers 1877–1902* (Cape Town, 1977).

10 *Reynolds's Political Instructor*, 23 February 1850, p. 123; Robert J. Hind, '"We Have No Colonies": Similarities Within the British Imperial Experience', *Comparative Studies in Society and History*, XXVI (1984), pp. 3–35, and Miles Taylor, '"Imperium et Libertas?" Rethinking the Radical Critique of Imperialism during the Nineteenth Century', *Journal of Commonwealth and Imperial History*, XIX (1991), pp. 1–23.

11 For the response of the radical and Liberal press to the Boer War, see Mark A. Hampton, 'The Fourth Estate: Theories, Images and Ideals of the Press in Britain 1880–1914' (unpublished Ph.D. thesis, Vanderbilt University, 1998), chap. 4.

12 C. S. Dawe, *King Edward's Realm: The Story of the Making of the Empire* (London, 1902), p. 10.

13 T. A. Coghlan, *A Statistical Account of the Seven Colonies of Australia* (1900), pp. 250, 290–91 and 297–8. These are contemporary estimates, rendered uncertain by the failure to enumerate the Aboriginal people.

14 Asa Briggs, *Victorian Cities* (London, 1963; re-printed, 1980), pp. 277–310.

15 Wendy Brady, 'Republicanism: An Aboriginal View' in *The Republican Debate*, eds Wayne Hudson and David Carter (Sydney, 1993), p. 145.

16 Ballads of transportation and exile circulated widely in the rural districts of Britain for many years; see Lilias Rider Haggard, ed., *I Walked By Night: Being the Life and History of the King of the Norfolk Poachers* (London, 1935), p. 76, and for transportation history more generally, Alan Atkinson, *The Europeans in Australia: A History* (Melbourne, 1997), chaps 5 and 12. For a specific case study of transportation, see Robert Fyson, 'The Transported Chartist: The Case of William Ellis 1842–47', in *The Chartist Legacy*, ed. Owen Ashton, Robert Fyson and Stephen Roberts (Woodbridge, 1999). And for a the culture of the transportees, see Paul Donnelly, 'A Bracelet of Bright Haire: Memory and Tokens of Love', in *Convict Love Tokens: The Leaden Hearts the Convicts Left Behind*, eds Michele Field and Timothy Millett (Adelaide, 1998), pp. 53–66.

17 Joyce, *Democratic Subjects*, p. 134.

18 David Fitzpatrick, *Oceans of Consolation: Personal Accounts of Irish Migration to Australia* (Cork, 1991), introduction and chaps 18–20, and Patrick O'Farrell, *The Irish in Australia* (Sydney, 1983).

19 For example, E. M. Johnstone, 'Violence Transported: Aspects of Irish Peasant Society', in *Ireland and Irish-America*, ed. O. MacDonagh and W. F. Mantle (New Hampshire, 1986), pp. 137–54, and Eric Richards, 'Irish Life and Progress in Colonial South Australia', *Irish Historical Studies*, XXVII (1991), pp. 216–36.

20 Following the attack, the British navy threatened to bombard Sydney; see *Age*, 13 March, 1868, p. 5, 16 March 1868, p. 5, and 17 March 1868, p. 6. The best account of Irish militants in Australia is Keith Amos, *The Fenians in Australia 1865–1880* (Melbourne, 1988), chap. 3.

21 Douglas Cole, '"The Crimson Thread of Kinship": Ethnic Ideas in Australia 1870–1914', *Historical Studies* (Australia), XIV (1969), pp. 511–25.

22 For the progress and principles of the Imperial Federation League, see *Imperial Federation*, 1 July 1887, p. 158.

23 Luke Trainor, *British Imperialism and Australian Nationalism: Manipulation, Conflict and Compromise in the Late Nineteenth Century* (Melbourne, 1994), chap. 2 and pp. 95–8.

24 J. Bassett, '"A Thousand Miles of Loyalty": The Royal Tour of 1901', *New Zealand Journal of History*, XXI (1987), p 125.

25 *Bulletin*, 15 May 1886.

26 Commenting on the recent jubilee, the *Republican* 4 July 1887 wrote: 'The days of our childhood are passed and the hour of our manhood is at hand.' (The masculinist character of the national movements at the time has been noted by Marilyn Lake, 'The Politics of Respectability: Identifying the Masculinist Context', *Historical Studies* (Australia), XXII (1986), pp. 116–31.)

27 There is a large body of work on imperial literature aimed at a young audience, but see in particular John M. Mackenzie, *Propaganda and Empire: The Manipulation of British Public Opinion 1880–1960* (Manchester, 1984), chaps 7–9, and Allan Warren, 'Citizens of the Empire: Baden-Powell, Scouts and Guides and an Imperial Idea 1900–1940', in *Imperialism and Popular Culture*, ed. John M. Mackenzie (Manchester, 1986), pp. 232–57.

28 M. Quartly, 'Mothers and Fathers and Brothers and Sisters: The A.W.A. and the A.N.A. and Gendered Citizenship', *Journal of Australian Studies*, XX (1993), p. 24.

29 Bruce Scates, 'We Are Not Aboriginal, We Are Australian: William Lane, Racism and the Construction of Aboriginality', *Labour History*, LXXII (1997), pp. 35–49, and McKenna, *The Captive Republic*, chaps 2–3.

30 Russel Ward, *The Australian Legend* (Oxford, 1958), chaps 1, 5 and 6, and Richard White, *Inventing Australia: Images and Identity 1688–1980* (Melbourne, 1981), chaps 1–3.

31 Geoffrey Boxall, *The Story of the Australian Bushrangers* (London, 1899), p. vi.

32 For example, Bruce Mansfield's analysis of the reading behind the contemporary pamphlet by the British émigré radical George Black, 'Why I Am A Republican' (Pamphlet, Sydney, 1888 and 1891) in 'The Background to Radical Republicanism in New South Wales in the 1880s', *Historical Studies* (Australia), V (1953), pp. 342–3.

33 *Boomerang*, 26 September 1894, p. 4, and *Truth* (Sydney), 27 September 1896, p. 4, and 18 October 1896, p. 4.

34 *Bulletin*, 1 January 1887.

35 *Truth* (Sydney), 29 November 1896, p. 4. See for John Norton, Michael Cannon, *John Norton 1858–1916: An Australian Populist* (Melbourne, 1981), pp. 3–10.

36 Norton's obituary is in *Truth*, 22 April 1916, pp. 5–6.

37 A. Thomson, 'The Early History of the Bulletin', *Historical Studies* (Australia), VI (1954), p. 129.

38 *Reynolds's Newspaper*, 30 July 1899, p. 2, and *Truth* (Sydney), 18 October 1896, p. 4, and 25 July 1897, p. 4.

39 For the unveiling of John Dunmore Lang's statue, see the *Bulletin*, 15 December 1888, and the *Sydney Morning Herald*, 10 December 1888; for the plinth of Victoria's statue used as a radical meeting place, see Trainor, *British Imperialism and Australian Nationalism*, pp. 66–80.

40 Mansfield, 'The Background to Radical Republicanism', p. 339.

41 *Bulletin*, 5 June 1886.

42 Robin Gollan, *Radical and Working Class Politics: A Study of Eastern Australia 1850–1910* (Melbourne 1960), p.119.

43 The Order of St Michael and St George were specially constituted for the colonies. Sir Robert Meade of the Colonial Office spoke of the ceremonial associated with it as 'a splendid tomfoolery'; see R. H. Meade, 'Commonplace Book', 24 April 1895, in the Clanwilliam Papers, Public Record Office, Northern Ireland.

44 Paul Rickard, *Australia: A Cultural History* (London, 1988), p. 113. There was similar opposition to Empire Day in Ireland; see David H. Hume, 'Empire Day in Ireland 1896–1962', in *An Irish Empire: Aspects of Ireland and the British Empire*, ed. Kevin Jeffrey (Manchester, 1996), pp. 149–62.

45 Kay Saunders, *Working in Bondage: The Origin and Basis of Unfree Labour in Queensland 1824–1916* (Brisbane, 1982) and *idem*, 'The Workers' Paradise: Indentured Labour in the Queensland Sugar Industry to 1920' in *Indentured Labour in the British Empire 1834–1920*, ed. Kay Saunders (London, 1984), pp. 213–29.

46 Raymond Markey, 'Race and Organized Labor in Australia 1850–1901', *Historian*, LVIII (1996), pp. 343–60.

47 *Queensland Figaro*, 6 October 1883.

48 Quoted in *Imperial Federation*, 1 July 1887, p. 152.

49 I. D. McNaughton, 'The Case of Benjamin Kitt', *Royal Historical Society of Queensland Journal*, IV (1951), pp. 535–58, and B. R. Penny, 'The Blake Case', *Australian Journal of Politics and History*, VI (1960), pp. 176–89.

50 *Sydney Morning Herald*, 24 November 1888.

51 *Truth* (Sydney), 10 April 1897, p. 4.

52 *Liberator*, 29 May 1897, p. 10330.

53 *Reynolds's Newspaper*, 28 September 1890, p. 3.

54 *Ibid.*, 30 July 1876, p. 3, and 24 July 1881, p. 2.

55 *Tomahawk*, 25 January 1868, p. 39.

56 Trainor, *British Imperialism and Australian Nationalism*, chaps 3, 8 and 12, and J. Mordike, *An Army for a Nation* (Sydney, 1992), chaps 1–3.

57 Black, *Why I Am A Republican*, p. 20.

58 *Republican*, 4 July 1887.

59 Barbara R. Penny, 'Australian Reactions to the Boer War: A Study in Colonial Imperialism', *Journal of British Studies*, VII (1967), pp. 97–130, and Alistair Thomson, *Anzac Memories: Living with the Legend* (Cambridge, 1995), chap. 2.

60 Eleke Boehmer, *Colonial and Post-Colonial Literatures* (Oxford, 1993).

61 John Docker, *The Nervous Nineties* (Melbourne, 1991), p. 235.

62 Graeme Davison, 'Sydney and the Bush: An Urban Context for the Australian Legend', *Historical Studies* (Australia), XVIII (1978), p. 199.

63 The subordination of women in a colonial context is demonstrated by a particularly brutal rape case at Mount Rennie on the outskirts of Sydney in 1886, in which a campaign for a commutation of the death sentence for the attackers became an expression of 'masculinist' Australian nationalism; see Trainor, *British Imperialism and Australian Nationalism*, p. 75.

64 Marilyn Lake, 'Australian Frontier Feminism and the Marauding White Man' in Midgly, ed., *Gender and Imperialism*, pp. 123–36.

65 Jill Roe, 'Chivalry and Social Policy in the Antipodes' in White and Russell, eds, *Memories and Dreams*, pp. 3–19.

66 Helen Irving, 'The Republic as a Feminist Issue', Feminist Review, LII (1996), pp. 87–101, and Marilyn Lake, 'Women and Nation in Australia: The Politics of Representation', *Australian Journal of Politics and History*, XLIII (1997), pp. 41–52.

67 L. J. Ljungdahl, ed., *Catherine Helen Spence: 'A Week in the Future'* (Melbourne, 1987), pp. 109–10.

68 Marilyn Lake, 'The Republic, the Federation and the Intrusion of the Political', in '"Vox Reipublicae": Feminism and the Republic', ed. Jeanette Hoorn and David Goodman, *Journal of Australian Studies Special Edition*, XLVII (1996), pp. 5–16.

69 Joseph Rayner Stephens, 'The Altar, The Throne and The Cottage' (Pamphlet, Stalybridge, 1868), p. 8, and his speech in the *Preston Herald*, 2 May 1868.

70 Helen Irving, 'Who Were the Republicans' in Headon, Warden and Gammage, eds, *Crown or Country*, pp. 71–2.

71 J. Chamberlain – Lord Salisbury, 22 Jan. 1900, JC 11, Chamberlain Papers, Australian Joint Copying Project M867.

72 Robin Gollan, 'Discovering our Republican Heritage' in Headon, Warden and Gammage, eds, *Crown or Country*, p. 86.

6 *'Lords of Misrule': Liberalism, the House of Lords and the Campaign Against Privilege 1870–1911*

1 For example, E. Allyn, *Lords versus Commons: A Century of Conflict and Compromise 1830-1930* (New York, 1931), pp. 116-21; Smith, *The House of Lords in British Politics*, chap. 9, and Andrew Adonis, *Making Aristocracy Work: The Peerage and the Political System in Britain 1884–1914* (Oxford, 1992), chaps 7–9.

2 *Justice*, 6 July 1895, p. 4.

3 *Christian Socialist*, 1 September 1884, pp. 56–7.

4 Stephen Reynolds and Bob and Tom Woolley, *Seems So! A Working-Class View of Politics* (London, 1911), pp. 132–3.

5 Cecil Chesterton, *Gladstonian Ghosts* (London, 1905), p. 173.

6 Biagini, *Liberals, Retrenchment and Reform*, chap. 5. Biagini's work draws heavily on the observations of Jephson, *The Platform*, vol. II, pp. 608–9.

7 *Freethinker's Magazine*, 1 October 1850, p. 129, and 1 July 1850, p. 42.

8 *Radical*, 1 September 1888, pp. 6–7

9 Carlile preached a holistic view of society that saw monarchy, aristocracy, and the church's prescriptive advice on sex and procreation as part of the same sanctimonious totality; see Michael Bush, *What is Love: Richard Carlile's Philosophy of Sex* (London, 1998), pp. 1–51.

10 *People's Paper*, 10 July 1858, p. 1.

11 Dilke's speech on the House of Lords at Birmingham Town Hall is typical of this tactic. In contrast to that at Bolton it passed off peacefully; see the *Birmingham Daily Post*, 8 December 1871, p. 4.

12 *Ibid.*, 7 December 1871, p. 5. Also see Charles Cattell, 'Abolition of the House of Lords' (Pamphlet, Birmingham, 1872).

13 *Reynolds's Newspaper*, 27 June 1897, p. 6.

14 *Ibid.*, 6 June 1897, p. 5. In the 1870s the *National Reformer* ran a similar column entitled 'Our Aristocracy'; see the *National Reformer*, 3 December 1871, p. 355; 25 February 1872, pp. 114–15, and 17 March 1872, p. 163. Also see the *Republican*, 1 September 1882, pp. 425–6; 1 October 1882, p. 439, and 1 September 1883, p. 521. For secularist hostility to the aristocracy see George Standring, 'The People's History of the Aristocracy' (Pamphlet, London, 1891).

15 *English Labourers' Chronicle*, 1 October 1881, p. 4.

16 Taylor, '"The Best Way to Get What He Wanted"', pp. 185–204.

17 *Loc. cit.* and *idem*, '"Commons-Stealers", "Land-Grabbers" and "Jerry-Builders"', pp. 383–407.

18 The case for Gladstone's later radicalism has been re-examined in Michael

Barker, *Gladstone and Radicalism: The Reconstruction of Liberal Policy in Britain 1885–1894* (Brighton, 1975), pp. 171–3, and D. M. Schreuder, 'The Making of Mr Gladstone's Posthumous Career: The Role of Morley and Knaplund as 'Monument Masons' 1903–1927' in *The Gladstonian Turn of Mind: Essays Presented to J. B. Comacher*, ed. Bruce Kinzer (Toronto, 1985), pp. 197–237.

19 *Single Tax*, 1 June 1898, p. 4. Similar sentiments were expressed by Keir Hardie in an obituary of Gladstone in the *Labour Leader*, 28 May 1898, pp. 178–9.

20 Disraeli famously quipped on the occasion of his elevation to the Lords, 'I am dead; dead but in the Elysium Fields.' See Smith, *The House of Lords*, pp. 142–3.

21 Quoted in Roy Jenkins, *Gladstone* (London, 1995), pp. 495–6, and Matthew, *Gladstone 1875–1898*, p. 177.

22 Anon., *Anecdotes of the Rt. Hon. W. E. Gladstone by an Oxford Man* (London, n.d.), p. 32.

23 Matthew, ed., *Gladstone Diaries*, vol. XIII, appendix 1, p. 431.

24 Matthew, *Gladstone 1875–1898*, p. 355.

25 Roy Jenkins, *Asquith* (London, 1964), pp. 227–8. Tory fears of imminent royal disintegration were apparently confirmed when a pamphlet, 'Bigamy Sanctified', by E. R. Mylius appeared in 1911 disputing the succession and suggesting that George V already had a wife before his marriage to Mary; see David Dutton, *Simon: A Political Biography of Sir John Simon* (London, 1992), p. 16.

26 J. E. Woolacott, *The House of Lords: A Lecture* (National Secular Society, 1884), p. 3.

27 A. Mackenzie, 'The Peers and the Franchise: The House of Lords' (Pamphlet, London, 1884), p. 10.

28 *Republican*, 1 September 1884, pp. 41–2.

29 'Publius', 'The House of Lords: What Shall We Do With It?' (Pamphlet, Manchester, 1884) and Anon., 'The Peers and the People: What Shall We Do With the House of Lords?' (Pamphlet, London, 1884).

30 Anon., 'The Peer's Plunder and the People's Poverty' (Liverpool Financial Reform Association, 1884), pp. 1–2.

31 *Times*, 23 August 1889, p. 7.

32 Lord Carrington, 'Recollections of My Life From Public School to Privy Seal', Autobiographical Fragment, Rosebery Papers, National Library of Scotland, (MSS 10229).

33 Robert Rhodes James, *Rosebery* (London, 1963; reprinted, 1995), chap. 10. For his objections to the Lords, see Lord Rosebery, 'The Reform of the House of Lords' (Pamphlet, Edinburgh, 1884), pp. 3–31.

34 *The Premier's Battle Cry: Mr. Asquith's Speech at the National Liberal Club* (*Yorkshire Observer*, 1910), p. 4.

35 David Lloyd George, *Better Times: Speeches by the Rt. Hon. David Lloyd George* (London, 1910), pp. 221–2.

36 E. R. Pearce-Edgcombe, 'The Last Function of the House of Lords' (Pamphlet, Manchester, 1884), p. 38.

37 For example, the lines 'The House of Peers, throughout the war/Did nothing in particular/And did it very well.' in W. S. Gilbert's *Iolanthe*, II (1882).

38 George A. Denison, 'Why Should the Bishops Continue to Sit in the House of Lords?' (Pamphlet, London, 1850), pp. 36–7.

39 Reynolds and the Woolleys, *Seems So!*, p. 304.

40 Kenneth O. Morgan, *David Lloyd George: Welsh Radical and World Statesman* (Cardiff, 1963), p. 44, and Martin Pugh, *Lloyd George* (London, 1988), pp. 49–50.

41 Anon., 'Peers v. the People: What's the Use of the House of Lords?' (Pamphlet, Manchester, 1884), pp. 17–18.

42 Pugh, *Lloyd George*, p. 54.

43 'Publius', 'The House of Lords?', p. 3. During the 'Peers versus the People' elections of 1910 Lloyd George was highly critical of the 'shooting estates'.

44 Pugh, *Lloyd George*, chaps 1–3.

45 See the *Birmingham Daily Post*, 14 October 1884, pp. 4–5; the *Newcastle Weekly Chronicle*, 18 October 1884, p. 3, and *Reynolds's Newspaper*, 19 October 1884, p. 2 and p. 4.

46 *Newcastle Weekly Chronicle*, 5 July 1884, p. 4.

47 David Lloyd George referred specifically to the 1832 House of Lords crisis in a speech at Walworth in 1909; see *Better Times*, p. 221.

48 *English Labourers' Chronicle*, 2 August 1884, pp. 2–4.

49 *Newcastle Weekly Chronicle*, 26 July 1884, p. 3. At a similar demonstration on Glasgow Green an iron cage was paraded with a radical dressed as a peer inside and a placard with the legend 'What the people would do with the peers'; see John Hodge, *Workman's Cottage to Windsor Castle* (London, 1931), p. 6.

50 H. C. G. Matthew, 'Disraeli, Gladstone and the Politics of Mid-Victorian Budgets', *Historical Journal*, XXII (1979), pp. 615–43.

51 Bruce K. Murray, *The People's Budget 1909–1910* (Oxford, 1980).

52 Election Leaflets, 1906–1910 (308 N6 V.108), MCRL.

53 Joan Smith, 'Labour Traditions in Glasgow and Liverpool', *History Workshop*, no. 17 (1984), pp. 32–56 and Graham Walker, *Thomas Johnstone* (Manchester, 1988), pp. 9–12.

54 Harold Storey, *The House of Lords: History of the Fight between the People and the Peers, Statement of Liberal Policy, Examination of the Government's Proposals* (Liberal Party, 1927), pp. 8–9.

55 'A Peer', 'The Peers and the Situation', *National Review*, LIV (1909), pp. 241–2.

56 The best guide to the historical principles of Liberalism is Alan Sykes, *The Rise and Fall of British Liberalism 1776–1988* (London, 1997), chap. 1.

57 R. H. Mottram, *East Anglia: England's Eastern Province* (London, 1933), p. 12.

58 Arthur G. Symonds, 'The House of Lords: Not a Second Chamber or Senate', Election Ephemera 1906–1910 (308 N6 V.108), MCRL.

59 A. Labouchère Thorold, *The Life of Henry Labouchère* (London, 1913), p. 217.

60 *Ibid.*, pp. 208–26.

61 *Justice*, 12 November 1887 and 14 July 1888.

62 The outline of the Newcastle proposals is in Simon Maccoby, *The English Radical Tradition 1763–1914* (London, 1952), vol. V.

63 *Northampton Mercury*, 29 June 1894, p. 5 and the *Northampton Herald*, 30 June 1894, p. 1.

64 William T. Stead, 'The General Election, 1895: The Poster in Politics', *Review of Reviews*, XII (1895), pp. 168–76.

65 John S. Ellis, 'Reconciling the Celt: British National Identity, Empire and the 1911 Investiture of the Prince of Wales', *Journal of British Studies*, XXXVII (1998), pp. 391–418.

66 See the work of the radical Liberal Harold Evans, *Our Old Nobility* (London, 1879; new edition, 1907), p. 1.

67 Frank Owen, *Lloyd George: His Life and Times* (London, 1954), p. 195.

68 Especially Logie Barrow and Ian Bullock, *Democratic Ideas and the British Labour Movement 1880–1914* (Cambridge, 1997), chaps 1–3.

69 The standard account is Ross McKibbin, *The Evolution of the Labour Party 1910–1924* (London, 1974), chaps 1–6, and the conclusion. An updated version

of this argument appears in *idem*, *Classes and Cultures: England 1918–1951* (Oxford, 1998).

70 Peter Clarke, 'The Social Democratic Theory of the Class Struggle' in *The Working Class in Modern British History*, ed. Jay Winter (Cambridge, 1983), pp. 3–18, and Stephen Fielding, Peter Thompson and Nick Tiratsoo, '*England Arise': The Labour Party and Popular Politics in 1940s Britain* (Manchester, 1995), chap. 4.

71 David Butler, 'By-elections and Their Interpretation' in *By-elections in British Politics*, eds Chris Cook and John Ramsden (London, 1997), pp. 1–12.

72 J. G. Swift MacNeill, *Titled Corruption: The Sordid Origin of Some Irish Peerages* (London, 1894).

73 *Republican*, 1 August 1884, p. 39.

74 William T. Stead, *Fifty Years of the House of Lords* (London, 1880; reprinted 1894), p. 63.

75 J. Ramsay MacDonald, *Tories and the House of Lords: An Exposure of Their Trickery* (Labour Party, 1910), pp. 14–16.

76 Corinne C. Weston, 'Salisbury and the Lords 1868–1895', *Historical Journal*, XXV (1982), pp. 103–29 and *idem*, *The House of Lords and Ideological Politics: Lord Salisbury's Referendal Theory and the Conservative Party 1846–1922* (American Philosophical Society, 1991).

77 Ian Bullock and Siân Reynolds, 'Direct Legislation and Socialism: How British and French Socialists Viewed the Referendum in the 1890s', *History Workshop*, no. 24 (1987), pp. 62–81; John Sketchley, 'Shall the People Govern Themselves?' (Pamphlet, London, 1896), pp. 10–13, and the *Labour Echo*, 13 April 1895, p. 4.

78 *New Age*, 19 September 1895, p. 396.

79 *Labour Leader*, 6 May 1910, p. 280.

80 Evans, *Our Old Nobility*, pp. 6–7. Some Labour pamphleteers alleged that peers acted as 'decoy-ducks' conferring a veneer of respectability on their firms in company board-rooms; see H. R. Stockman, *Labour and the Lords: An Indictment* (Labour Party, 1909), pp. 10–11.

81 *New Age*, 10 October 1895, p. 17. In 1911 Cecil Chesterton suggested that new peers should be made up of dockers and workers, rather than employers or wealthy contributors to Liberal Party funds; see *ibid.*, 30 March 1911, p. 512.

82 *Labour Echo*, 13 April 1895, p. 4. Also see the *Republican*, 1 September 1883, pp. 521–2 on the question of 'capitalists' in the House of Lords.

83 *Bradford Observer*, 30 October 1894, p. 6.

84 *Ibid.*, 29 October 1894, p. 4.

85 *Labour Leader*, 28 May 1898, pp. 178–9.

86 Pugh, *Lloyd George*, p. 51 and p. 185.

87 For an excellent attempt to understand popular responses to the 1912 sinking of the Titanic in terms of a Progressivist discourse see Steven Biel, '*Down With the Old Canoe': A Cultural History of the Titanic Disaster* (New York, 1998), chaps 2–4.

88 David Spring, 'Land and Politics in Edwardian England', *Agricultural History*, LVIII (1984), pp. 17–42 and Sykes, *Rise and Fall of British Liberalism*, p. 159.

89 *Ibid.*, pp. 158–9.

90 'The Peers and the Land', election ephemera 1906–1910 (308 N6 V.108) MCRL. For the original speech see the *People's Paper*, 8 November 1856, p. 1 and p. 4.

91 See Ursula Vogel, 'The Land Question: A Liberal Theory of Communal Property', *History Workshop*, no. 27 (1989), pp. 106–35 and Michael Tichelar, 'Socialists, Labour and the Land: The Response of the Labour Party to the Land Campaign of Lloyd George Before the First World War', *Twentieth Century History*, VIII (1997), pp. 127–44.

92   Roy Douglas, 'God Gave the Land to the People', in *Edwardian Radicalism 1900–1914*, ed. A. J. A. Morris (London, 1974), pp. 148–61, and Pugh, *Lloyd George*, pp. 63–6.

93   Vogel, 'The Land Question', p. 109.

94   *Reynolds's Newspaper*, 20 January 1884, p. 3.

95   A. R. Wallace, *The 'Why' and the 'How' of Land Nationalisation* (Land Nationalisation Society, London, 1883), pp. 5–7; Richard Pankhurst, *The Land and the Nation* (Manchester Statistical Society, 1884), and Joseph Hyder, *The Case for Land Nationalisation* (London, 1913), pp. 42–4.

96   Tom Johnstone, *Our Scots Noble Families* (Glasgow, 1909).

97   Labouchère Thorold, *Life of Henry Labouchère*, chaps 7 and 8.

98   *Reynolds's Newspaper*, 27 July 1884, p. 1.

99   *Single Tax*, 1 January 1898, p. 3.

100 John Osmond, *The Divided Kingdom* (London, 1988), p. 186, and Roland Quinault, 'The Cult of the Centenary c.1784–1914', *Historical Research*, LXXI (1998), pp. 303–23.

101 *Review of Reviews*, XII (1895), pp. 7–8.

102 Roger Howell, 'Who Needs Another Cromwell? The Nineteenth Century Image of Oliver Cromwell', in *Images of Oliver Cromwell*, Richardson, ed., p. 97, and J. F. Battick and N. C. Klimavicz, 'Much Ado About Oliver: The Parliamentary Dispute Over Cromwell's Statue', *History Today*, XXIV (1974), pp. 406–12.

103 Kenneth Rose, *George V* (London, 1985).

104 *Observer*, 16 August 1914 and Peter Fleming, *Invasion 1940* (London, 1957), pp. 258–9.

105 Charles A. Glyde, 'Britain's Disgrace: An Urgent Plea for Old Age Pensions' (Pamphlet, Bradford, 1903), p. 6.

106 *Ibid.*, p. 19.

107 Sims, *Sixty Years' Recollections*, p. 135.

108 Chesterton, *Gladstonian Ghosts*, pp. 169–71.

109 Allyn, *Lords versus Commons*, p. 221, and for Labour policy towards the Lords more generally J. P. Morgan, *The House of Lords and the Labour Government 1964–70* (Oxford, 1975).

110 Quoted in Dermot Keogh, *Jews in Twentieth-Century Ireland* (Cork, 1998), p. 59.

111 Brian O'Higgins, ed., *The Voice of Banba: Songs, Ballads and Satires* (Dublin, 1931), p. 85. Also see in the same volume 'A Loyal Come All Ye' (p. 37) and 'To the Marys of Ireland' (p. 51).

112 *Manchester Evening News*, 7 July 1913, p. 3, and 8 July 1913, p. 4.

113 *Ibid.*, 14 July 1913, p. 2.

114 *Commonweal*, 24 June 1893, p. 2, and 22 July 1893, p. 1.

115 *Ibid.*, 8 July 1893, p. 1

116 *Manchester Evening News*, 9 July 1913, p. 4.

7 The Labour Party and the Failure of English Republicanism 1919–99

1   Quoted in Prochaska, *Royal Bounty*, p. 208, and in Herbert Morrison, *Government and Parliament: A Survey from the Inside* (Oxford, 1954), p. 105.

2   *New Illustrated*, 21 June 1919, p. 329.

3   Paul Fussell, *The Great War and Modern Memory* (Oxford, 1975), chaps 4–6, and Jay Winter, *Sites of Memory and Sites of Mourning: The Great War in European Cultural History* (Cambridge, 1995), chaps 2 and 3.

4   Gerald J. DeGroot, *Blighty: British Society in the Era of the Great War* (London, 1996), chaps 15 and 16.

5 *New Illustrated*, 24 May 1919, p. 4.

6 Frank Prochaska, 'The Head that Wears the Crown: Republicans and the Monarchy, Past, Present – and Future', *Times Literary Supplement*, 26 July 1996, pp. 14–15.

7 John Stevenson, 'The United Kingdom', in *The Working Class and Politics in Europe and America 1929–1945*, eds Stephen Salter and John Stevenson (London, 1990), pp. 125–53.

8 Wells's last published correspondence returned to this issue; see H.G. Wells, 'A Republican's Faith', *New Statesman and Nation*, XXVIII (1944), p. 421 and *idem, Travels of a Republican Radical in Search of Hot Water* (London, 1939), pp. 28–39.

9 The account of Hardie's life which most strongly highlights his republicanism is Iain McLean, *Keir Hardie* (London, 1975), pp. 47–9, 132 and 167–8.

10 Taylor, *The Troublemakers*, p. 113.

11 *Labour Leader*, 20 May 1910, p. 305 and p. 311.

12 Taylor, *The Troublemakers*, p. 153.

13 Kenneth O. Morgan, 'England, Britain and the Audit of War', *Transactions of the Royal Historical Society*, VII (1997), pp. 131–53.

14 Correspondence in *Forward*, 27 June 1953, p. 5. Since the 1980s the Scottish National Party has resumed its attempts to reclaim the Scottish Covenanting and republican tradition for a nationalist posture; see *Jacobites or Covenanters: Which Tradition?* (Scottish Republican Forum, 1994).

15 Herbert Morrison, *An Autobiography* (London, 1960), p. 129.

16 Martin Pugh, *The Making of Modern British Politics 1867–1939* (London, 1982), chaps 11–13.

17 *Daily Herald*, 9 January 1924, p. 6. For Drinkwater's attempt to revive the cult of the liberal reforming Cromwell, see John Drinkwater, *Cromwell: A Character Study* (London, 1927), p. 15.

18 *Daily Herald*, 6 March 1924, p. 1.

19 Viscount Philip Snowden, *An Autobiography* (London, 1934), vol. II, p. 952; Morrison, *Government and Parliament*, pp. 91–4 and Jonathan Freedland, *Bring Home the Revolution: How Britain Can Live the American Dream* (London, 1998), pp. 191–3.

20 Morrison, *An Autobiography*, pp. 158–9.

21 *Idem, Government and Parliament*, p. 105.

22 Joseph Clayton, *The Rise and Decline of Socialism in Great Britain 1884–1924* (London, 1926), pp. 229–40.

23 Robert Rhodes James, ed., *Chips: The Diaries of Sir Henry Channon* (London, 1967), p. 60.

24 This point is made effectively in David Marquand, *Ramsay MacDonald* (London, 1977; new edition, 1997).

25 Hodge, *Workman's Cottage to Windsor Castle*, p. 1.

26 Margaret Cole, ed., *Beatrice Webb's Diaries 1924–32* (London, 1956), p. 79.

27 Morrison, *An Autobiography*, p. 113.

28 T. A. Jackson, *The Jubilee – and How* (Communist Party, 1935), p. 5.

29 See Robert Skidelsky, *Politicians and the Slump: The Labour Government of 1929–31* (London, 1967; new edition, 1994), chap. 3.

30 MacNeill Weir, *The Tragedy of Ramsay MacDonald*, pp. vii–xii, invokes Joseph Chamberlain's cynicism of the wild enthusiasts 'tamed to the treasury bench'. Also J. Scanlon, *The Decline and Fall of the Labour Party* (London, 1932).

31 James, ed., *Chips*, p. 140.

32 The black legend of Ramsay MacDonald's 'betrayal' found a lasting place in popular literature; see Howard Spring, *Fame is the Spur* (London, 1940).

33 Elizabeth Longford, *Elizabeth R: A Biography* (London, 1983), p. 264.

34 Philip Ziegler, *King Edward VIII* (London, 1990), pp. 214–20.

35 Willlie Hamilton, *My Queen and I* (London, 1975), pp. 106–8.

36 *Labour Party Annual Report, 1923* (London, 1924), pp. 250–51.

37 John Vaizey, *Education in a Class Society: The Queen and Her Horses Reign* (Fabian Society, 1962), p. 2.

38 Frances, Countess of Warwick, *Discretions* (New York, 1931), p. 261.

39 *Forward*, 2 May 1953, p. 5.

40 *Daily Herald*, 3 December 1936.

41 *Times*, 5 December 1936.

42 Kingsley Martin, *The Magic of Monarchy* (London, 1936), pp. 74–9.

43 Edward Short, *Whip to Wilson: The Crucial Years of Labour Government* (London, 1989), p. 64.

44 Stuart Bell, *How to Abolish the Lords* (Fabian Society, 1981), pp. 9–10.

45 Richard Holme, 'The Lords: The Not Contents Have It', *New Statesman*, 3 June 1988, pp. 10–12.

46 Ben Pimlott, *Harold Wilson* (London, 1992), pp. 685–90.

47 Short, *Whip to Wilson*, p. 66.

48 Anthony Barnett, 'End of the Affair', *New Statesman and Society*, 5 April 1996, pp. 20–23.

49 For example, Denis Healey, *The Time of My Life* (London, 1989), pp. 89–91.

50 Paul Richards, *Long to Reign Over Us?* (Fabian Society, 1996).

51 Ina Zweiniger-Bargielowska, 'Royal Rations', *History Today*, XLIII (1993), pp. 13–15, and idem, *Austerity in Britain: Rationing and Controls on Consumption 1939–1954* (Oxford, 1994).

52 John Grigg, 'The Monarchy Today', *English and National Review*, CXLIX (1957), pp. 61–6. Also see Grigg's reply to his critics 'The Rumpus – And After', *ibid.* (August, 1957), pp. 106–19.

53 Sylvia Street, *British National Cinema* (London, 1997).

54 Asa Briggs, *The History of Broadcasting in the United Kingdom* (Oxford, 1996), vol. V, *passim*.

55 Joanna Bourke, *Working-Class Cultures in Britain: Gender, Class and Ethnicity 1890–1960* (London, 1994), pp. 186–9 and Samuel, *Island Stories*, pp. 172–93.

56 *Manchester Guardian*, 3 June 1953, pp. 3–4.

57 *Ibid.*, pp. 2, 10.

58 Edward Shils and Michael Young, 'The Meaning of the Coronation', *Sociological Review*, I (1953), pp. 63–81.

59 *Manchester Guardian*, 3 June 1953, p. 10.

60 N. Birnbaum, 'Monarchs and Sociologists: A Reply to Professor Shils and Mr. Young', *Sociological Review*, III (1955), pp. 5–23.

61 John Pudney, ed., *The Queen's People; Photographs by Izis Bidermanas* (London, 1953), pp. 10–11.

62 Birnbaum, 'Monarchs and Sociologists', p. 17.

63 The evidence from the Mass Observation archive on the coronation is summarized in Philip Ziegler, *Crown and People* (London, 1978), chap. 5.

64 Birnbaum, 'Monarchs and Sociologists', p. 19.

65 Edgar Wilson, *The Myth of British Monarchy* (London, 1989), p. 44.

66 Harrison, *Transformation of British Politics*, chap. 12.

67 See John Tulloch and Manuel Alvarado, *Doctor Who: The Unfolding Text* (London, 1983), pp. 43–50.

68 *Eagle*, 29 May 1953, p. 7 and p. 8.

69 Griel Marcus, *Lipstick Traces: A Secret History of the Twentieth Century* (London, 1991), pp. 34–5 and 199–200. Also see Jon Savage, *England's Dreaming: The Sex Pistols and Punk Rock* (London, 1993), and *idem*, 'Pointing Pistols at the Throne', *Guardian*, 2 June 1993, p. 4

70 Imogen O'Rourke, 'Never Mind the Pollocks', *ibid.*, 27 January 1998, p. 9.

71 Christopher Hird, 'Myths, Lies and the Royals', in *After Diana: Irreverent Elegies*, ed. Mandy Merck (London, 1998), pp. 199–205.

72 Tim Hames and Mark Leonard, *Modernizing the Monarchy* (Demos, 1998), pp. 10–11.

73 Tom Nairn, *The Enchanted Glass: Britain and Its Monarchy* (London, 1988), pp. 213–315.

74 *Daily Mail*, 23 September 1998, p. 4 and p. 8.

75 Eric Hobsbawm, 'Another Forward March Halted', *Marxism Today*, 1 October 1989, pp. 14–19.

76 Woodrow Wyatt's diaries seem to confirm rumours of antagonism between Mrs Thatcher and the Palace current at the time; see the *Guardian*, 5 October 1998, p. 8.

77 John Lloyd and Caroline Daniel, 'New Labour, New Monarchy', *New Statesman*, 14 June 1996, pp. 16–19, and Simon Heffer, 'The Royals Fight Back', *New Statesman*, 29 August 1998, pp. 15–16.

78 Vernon Bogdanor, 'Mirror for a Multicultural Age? How Proposed Constitutional Reforms Will Affect the Monarchy', *Times Literary Supplement*, 31 July 1998, pp. 13–14.

79 *Guardian*, 26 September 1998, p. 12.

80 Anthony Barnett, 'Empire State', *New Statesman and Society*, 26 July 1994, pp. 20–21.

81 Mark Goldie, 'The Bill of Rights, 1689 and 1998', *History Today*, XLVIII (1998), pp. 10–12.

82 Hames and Leonard, *Modernizing the Monarchy*, pp. 21–34.

83 Ben Pimlott, 'The A-Word Won't Go Away', *Observer*, 8 November 1998, p. 13.

84 Quoted in Tom Nairn, 'Nations: Breaking Up is Hard to Do', *Marxism Today*, Special Issue, October 1998, pp. 40–43.

Conclusion: The Future of the Monarchy?

1 Sue Townsend, *The Queen and I* (London, 1992), pp. 313.

2 It was referred to only in the quality dailies; see the *Independent*, 29 January 1999, p. 4, and the *Guardian*, 6 February 1999, p. 3.

3 Justin Champion, 'Reign, Reign, Go Away', *Times Higher Education Supplement*, 16 December 1994, p. 16.

4 In a supreme display of kitsch, the remains of William Annetts, founder of the Sealed Knot, were blown from the mouth of a cannon after his death in 1998; see the *Independent*, 12 January 1998, p. 2.

5 This is in part the popular perception of British government more generally, see Weir and Beetham, *Political Power and Democratic Control in Britain*, pp. 25–6.

6 This point is made well in John Baxendale and Christopher Pawling, *Narrating the Thirties: A Decade in the Making, 1930 to the Present* (London, 1996), chap. 6.

7 Andrew Morton, *Diana: Her True Story* (London, 1992), especially pp. 155–70 and the appendix.

8 *Guardian*, 18 February 1999, p. 7

9 *Picture Post*, 25 April 1953, pp. 13–15.

10 Vernon Bogdanor, 'Mirror for a Multicultural Age: How Proposed Constitutional Reforms Will Affect the Monarchy', *Times Literary Supplement*, 31 July 1998, p. 13.
11 Antony Taylor and Luke Trainor, 'Monarchism and Anti-Monarchism: Anglo-Australian Comparisons 1870–1901', *Social History*, 24 (1999), pp. 158–73, and Antony Taylor, 'Republican Ruminations from Down Under', *History Today*, 45 (1995), pp. 6–9.
12 *Guardian*, 28 September 1993, p. 2.
13 Peter Browne, 'Coming Out for the Republic', *New Statesman*, 13 February 1998, pp. 26–7.
14 For example, Les Murray, *The Boys Who Stole the Funeral: A Novel Sequence* (Sydney, 1980), p. 47.

Select Bibliography

This bibliography is not an exhaustive account of the materials cited in this work. What follows nevertheless provides an introduction to the main primary and secondary sources available on monarchy, opposition to it, and the role of anti-monarchism in popular politics from the 1790s onwards.

Manuscript Sources

Charles Bradlaugh Papers, National Secular Society Archive, Bishopsgate Institute, London
Home Office Disturbance Books, Public Record Office (HO 45/9269/9391)
George Howell Collection, Bishopsgate Institute, London
Manchester Central Reference Library, Language and Literature Library, Pearson Collection of Nineteenth Century Ballads

Newspapers

Bee-Hive 1866–71
Commonwealth 1865–67
Freethinker's Magazine 1850–51
Justice 1885–98
Labour Leader 1898–1912
National Reformer 1868–84
New Age 1895–7
Newcastle Weekly Chronicle 1868–85
Northern Star 1845–50
People's Advocate 1875–7
People's Paper 1852–7
Radical 1887–8
Reynolds's Newspaper 1850–1901
Republican 1870–71
Republican 1881–5

Contemporary Printed Sources

Adams, W. E., *Memoirs of a Social Atom* (London, 1903), vols 1–2
Asquith, H. H., *The Premier's Battle Cry* (*Yorkshire Observer*, 1910)
Axon, W. E. A., 'The Mayor of Manchester and His Slanderers' (Pamphlet, Manchester, 1877)
Black, George, *Why I am a Republican* (Australian Republican League, Sydney, 1888)
Bradlaugh, Charles, *The Impeachment of the House of Brunswick* (National Secular Society, 1871)
Carnegie, Andrew, *Triumphant Democracy or Fifty Years' March of the Republic* (London, 1886)

Carnegie, Andrew, *Autobiography* (London, 1920)

'Casey', *Who Are the Bloodsuckers?* (Independent Labour Party, 1905)

Chatterton, Daniel, 'Chatterton's Letter to the Prince of Wales and All Other Aristocratic and Royal Paupers' (Pamphlet, London, 1882)

Chesterton, Cecil, *Gladstonian Ghosts* (London, 1905)

Cowen, Joseph, 'Speech on the Royal Titles Bill' (Pamphlet, Newcastle, 1876)

Cox, John Charles, 'The Cost of the Royal Household, Royal Annuities and Crown Lands' (Pamphlet, London, 1872)

Dilke, Charles Wentworth, 'The Cost of the Crown' (Pamphlet, London, 1871)

Dilke, Charles Wentworth, *Problems of Greater Britain* (London, 1890), vol. 1.

Finlen, James, 'A Warning and an Example Dedicated to the Dynasties of Christendom: Maximilian, His Life and Death' (Pamphlet, London, 1867)

Froude, James A., *Oceana: Britain and Her Colonies* (London, 1886)

Glyde, Charles, A., 'Britain's Disgrace: An Urgent Plea for Old Age Pensions' (Pamphlet, Bradford, 1903)

'God Save the Queen! A Few Last Words on the Royal Titles Bill by a Loyal Subject and True Englishman' (Pamphlet, London, 1876)

Hodge, John, *Workman's Cottage to Windsor Castle* (London, 1931)

Howe, Joseph, *Twenty-Five Years' Fight With the Tories* (Leeds, 1907)

Jackson, T.A., *The Jubilee – And How* (Communist Party, 1935)

Lloyd George, David, *Better Times: Speeches by the Rt. Hon. David Lloyd George* (London, 1910)

Mackenzie, A., 'The Peers and the Franchise: The House of Lords' (Pamphlet, London, 1884)

Morrison Davidson, J., *Lives of Eminent Radicals In and Out of Parliament* (London, 1880)

Odger, George, 'Odger's Monthly Pamphlets on Current Events No. 1: Republicanism Versus Monarchy' (Pamphlet, London, 1872)

Sargant, W.L., 'The Princess and Her Dowry' in *idem, Essays of a Birmingham Manufacturer* (London, 1871), vol. III, pp. 167–94.

Sims, Gerald R., *My Life: Sixty Years' Recollections of Bohemian London* (London, 1917)

St Clair, S., 'A Sketch of the Life and Labours of John de Morgan' (Pamphlet, Leeds, 1880)

Taylor, Peter A., 'The Dowry for the Princess Louise' (Pamphlet, London, 1871)

Whiteing, Richard, *My Harvest* (London, 1915)

Woolacott, J. E., 'The House of Lords: A Lecture' (Pamphlet, Manchester, 1884)

Wright, Thomas, *Our New Masters* (London, 1873)

Articles in Books and Journals

Arblaster, Anthony, 'The Fall of the House of Windsor', *New Left Review*, no. 208 (1994), pp. 127–32.

Arnstein, Walter L., 'Queen Victoria Opens Parliament: The Disinvention of Tradition', *Historical Research*, CXIII (1990), pp. 178–94

Belchem, John, 'Republicanism, Popular Constitutionalism and the Radical Platform in Early Nineteenth Century England', *Social History*, VI (1981), pp. 1–32

Belchem, John, and Epstein, James, 'The Nineteenth-Century Gentleman Leader Revisited', *Social History*, XXII (1997), pp. 174–93

Biagini, Eugenio, and Reid, Alistair, 'Currents of Radicalism' in *Currents of Radicalism: Popular Radicalism, Organised Labour and Party Politics in Britain 1850–1914*, eds Biagini and Reid (Cambridge, 1990), pp. 1–19

Cannadine, David, 'The Context, Performance and Meaning of Ritual: The British Monarchy and the "Invention of Tradition", c.1820–1977', in *The Invention of Tradition*, eds Eric Hobsbawm and Terence Ranger (Cambridge, 1983), pp. 101–64

Chase, Malcolm, 'From Millennium to Anniversary: The Concept of Jubilee in Late Eighteenth Century and Nineteenth Century England', *Past and Present*, no. 129 (1990), pp. 132–47

Connors, Jane, 'The 1954 Royal Tour of Australia', in *Memories and Dreams: Reflections on Twentieth Century Australia*, eds Richard White and Penny Russell (Melbourne, 1997), pp. 172–85

D'Arcy, Feargus A., 'Charles Bradlaugh and the English Republican Movement', *Historical Journal*, XXV (1982), pp. 367–83

Epstein, James, 'Radical Dining, Toasting and Symbolic Expression in Early Nineteenth Century Lancashire: Rituals of Solidarity', *Albion*, XX (1988), pp. 271–91

Gossman, N.J., 'Republicanism in Nineteenth Century England', *International Review of Social History*, VII (1962), pp. 47–60

Hammerton, Elizabeth, and Cannadine, David, 'Conflict and Consensus on a Ceremonial Occasion: The Diamond Jubilee in Cambridge in 1897', *Historical Journal*, XXIV (1980), pp. 111–46

Harling, Philip, and Mandler, Peter, 'From Fiscal-Military State to *Laissez-Faire* State 1760–1850', *Journal of British Studies*, XXXII (1993), pp. 44–70

Harcourt, Freda, 'Gladstone, Monarchism and the "New Imperialism" 1868–1874', *Journal of Imperial and Commonwealth History*, XIV (1985), pp. 20–51

Irving, Helen, 'The Republic as a Feminist Issue', *Feminist Review*, LII (1996), pp. 87–101

Kemnitz, Thomas Milton, 'Matt Morgan of *Tomahawk* and English Cartooning', *Victorian Studies*, XIX (1975), pp. 5–32

Kuhn, William M., 'Ceremony and Politics: The British Monarchy 1871–72', *Journal of British Studies*, XXVI (1986), pp. 133–62

——, 'Queen Victoria's Civil List: What Did She Do With It?', *Historical Journal*, XXXVI (1993), pp. 642–65

Nicholls, David, 'The New Liberalism - After Chartism?', *Social History*, XXI (1996), pp. 355–64

Spearritt, Peter, 'Royal Progress: The Queen and Her Australian Subjects', in *Australian Cultural History*, eds S. L. Goldberg and F. B. Smith (Cambridge, 1998), pp. 138–57

Taylor, Antony, '*Reynolds's Newspaper*, Opposition to Monarchy and the Radical Anti-Jubilee: Britain's Anti-Monarchist Tradition Reconsidered', *Historical Research*, LXVIII (1995), pp. 318–37

——, 'Anti-Monarchism and the English Radical Tradition 1850–1872', in *Re-reading the Constitution: New Narratives in the Political History of England's Long Nineteenth Century*, ed. James Vernon (Cambridge, 1996), pp. 154–78

Taylor, Miles, 'Imperium et Libertas? Rethinking the Radical Critique of Empire During the Nineteenth Century', *Journal of Imperial and Commonwealth History*, XIX (1991), pp. 1–23

Books

Ashton, Owen, *W.E.Adams, Chartist, Radical and Journalist 1832–1906* (Whitley Bay, 1991)

Baer, Marc, *Theatre and Disorder in Late Georgian London* (Oxford, 1992)

Barnett, Anthony (ed.), *Power and the Throne: The Monarchy Debate* (London, 1994)

Barrow, Logie, and Bullock, Ian, *Democratic Ideas and the British Labour Movement 1880–1914* (Cambridge, 1997)

Belchem, John, *Popular Radicalism in Nineteenth Century Britain* (London, 1996)

Biagini, Eugenio, *Liberty, Retrenchment and Reform: Popular Liberalism in the Age of Gladstone 1860–1880* (Cambridge, 1992)

Bogdanor, Vernon, *The Monarchy and the Constitution* (Oxford, 1995)

Breuilly, John, *Labour and Liberalism in Nineteenth Century Europe: Essays in Comparative History* (Manchester, 1992)

Cannadine, David, *History in Our Time* (New Haven and London, 1998)

Clark, Anna, *The Struggle for the Breeches: Gender and the Making of the British Working Class* (Berkeley, 1995)

Colley, Linda, *Britons: Forging the Nation 1707–1837* (New Haven and London, 1992)

Epstein, James, *Radical Expression: Political Language, Ritual and Symbol in England 1790–1850* (Oxford, 1994)

Fielding, Steven, Thompson, Peter, and Tiratsoo, Nick, *'England Arise': The Labour Party and Popular Politics in Wartime Britain* (Manchester, 1995)

Finn, Margot, *After Chartism: Class and Nation in English Radical Politics 1848–1874* (Cambridge, 1993)

Fruchtman, Jack, *Thomas Paine: Apostle of Freedom* (London, 1994)

Hall, Alex, *Scandal, Sensation, and Social Democracy: The SPD Press and Wilhelmine Germany 1890–1914* (Cambridge, 1977)

Hall, Phillip, *Royal Fortune: Tax, Money and the Monarchy* (London, 1992)

Hames, Tim and Leonard, Mark, *Modernising the Monarchy* (Demos, 1998)

Hamilton, Willie, *My Queen and I* (London, 1975)

Haseler, Stephen, *The End of the House of Windsor: Birth of a British Republic* (London, 1993)

Hitchens, Christopher, *The Monarchy: A Critique of Britain's Favourite Fetish* (London, 1990)

Jenkins, Roy, *Sir Charles Dilke: A Victorian Tragedy* (London, 1958)

Joyce, Patrick, *Visions of the People: Industrial England and the Question of Class 1848–1914* (Cambridge, 1991)

Joyce, Patrick, *Democratic Subjects: The Self and the Social in Nineteenth Century England* (Cambridge, 1994)

Karsten, Peter, *Patriot Heroes in England and America: Political Symbolism and Changing Values Over Three Centuries* (Madison, 1978)

Keane, John, *Tom Paine: A Political Life* (London, 1995)

Kuhn, William M., *Democratic Royalism: The Transformation of the British Monarchy 1861–1914* (London, 1996)

Marsh, Peter, *Joseph Chamberlain: Entrepreneur in Politics* (New Haven and London, 1994)

McCalman, Ian, *Radical Underworld: Prophets, Revolutionaries and Photographers in London 1795–1840* (Oxford, 1988)

McKenna, Mark, *The Captive Republic: A History of Republicanism in Australia 1788–1996* (Cambridge, 1996)

Merck, Mandy (ed.), *After Diana: Irreverent Elegies* (London, 1998)

Morris, Marilyn, *The British Monarchy and the French Revolution* (New Haven and London, 1998)

Munich, Adrienne, *Queen Victoria's Secrets* (New York, 1996)

Nicholls, David, *The Lost Prime Minister: A Life of Sir Charles Dilke* (London, 1995)

Matthew, H.C.G., *Gladstone 1809–1874* (Oxford, 1986)

——, *Gladstone 1875–1898* (Oxford, 1995)

Mackenzie, John M., *Propaganda and Empire: The Manipulation of British Public Opinion 1880–1960* (Manchester, 1987)

McWilliam, Rohan, *Popular Politics in Nineteenth Century England* (London, 1998)

Murray-Brown, Jeremy (ed.), *The Monarchy and its Future* (London, 1969)

Nairn, Tom, *The Enchanted Glass: Britain and its Monarchy* (London, 1988)

Parry, Jonathan, *The Rise and Fall of Liberal Government in Victorian Britain* (New Haven and London, 1993)

Prothero, Iorwerth, *Radical Artisans in England and France 1830–1871* (Cambridge, 1997).

Pugh, Martin, *The Making of Modern British Politics 1867–1939* (London, 1982)

Martin, Kingsley, *Britain in the Sixties: The Crown and the Establishment* (London, 1962)

Pimlott, Ben, *The Queen: A Biography of Elizabeth II* (London, 1997)

Prochaska, Frank, *Royal Bounty: The Making of a Welfare Monarchy* (New Haven and London, 1995)

Richards, Thomas, *The Commodity Culture of Victorian England: Advertising and Spectacle 1851–1914* (New York, 1990)

Rickard, John, *Australia: A Cultural History* (London, 1988)

Samuel, Raphael, *Island Stories: Unravelling Britain* (London, 1998).

Royle, Edward, *Radicals, Secularists and Republicans: Popular Freethought in Britain 1866–1915* (Manchester, 1980)

Searle, G. R., *Country Before Party: Coalition and the Idea of National Government in Modern Britain 1885–1997* (London, 1995)

Smith, E. A., *The House of Lords in British Politics and Society 1815–1911* (London, 1992)

Smith, F. B., *Radical Artisan: William James Linton 1812–1897* (Manchester, 1973)

Sykes, Alan, *The Rise and Fall of British Liberalism 1776–1998* (London, 1997)

Thompson, Dorothy, *Queen Victoria: Gender and Power* (London, 1990)

Todd, Nigel, *The Militant Democracy: Joseph Cowen and Victorian Radicalism* (Whitley Bay, 1991)

Trainor, Luke, *British Imperialism and Australian Nationalism: Manipulation, Conflict and Compromise in the Late Nineteenth Century* (Cambridge, 1994)

—— (ed.), *Republicanism in New Zealand* (Palmerston North, 1996)

Tribe, David, *President Charles Bradlaugh MP* (London, 1971)

Vernon, James, *Politics and the People: A Study in English Political Culture c.1815–1867* (Cambridge, 1993)

Ziegler, Philip, *Crown and People* (London, 1978)

Theses

Hampton, Mark, 'The Fourth Estate: Theories, Images and Ideals of the Press in Britain 1880–1914' (unpublished Ph.D. thesis, Vanderbilt University, 1997)

McWilliam, Rohan, 'The Tichborne Claimant and the People: Investigations into Popular Culture' (unpublished D.Phil. thesis, University of Sussex, 1990)

Smith, M. P., 'Republicanism in Victorian Britain' (unpublished Ph.D. thesis, University of Toronto, 1979)

Photographic Acknowledgements and Picture Sources

The author and publishers wish to express their thanks to the following sources of illustrative material (illustration numbers are **in bold**) and/or permission to reproduce it:

Birmingham Public Library: **27** (*Dart*, 1 May 1880); **30** (*Dart*, 22 May 1880); **62**.

British Library, London: **17** (*The Republican*, 1 February 1882, vol. VII); **43** (*Radical*, 1 July 1887).

The Guardian Archives: **74** (*The Guardian*, 3 June 1953).

Cliff Harrison: **68** (*New Illustrated*, 17 May 1919).

Image Library, State Library of New South Wales: **50** (*Bulletin*, 23 May 1885); **51** (*Bulletin*, 23 July 1887); **53** (*Bulletin*, 27 February 1886); **56** (*Bulletin*, 30 July 1887).

The Manchester Central Libraries: **1**; **2**, **5** (*The Political House that Jack Built*, London, 1819); **3** (*The Real or Constitutional House that Jack Built*, London, 1819); **6** (*A Frown from the Crown, or the Hydra Destroyed*, London, 1820); **12** (*Fun*, 28 September 1892); **14** (*Fun*, 30 March 1872); **18** (*Illustrated Police News*, 16 December 1871); **21** (*The Tomahawk Christmas Almanack*, 1868); **23** (*Tomahawk*, 8 June 1867); **24** (*Fun*, 25 February 1871); **25** (*Judy*, 26 April 1871); **26** (*Illustrated Police News*, 9 March 1872); **31** (*Judy*, 22 November 1871); **32** (*The Graphic*, 17 February 1872); **47** (*Illustrated Australian News*, 30 August 1879); **49** (*Illustrated Australian News*, 25 June 1887); **54** (*Tomahawk*, 25 January 1868); **69** (George Haw, *From Workhouse to Westminster: The Life Story of Will Crooks*, London, 1907); **70** (*Punch*, 30 January 1924).

Manchester Central Library, Local Studies Division: **28**, **29**.

National Museum of Ireland, Dublin: **45**.

National Museum of Labour History, Manchester: **65**.

Nicholas Treadwell Gallery, London: **79**.

Oldham Public Library: **39**, **40**, **44**.

University of Warwick Library: **9** (*Punch*, 1848, vol. XIV); **10** (*Punch*, 1844, vol. VII); **11** (*Punch*, 1847, vol. XIII); **13** (*Punch*, 30 May 1857, vol. XXXIII); **16** (*Illustrated London News*, 4 August 1866); **19** (*Punch*, 8 April 1871); **20** (*Punch*, 30 November 1867); **33** (*Illustrated London News*, 9 December 1871); **41** (*Illustrated London News*, 7 January 1888); **52**, **57** (*Punch*, 6 April 1910) and **61** (*Single Tax*, 1 June 1898).

Courtesy of the author: **4** (*The Royal History of England*, London, 1878); **7**, **8**, **22** (O. F. Walton, *Pictures and Stories from Queen Victoria's Life*, London, 1901); **15** (O. Paxton Hood, *Oliver Cromwell: His Life, Time, Battlefields and Contemporaries*, London, 1895); **34**, **37**, **42** (Herbert Maxwell, *Sixty Years a Queen*, London, 1887); **35** (*Le Rire*, 2 February 1901); **36**, **58** (*Bits of Beaconsfield: A New Series of Disraeli's Curiosities of Literature*, Manchester, 1880); **46** (*The Children's Friend*, 1909, vol. XLVIII); **55** (*The Anzac Book*, Melbourne, 1916); **59** (Robert Banks, *The Right Honourable W. E. Gladstone and Hawarden Castle and Village*, Manchester, 1898); **60** (*Gladstone Almanack*, Edinburgh, 1885); **64** (*The Premier's Battle-Cry* (*Yorkshire Observer*, 1910);

63, 66 (*Chatterbox* annual, 1911); **67** (Brian O'Higgins, *The Voice of Banba: Songs, Ballads and Satires*, Dublin, 1931); **71** (T. A. Jackson's *The Jubilee – And How*, Communist Party, 1935); **75** (special coronation supplement to the *Eagle*, 29 May 1953); **76**; **77** (supplement to *England*, 17 December 1887).

Index